PRAISE FOR THE VOLUME

The Ethics of Personal Data Collection in International Relations is a far-reaching exploration of how to combine people-centred and state-centred perspectives on global politics. Mazzucelli, Keith, and Hollifield have commissioned work from a number of new, fresh voices, scholars and experts who are able to connect a set of issues – ethics, data collection and inter-state relations – that are not often considered together. Moreover, the frame of inclusionism integrates domestic and international considerations in a promising way. This is highly original work.
—Anne-Marie Slaughter, Bert G. Kerstetter '66 University Professor Emerita of Politics and International Affairs, Princeton University

Mazzucelli, Keith, and Hollifield are breaking new ground in academic and policy research with the publication of *The Ethics of Personal Data Collection in International Relations*. This volume integrates cutting-edge case analyses at the nexus of timely ethical concerns, data collection methods and international relations concepts. Furthermore, the introduction of a new frame of reference in the literature, inclusionism, has the potential to address sources of alienation and polarization, which increasingly mark civil societies worldwide, in spiritually transformative ways.
—David M. Elcott, Taub Professor of Practice in Public Service and Leadership, Robert F. Wagner Graduate School of Public Service, New York University

The Ethics of Personal Data Collection in International Relations is a timely contribution to a most urgent governance challenge of our time. The uses and misuses of data collection are amplified by the global scale of public policy making in the era of COVID-19. As commercial and political interests assert their agendas, countervailing normative duties and restraints remain to be defined and empowered. Mazzucelli, Keith, and Hollifield set a new agenda in this wide-ranging and thorough volume, particularly with their focus on the essential issue of inclusionism. This book is sure to guide the field of international relations in a fruitful new direction.
—Joel H. Rosenthal, president, Carnegie Council for Ethics in International Affairs

The Ethics of Personal Data Collection in International Relations is an exciting and inspiring volume that deals with some of the most pressing issues of global concern affecting societies during the COVID-19 pandemic, including collection and use and misuse of data, fake news, alienation, and polarization. It has the merit of bringing together scholars and researchers who present case studies referring to both the Western and the non-Western worlds, including China, India, Iran and Taiwan. A further merit is the introduction of a new and less explored International Relations paradigm, inclusionism, as the key to dealing with the sources of polarization and marginalization/alienation that characterize current societies and risk compromising the 'future of democracy in the face of the rising tide of authoritarianism'. Indeed, as Mazzucelli, Keith, and Hollifield underline in their Introduction, the 'thread running through the chapters highlights the inadequacy of current international relations models to account for the practical effects of information technology innovation, especially in situations where domestic and international strategies overlap'. This volume is a fundamental contribution to the literature on its subject and an enriching read for both scholars and advanced students of International Relations.

—Barbara Onnis, professor of International Politics of Asia, Department of Social and Political Sciences, University of Cagliari

The Ethics of Personal Data Collection in International Relations

ANTHEM ETHICS OF PERSONAL DATA COLLECTION

The **Anthem Ethics of Personal Data Collection** series publishes scholarly works at the intersection of data, ethics and digital technology in the 21st century. This series introduces the personal data movement by highlighting innovative research in public health, violence against women in public spaces, the energy sector, sexual violence in conflict, vocational training, insurance policy underwriting, individual control of enterprise data sharing, and data as labor. The series focuses primarily on the ethical concerns regarding personal data as a natural resource in the era of digital revolution.

Series Editors

Colette Mazzucelli – New York University, USA
James Felton Keith – Keith Institute, USA

Titles in the series

Personal Data Collection Risks in a Post-Vaccine World
Regulating Cross-Border Data Flows
The Ethics of Personal Data Collection in International Relations
Hacking Digital Ethics
The Domains of Identity

The Ethics of Personal Data Collection in International Relations

Inclusionism in the Time of COVID-19

Edited by
Colette Mazzucelli, James Felton Keith,
and C. Ann Hollifield

Anthem Press
An imprint of Wimbledon Publishing Company
www.anthempress.com

This edition first published in UK and USA 2023
by ANTHEM PRESS
75–76 Blackfriars Road, London SE1 8HA, UK
or PO Box 9779, London SW19 7ZG, UK
and
244 Madison Ave #116, New York, NY 10016, USA

© 2023 Colette Mazzucelli, James Felton Keith, and C. Ann Hollifield
editorial matter and selection; individual chapters © individual contributors

The moral right of the authors has been asserted.

All rights reserved. Without limiting the rights under copyright reserved above,
no part of this publication may be reproduced, stored or introduced into
a retrieval system, or transmitted, in any form or by any means
(electronic, mechanical, photocopying, recording or otherwise),
without the prior written permission of both the copyright
owner and the above publisher of this book.

British Library Cataloguing-in-Publication Data
A catalogue record for this book is available from the British Library.

Library of Congress Control Number: 2022949636

ISBN-13: 978-1-83998-812-7 (Pbk)
ISBN-10: 1-83998-812-6 (Pbk)

Cover Image: Designed by Marc Nelson in
Artistic Collaboration with Colette Mazzucelli

This title is also available as an e-book.

CONTENTS

Acknowledgments   ix

Foreword by Prof. Dr. Azza Karam—Secretary-General, Religions for Peace   xiii

Word Clouds by Leslie Elizabeth Prosy, New York University   xvii

Introduction: Non-Western versus Western Reflections on the Ethics of Personal Data Collection in a Variegated "Chessboard-Web" Ecosystem   1
Colette Mazzucelli, James Felton Keith, and Andrea Adams

Part I

Chapter 1. Information Technology: National Security Savior or Civil Rights Disaster   21
Celeste Brevard

Chapter 2. Is This Chapter "Fake News"?: Exploring the Possibilities of Regulating Online Disinformation while Preserving the Right to Freedom of Expression in Europe   47
Sophia Ehmke

Chapter 3. Geopolitics, Personal Data Collection, and Globalization: Iran's Response to COVID-19   69
Megan Cameron

Part II

Chapter 4. Taiwan's Response to the COVID-19 Pandemic: A Social Constructivist Analysis of Identity Differentiation with the People's Republic of China   93
Jasmine C. Lee

Chapter 5. Reeducation Camps in Xinjiang, China: An Intersectional Constructivist Approach   115
Mary Davis

Part III

Chapter 6. Smartphones and Data Privacy Ethics: International Regulations in a "Chessboard-Web" Environment 131
Andrea Adams

Chapter 7. Ethical Considerations around Crowdsourcing Stories of Sexual Abuse and Harassment in Public Spaces: The Safecity India Story 155
Suzanne Goodney Lea and Elsa Marie D'Silva

Chapter 8. Protecting Privacy in a Sexual Assault Prevention Program 171
Lynne Chandler-Garcia and John C. Riley

Conclusion 189
Colette Mazzucelli, James Felton Keith, and Andrea Adams

Afterword by Dean Joshua Cooper—International Training Center for Teaching Peace and Human Rights (Geneva) 199

List of Contributors 203

Index 209

ACKNOWLEDGMENTS

This edited volume builds on the research made possible by the cooperation between Nathaniel Raymond, formerly of the Harvard Humanitarian Initiative and presently a lecturer at Yale University, and Colette Mazzucelli, New York University (NYU) and Pioneer Academics. Colette and Nathaniel brought together a community of researchers and practitioners in Bosch workshops at NYU in New York and NYU in Washington, DC, including Kristin Bergtora Sandvik, Karen Naimer, Christoph Koettl, Stefan Schmitt, Jay Aronson, Ziad Al Achkar, and Charles Martin-Shields. Colette thanks Professors Douglas Irvin-Erickson and Yasemin Irvin-Erickson, George Mason University, for the cooperation that led to a cutting-edge Special Issue of *Genocide Studies and Prevention* (GSP), "Information and Communications Technologies in Mass Atrocities Research and Response," published in 2017. The pedagogically inspired volume *Genocide Matters: Emerging Issues and On-Going Perspectives* (Routledge, 2013), edited by our colleagues, Professors Joyce Apsel, NYU, and Ernesto Verdeja, University of Notre Dame, resonates strongly as we nurture the research in our community.

The cover of this edited volume designed by Marc Nelson and Colette Mazzucelli speaks to the origins of the GSP research, which is grounded in concerns related to structure and agency in an era when transnational migration, the global pandemic, and climate change influence the nature of conflict and raise awareness regarding the ethics of personal data collection. Our artistic sensitivity and that of the contributors pertains to the protection of the most vulnerable from the misuses of data, particularly concerning its collection in the most fragile conflict environments. The research support to connect the Special Issue and this edited volume provided by Laura Salter, Annika Squires, and Nicole Scartozzi of NYU and Megan Cameron of York University is most sincerely appreciated, as are the insights provided by Edward Ablang, Harvard University, and Megan Araghi, SOAS University of London.

The contributors to this volume come from diverse regions in our world. Their analyses shed light on local contexts across continents. Colette expresses appreciation to this volume's peer reviewers Professors Nanette Levinson, codirector, Internet Governance Lab, School of International Service, American University, and Corri Zoli, director of research, Institute for Security Policy & Law, Syracuse University College of Law/Maxwell School of Citizenship & Public Affairs, for their constructive suggestions to Anthem Press. For the inspiring foreword and afterword, respectively, Colette thanks Prof. Dr. Azza Karam, secretary general, Religions for Peace, New York, and Dean Joshua Cooper, International Training Center for Teaching Peace and Human Rights (Geneva).

Colette is also grateful to fellow Bosch alumna Professor Emerita C. Ann Hollifield for her outstanding editing, James Felton Keith for his specific ideas pertaining to Inclusionism, Professor Andrea Adams for her extraordinary dedication to the larger project that inspires this research, and Shirley Cloyes DioGuardi for her tireless humanitarian engagement. In addition, Colette expresses her appreciation to Tina Lam, Nicolette Teta, and Dr. Michael John Williams for their support related to the Bosch–NYU workshops. The authors who wrote chapters for a companion volume to this one also shared their insights to enrich our community dialogue. Colette thanks Laura Salter, Jakub Wojciech Kibitlewski, Thynn Thynn Hlaing, Emilie Greenhalgh Stammer, Professors Christian Rossi, David C. Unger, András László Pap, and Mary Kate Schneider, as well as Charles Martin-Shields and Ziad Al Ackhar. For the inspiring foreword and afterword, respectively, to that companion volume, Colette thanks President Emeritus Professor John Sexton, NYU, and Special Advisor Annette Richardson, UN Women.

Anthem Press has provided consistent support as the Ethics of Personal Data Collection Series emerged over the past several years starting with Kaliya Young's *The Domains of Identity*, published in 2020, and followed by Andréa Belliger and David J. Krieger's *Hacking Digital Ethics*, published in 2021. We look forward to Bryan Mercurio and Ronald Yu's *Regulating Cross-Border Data Flows: Issues, Challenges and Impact*, to be published in 2022. Our appreciation as editors is expressed to Tej P. S. Sood, publisher; Megan Greiving, senior acquisitions editor; and the Anthem Press marketing and sales teams. Colette dedicates this volume to her late mother, Adelina Maria De Ponte Mazzucelli, who urged her to ask questions from an early age, and to her father, Silvio Anthony Mazzucelli, who encourages her writing. Colette's orange tabby, Ginevra "Cuddles" Pario, is a loving feline companion in the midst of fact checking and creative writing.

Ann acknowledges with deep appreciation the Robert Bosch Foundation and the Robert Bosch Foundation Alumni Association's support for the conferences and collaborations that led directly to the creation of this volume. Across its long history, the Bosch Foundation has made fostering international understanding and cooperation a central part of its philanthropic mission. As a grateful alumna of the Bosch Fellowship Program, Ann thanks this volume's community of authors for the pleasure of working together to share the knowledge in the chapters that comprise this important and thought-provoking book.

For James, the journey toward Inclusionism started while seeking a moral regard that could sustain him in a world torn between a culture's truth and data's transparency. He is so thankful to everyone who listened as he tried to figure out how he meant what he was thinking. More specifically, James needs to thank an old mentor and former US Special Forces soldier, Earl Winters, for giving him a more realistic view of the incentives that threaten our communal and individual agency. He thanks his parents, Tawana and Steven Rogers, for giving him enough stability to try anything. Lastly, but most importantly, James thanks his husband, Andy Tarradath, for giving him enough encouragement to come out as the person that he is going to be tomorrow. In the middle of a global pandemic, Andy helped James realize that the communal rights we fight for must be built on human rights that allow our communities enough space to identify all of our individual participants.

Andrea first recognizes God for bringing her into this mission and on this journey with the Safecity team. Andrea thanks Suzanne Goodney Lea and Elsa Marie D'Silva for allowing her to contribute to their amazing work by providing a voice for victims using the Safecity crowd mapping app. Suzanne and Elsa welcomed Andrea's ideas and encouraged the expansion of her work surrounding ethics that became a chapter in this volume. Being a part of the Red Dot Global network has been a blessing and impacted Andrea's awareness and understanding of the needs and opportunities to support a global community by infusing ethics with technology. It is through this relationship that Andrea met Colette Mazzucelli. Colette's scholarship and leadership in crafting a narrative that intertwines the messages of the contributing authors around an emerging voice for international relations are groundbreaking. Andrea cherishes Colette's kindness and willingness to embrace her as a full contributor. Andrea also wishes to thank Ann Hollifield for elevating the direction and focus of her work and James Felton Keith for his generous sharing of strategic insights as well as Dr. Angelyn Flowers for her ongoing support and mentorship. Lastly, Andrea thanks her life partner, best friend, husband, and love of her life, Nigel, for his continued wisdom, encouragement, and support.

This volume is a testament to the vision in grantmaking and the life-changing experiences offered by the Robert Bosch Stiftung Gmb since its transatlantic Fellowship Program began in the 1980s. Although the Fellowship Program is ending, its legacy endures in this volume and the on-going research in community that the Bosch-NYU Workshops make possible.

FOREWORD

Prof. Dr. Azza Karam,
Secretary-General, Religions for Peace

How can spiritual transcendence safeguard peace in any community, let alone our planetary universe?

Fifty-one years ago, leaders of different religious institutions from around the world, representing all Christian denominations and their Islamic/Muslim counterparts together with representatives from diverse faith communities, including Hindu, Buddhist, Jain, Sikh, Zoroastrian, and Baha'i, came together with two purposes in mind. The first was to assemble to advocate, as one spiritual and religious voice, for a holistic peace—not just the absence of war: rather, seeking to prevent the very causes that lead to conflicts in the first place, including the escalating nuclear arms race and proxy wars, poverty, rampant human rights violations, and the decline of the primacy of the rule of law around the world.

The second purpose, what would become Religions for Peace, aimed to put words into actions, by practically working together at the national, regional, and global levels. From the latter inclination Inter-Religious Councils (IRCs) were born. This would be a structure that basically would convene the religious leaders from all faith institutions in any one country and serve as a space for these leaders to meet as equals, regardless of numerical, historical, or demographic religious dynamics. In other words, in the majority or minority, old or new, monotheistic/Abrahamic, or not, these faith leaders would meet as equals. For what purpose? To speak as one about the rights of all; to struggle as one for the rights—and dignity—of all; to ensure that no one is left behind. To hold accountable government and governance and to be the partner of all other secular civil society actors. These were the faith-based and faith-inspired civic actors working for the rights of all: yet with a special focus on the most vulnerable. In short, theirs is a human rights mission and a human-rights-based approach. Far from attempting to equalize or generalize the commonalities between each religion, this form of "interfaith dialogue" is more an attempt to translate deeply shared faith inspiration into common action destined for the most vulnerable anywhere.

This interfaith movement was mobilized owing to incendiary rhetoric and the near catastrophic increase in nuclear arsenals. Sensing respective governments and multilateral (intergovernmental) entities alike were unable even to speak the language of peace, religious leaders felt an imperative to provide the alternative narrative and exemplify the actions needed to hold humanity together in peace. Soon after its founding, a Religions for Peace IRC was quick to take shape in South Africa, where the anti-apartheid struggle was a powerful call to action, and in Japan, China, and Korea, where the real fears of a nuclear holocaust were an epicenter. Together, these religious actors were able to effect changes in the hearts and minds of many people. In fact, the South African IRC just about disbanded after its members were handpicked by the new democratically elected government of South Africa. In Korea and Japan, secular dogmatism combined with growing and powerful economies, which meant a reversal of any respect for a tendency to take religious voices too much into account.

Our world today, at best, resembles the calamitous dynamics of the 1970s in terms of governmental and intergovernmental ineptitudes. At worst, threats facing our world at present are significantly amplified by our very environment, Planet Earth, struggling to survive. Today we deal not only with a global pandemic: its moral, financial, and cultural ramifications abound. The novel coronavirus hit our world at a time when each and all our institutions, political, economic, financial, and social, are lame, or limping along, with their credibility tarnished by all manner of human weaknesses. Not least of these is an amplification of multiple forms of intersecting discrimination combined with a deficit of ideology as well as leadership. Our religious institutions are as tarnished as all others. Some suffer from a ludicrous sense of territoriality, internal and externally oriented struggles for power and influence amid theological disputes, racism, sexism, political corruption—the list is endless. Our institutions, created to be the means of liberation, egalitarianism, economic and financial sustainability, and accountability, have become, possibly, our Achilles' heel. If the multigovernment is struggling, it is because of the Darwinian prevalence of the survival of the fittest—rather than the ethos of collaboration and connectivity.

Before we believe that we have no more on which to rely or that all is lost, we must realize one simple, yet glaring, reality: this is the case for institutions that work in silos. Even gangs, weapons, and the drug trade are more efficient, lethally so, when alliances are made. Forms of human intelligence succeed better when intelligence services work together. The world wars ended when the stronger and better coordinated allies worked more and more efficiently with one another. This is a reality that stares us in the face. Yet, we fail to see this reality. Each of the religious institutions that have existed, literally for centuries, is struggling today—apart. Even when these institutions successfully come together ecumenically, this is not enough. Our world of faith is not just Christian. Our world is multifaith. Nonetheless, our actions, or rather the actions of our institutions, are siloed.

In South Korea and Japan, the Religions for Peace IRCs, as with the other 90 countries where this movement grew over the last half century, are today serving millions in diverse communities, having increased their work at both advocacy and service delivery levels during the COVID-19 response. Each calamity—from HIV and AIDS to Ebola, from civil war to border tensions, from natural humanitarian disasters to man-made wars—has been a call to action to serve their communities together. Examples abound, including multiple forms of reconciliation between Indigenous Peoples and Christian Churches taking place in Latin America and Africa, as interfaith efforts to save the natural habitat of the former and the very lungs of our earth—the Rainforests—are being realized, at national as well as multiple local levels.

The influence and aspirational work of nonstate actors, such as multifaith and peacekeeping groups, has always been a critical aspect of international relations, though not necessarily the focus of nation-states. Nation-states have left this work to international and transnational collaborators like the United Nations, the European Union, and other nongovernmental organizations. Despite the efforts of these organizations, the evolution of nationalism threatens to undermine their collaborative efforts across borders. These efforts notwithstanding, the real danger of the COVID-19 pandemic, nationalistic rhetoric, and the corresponding social media news cycles is a mutually reinforcing dynamic. This is a dynamic that acts to influence and fuel domestic responses against nation-states while simultaneously impacting transnational peacebuilding and conflict mitigation initiatives. This edited volume highlights the uneven uses and abuses of personal data by different regimes around the world, which, in turn, give this dynamic its own character and specificity.

As the chapters that follow ably discuss, our world comprises individuals vulnerable to surveillance capitalism (Zuboff, 2019), as explored by various authors in the pages ahead, and "secular dogmatism" (Sexton, 2019), which is analyzed in a companion volume edited by Mazzucelli, Keith, and Hollifield with Adams and Grichting. These vulnerabilities contribute to increasing polarization in societies. In this context, multifaith work is an enactment of spiritual transcendence, which seeks to safeguard peace in communities, by serving one beating heart at a time.

References

Sexton, J. (2019) *Standing for Reason. The University in a Dogmatic Age*. New Haven, CT: Yale University Press.
Zuboff, S. (2019) *The Age of Surveillance Capitalism: The Fight for a Human Future at the New Frontier of Power*. New York: Public Affairs.

WORD CLOUDS

Introduction: Non-Western versus Western Reflections on the Ethics of Personal Data Collection in a Variegated "Chessboard-Web" Ecosystem

Chapter 1. Information Technology: National Security Savior or Civil Rights Disaster

Chapter 2. Is This Chapter "Fake News"?: Exploring the Possibilities of Regulating Online Disinformation while Preserving the Right to Freedom of Expression in Europe

WORD CLOUDS

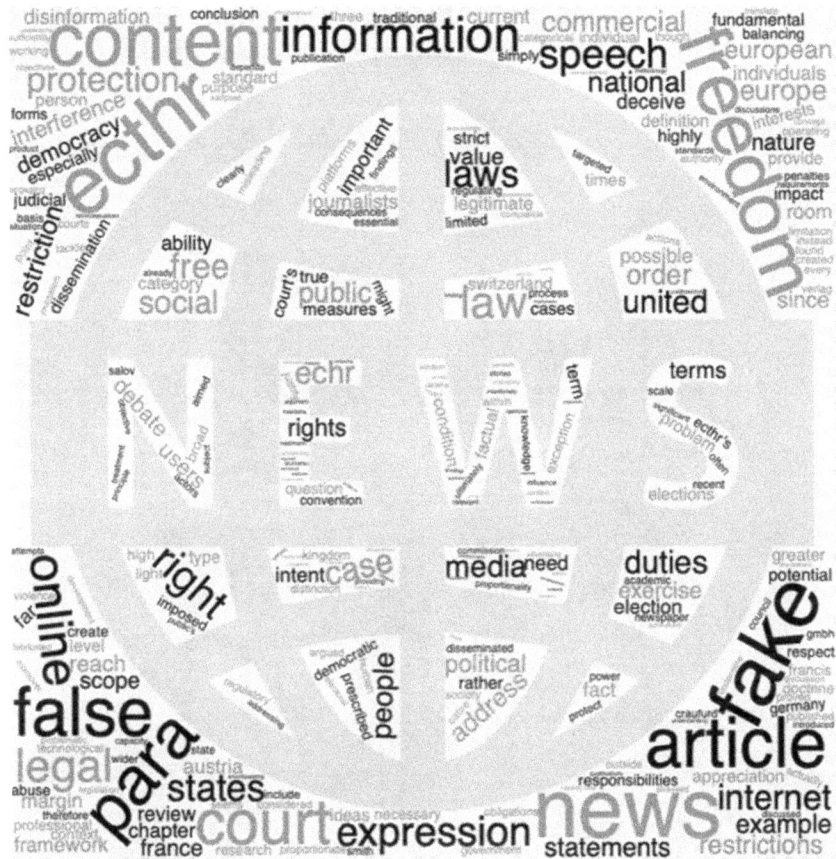

Chapter 3. Geopolitics, Personal Data Collection, and Globalization: Iran's Response to COVID-19

WORD CLOUDS

Chapter 4. Taiwan's Response to the COVID-19 Pandemic: A Social Constructivist Analysis of Identity Differentiation with the People's Republic of China

Chapter 5. Reeducation Camps in Xinjiang, China: An Intersectional Constructivist Approach

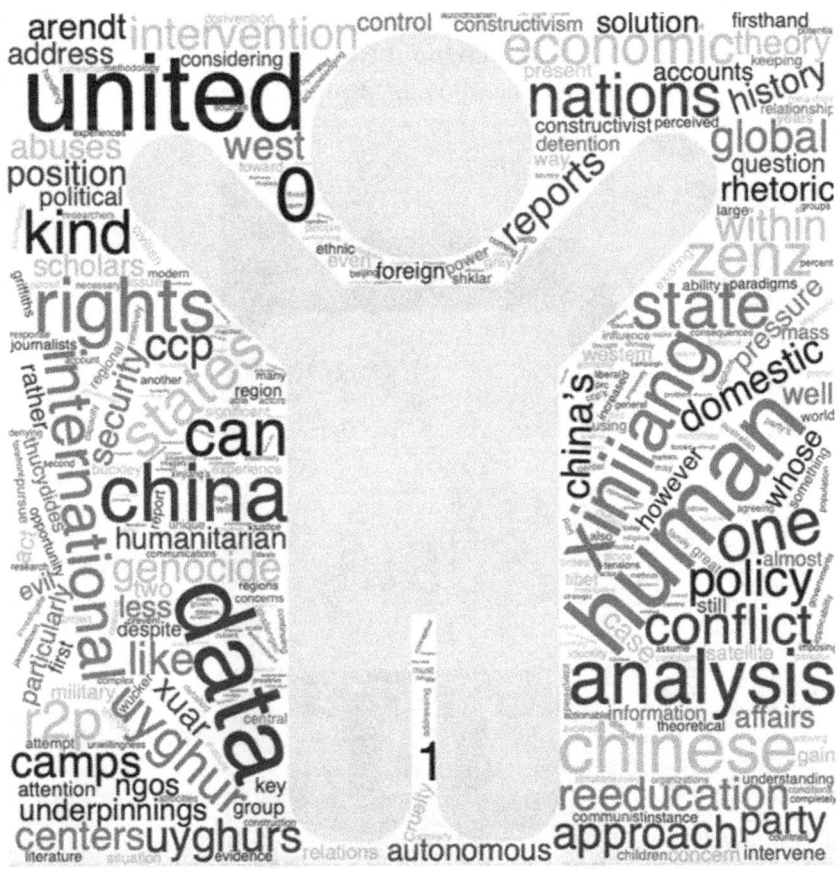

Chapter 6. Smartphones and Data Privacy Ethics: International Regulations in a "Chessboard-Web" Environment

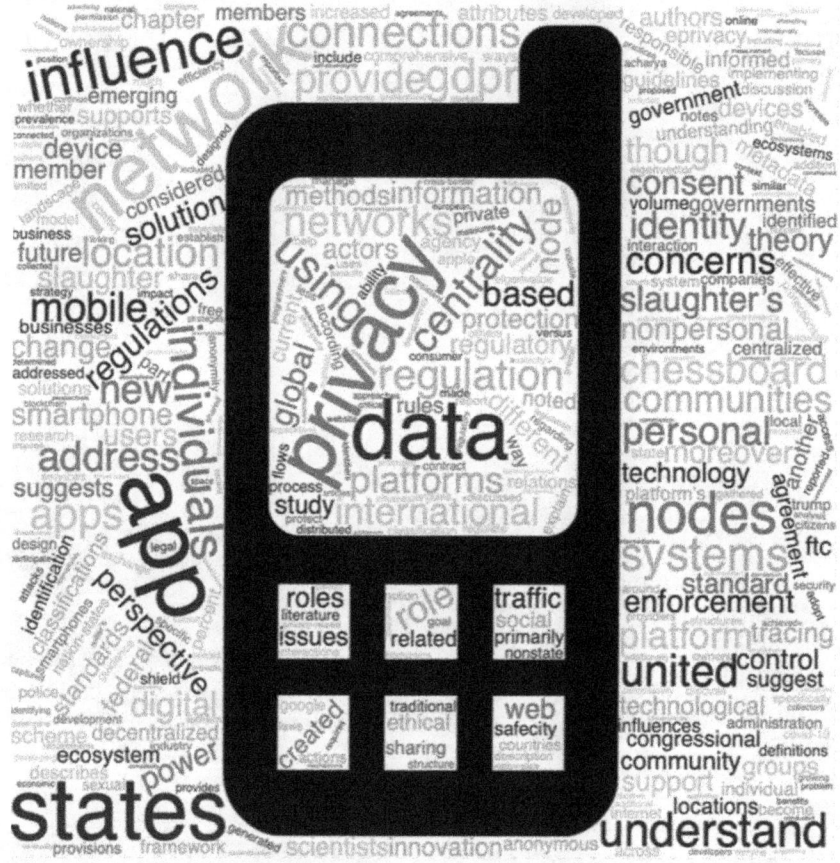

Chapter 7. Ethical Considerations around Crowdsourcing Stories of Sexual Abuse and Harassment in Public Spaces: The Safecity India Story

Chapter 8. Protecting Privacy in a Sexual Assault Prevention Program

Conclusion

INTRODUCTION

NON-WESTERN VERSUS WESTERN REFLECTIONS ON THE ETHICS OF PERSONAL DATA COLLECTION IN A VARIEGATED "CHESSBOARD-WEB" ECOSYSTEM

Colette Mazzucelli, James Felton Keith, and Andrea Adams

The emphasis on the ethics of personal data collection in this edited volume provides various case studies the occasion to bring race and gender to the forefront once again as lenses to understand international relations. The myth of the founding of international relations in 1919, analyzed by Acharya and Buzan (2019) a century later, is one that obfuscates the influence of race relations as well as gender in the early development of the discipline during the mid-nineteenth and early twentieth centuries. These case studies broaden the ways we understand international relations in the West and, as importantly, in the non-Western space given the countries that are the subjects of analysis: China, Iran, Taiwan, and India, as well as the European Union (EU) and the United States. Mainstream international relations theory does not fully capture the evidence of cyber-based, technology-driven activity, which influences the decisions leaders make impacting the lives of billions of people across the planet. As the contributors focus on the relevance of race and gender across cases, this volume underlines our concerns about the future of democracy in the face of the rising tide of authoritarianism around the world. The plight of the world's largest and most plural democracy, India, under the Modi government; the increasingly aggressive nature of China under President Xi Jinping; as well as the impact of Trumpism in the United States during the Biden presidency make these concerns, which place illiberalism at the center of developments, pressing as well as timely.

The supreme tension in the post-pandemic experience is inherent in the ways in which emerging powers once categorized in the Third World, notably

Brazil and India, are driving the spread of COVID-19. Public health in developing states has become a major influence in the civil society dimension of globalization. This evolution prompts us to consider the need for an international relations lens, inclusionism, which picks up where environmental stewardship (Acharya and Buzan, 2019, pp. 212–15), with its focus on climate justice and shared fate concerns, leaves off. This lens has COVID-19 as a reference point given the pandemic's truly global nature in modern times impacting most states in the world except North Korea and a small number of island countries. As we bear witness to what the authors term a "pandemic differential," it is evident looking ahead that the developing world is likely to experience COVID-19 and its mutations in quite different ways from the developed world. In terms of conflict analysis, the pandemic asks us to focus on an immersion in the local. This focus is more pressing because "'remaining undiscovered' and ignoring the outside, as strategies open to local cultures" (Paolini in Darby, 1997), to resist Western hegemony, is not an option in the post-pandemic era. For this reason, our initial aim in this volume is to share analyses that speak to non-Western, local experiences. Looking beyond Western models to explore non-Western perspectives that create "homegrown" theories is critical to expanding relational variations of power and influence (Ersoy, 2018). Using non-Western perspectives expands the international relations inquiry to include other concepts of influence as variables of study, thereby questioning assumptions concerning man's conflict with nature. The expansion into non-Western international relations inquiry requires a longer-term assessment of inclusionism to explain the significance of the pandemic's uneven impact on the developing world. Likewise, the implications for globalization of the nexus between climate change and the variants of the novel coronavirus (Preidt, 2021) must be considered.

This volume's relevance may be explained, first and foremost, during a time of unprecedented loss of life around the world each day. The data, which is oftentimes incomplete and misleading, nonetheless reveals the state as deficient as well as negligent in its response to social healthcare needs. This volume attests to the fact that pressing global public health concerns are ever present as subjects of societal discourse and debate in developed and developing states. Moreover, the COVID-19 pandemic makes the omission of the ethics of personal data collection analysis in the international relations literature even more salient given the rise of contact tracing and increased uses of mobile phone apps to track citizens by states and firms across the globe, as this volume's chapters analyzing the responses to COVID-19 in Iran and Taiwan explain.

For this reason, dialogue connecting research and practice is necessary to identify ways to address these emerging challenges at the conceptual, economic, legal, political, and social levels. The perspectives of researchers and the experience of practitioners must come together to bring the discussion forward. In response to this plea, a community of research-practitioners remains in dialogue after two Bosch workshops at New York University to define the contents of case studies in this volume. The responsibility of this research-practitioner community is to grapple with specific issues that define the state of the discipline in personal data collection ethics. Case studies, including prominent uses of crowd mapping platforms and mobile telephony apps, document legal and human rights concerns in remote areas. Field research speaks to cases ranging from an analysis of Iran's response to the COVID-19 pandemic to the exploitation of personal data collection to perpetuate modern slavery through reeducation camps in the People's Republic of China (PRC) to crowd mapping stories of physical abuses in public spaces by Safecity in India.

This volume's addition to the literature is in the innovative connections made between international relations and conflict analysis. In our reflections on international relations a basic distinction remains normatively valid, as Hoffmann analyzed (1960) over half a century ago. As he writes,

> It is the very lack of a supreme and generally accepted authority which explains why the rules of the game in world politics differ so sharply from the rules of domestic politics: the overriding loyalty of the groups into which the world has been divided, belongs to the group rather than to the world. […] Even in the period when those groups had a common ideal transcending their boundaries, such as "the majestic conception of the unity of the Christian community," political authority remained fragmented; the common ideal, at best, was no more than a restraint on the actions of the groups—not the expression of a supreme temporal power. Hence […] the striking differences between domestic law and international law, whose elaboration, interpretation, and enforcement continue to depend on the will and consent of its very subjects. Hence also the difference in perspective between the fields of world politics and "domestic" political science. (p. 2)

In thinking about the environment of the post-pandemic world, the authors of this introduction recognize the urgency to focus more purposefully on what may be defined less strictly as the international system, in Waltz's third image (1959), and more inclusively as the distributed ecosystem (Mazzucelli, 2020). This alternative third image is elaborated more in the context of case studies that are featured in a companion volume edited by Mazzucelli, Keith, and Hollifield. The distributed ecosystem as alternative third image speaks directly to the impact experienced around the world of man's war against nature, of which the COVID-19 pandemic is the latest illustration. Nonetheless, in the post-pandemic era, what has been true since the last century is even more relevant. Hoffmann's reflections on the discipline of international relations in 1960 still resonate strongly, albeit with greater tensions between increasingly multiethnic states, in which the indigenous figure more prominently when considering the "domestic experience" and the consistently uneven allocation of resources in the distributed ecosystem:

> One of the crucial features and paradoxes of politics today is that whereas internal politics are conditioned and affected by world problems more than ever before, the foreign policies of nations remain largely dictated by the domestic experience and by the nation's image of itself. World problems become domestic issues, but the nation's reaction to these issues and the nation's conduct on the world stage can often be explained only by internal history and by the values developed in those happier days when the outside world did not press so heavily on each country. (p. 4)

Realists from Kissinger to Waltz frame international relations in the twenty-first century in terms of the relationship between an emerging China and a United States whose power is analyzed relative to the "rise of the rest," to cite Zakaria (2009) in the literature. While classical realists, including Kissinger, reference the nature of leadership and the relations between state leaders, particularly Chinese President Xi Jinping and American President Joseph Biden, structural realists posit that the anarchical nature of the international system, in which there is "no common power" (Lieber, 2000), makes war among states an omnipresent condition in the state of nature.

The nature of competition between the PRC and the United States occurs at the apex of the international system, thereby influencing the dynamics of all other actors in a top-down, vertically oriented rivalry, which is driven simultaneously by economics, culture, demographics, geostrategy, ideology, politics, and technology. The Davis and Lee chapters in this volume contrast an illiberal response to exploit personal data collection to perpetuate modern-day slavery in the PRC (Ochab, 2020), with the democratic response through a combination of strong civic participation and technology, including contact tracing, personal data collection, and data transparency, by Taiwan to contain the spread of the novel coronavirus and minimize its impact on the daily lives of its people. Lee's analysis of the Taiwanese policy response is an important case to consider at the horizontal intersection of personal data, global pandemic, and social protests, which cuts into the vertical axis of China–US relations. The protests are relevant in Taiwan given their rise in recent years on the island in response to several fundamental public concerns: namely, "worsening economic inequality; opaque, unjust, and unaccountable governing institutions and procedures; and a growing but threatened sense of Taiwanese identity" (Ho, 2018). Lee utilizes a social constructivist lens to underline the ways in which personal data collection in the context of the COVID-19 pandemic illustrates Taiwan's distinct identity relative to the PRC. Her analysis speaks directly to the grassroots activist legacy of the 2014 Sunflower Movement. In contrast, the chapter by Davis highlights the asymmetric dimensions of power exercised by the PRC state apparatus (Ochab, 2020).

During a New York University MA Program in International Relations Virtual Open House, including Dr. Shinasi Rama, chief of Mission Robert Dry, Dr. Colette Mazzucelli, and Dr. Patty Chang, our discussion involved reference by Dr. Chang to the ways in which sexual violence in conflict is a horizontal issue that cuts across the vertical agenda of China–US relations in the context of her work at the United Nations. This observation came after Dr. Mazzucelli's initial comments regarding the importance of gender concerns on the international agenda. It is no coincidence that in an initial journal publication grounding this research, a Special Issue of *Genocide Studies and Prevention* conceived by Nathaniel Raymond and Colette Mazzucelli, their colleagues, Karen Naimer, Widney Brown, and Ranit Mishori, discuss the design, development, and deployment of MediCapt, a mobile app to document forensic evidence of sexual violence in conflict, using the Democratic Republic of the Congo as a case study (Naimer et al. in Mazzucelli and Visvizi, 2017).

In this volume, the chapter by Lea and D'Silva focuses on Safecity.in, which has devised an innovative solution to shed light on a persistent problem: the sexual harassment and assault of individuals—mostly, although not entirely, women—in public places. The chapter authored by Adams explores in a groundbreaking manner the question of how to create informed consent within an app that collects social data. The relevance of her analysis to the design of the mobile app for Safecity.in is noteworthy in terms of the ethics of personal data collection, particularly as its use evolves from crowdsourcing testimonies of women and men who have been abused in public spaces, as well as the legal changes taking place in India resulting from social protests on behalf of women's rights, to its implementation in the time of COVID-19, thereby illuminating the mounting cases of domestic violence in South Asia and in countries around the world.

Questions to Raise in the Literature

There are three questions that orient the analysis in this volume, which the respective case studies address. Our first question is, how do various actors, in what has been termed "global international society" (GIS) 1.2 by Acharya and Buzan, lay the foundation to expand on the Web methodology Slaughter (2018) introduces? In this context, GIS 1.2 means states, networks, and societies analyzed from 2008 onward given the changes taking place in the core and the periphery since the global financial crisis.

In Acharya and Buzan, the post-Western lens describes GIS 1.2 as the transition between Western-dominated, core–periphery structures and a post-Western transition/crisis period. In this period, "core" and "periphery" nations' interactions reflect changing power dynamics where new patterns emerge in the international relations space. Concerning privacy, their explanation might suggest that peripheral states' choice not to adopt Western privacy models is either a rejection of Western norms or the nation's relative global position (economy and power), which protects its decision to establish its own standard. However, core nations continue to lead in designing models. In 2018, the EU's Global Data Privacy Regulation (GDPR) represented the most recent agreement governing transborder data privacy protection; however, this protection only covers EU member states even though data regularly travels between and among all nations. Though nation-states have reasons to secure transborder protection agreements, they seem destined to deal with unregulated data traffic without the force of existing national agreements. These countries must alternatively contend with regulating organizations and companies that conduct business within their borders. Traditional, Western-dominant, international relations theory is likely to explain a nation-state's inability to establish privacy regulation as a failure to negotiate with a more powerful opponent. This volume asks the reader to reflect as well on different theoretical explanations reasoning from the local perspective on the periphery "at the edge of international relations" (Darby, 1997).

The post-Western perspective of Acharya and Buzan includes the contributions myriad societies, cultures, and values make, thereby reflecting the nation-state's accumulation of power, wealth, and influence in all sectors. Their analysis captures identities, networks, and influences contributing to a comprehensive international relations story. Their review explains the consequences of varying nation-state behavior and uncovers interdependent influences between states and peoples. Even if nationalism still explains much of nation-states' self-interested, power-based behavior (Basrur and Kliem, 2021), Acharya and Buzan's new foci represent a novel understanding of regional and peripheral nation-states and emerging nonstate influences on the global landscape. Their perspective outlines a global capitalistic environment, set in different ideological settings under the backdrop of rising migration, population density, recaptured cultural identities, and shared-fate global concerns.

They assert that the most critical influence is the unending, rapid technological advancement of the Internet established by private data platforms and data scientists. Some civil nonstate actors are powerful enough to make agreements with nation-states, while uncivil nonstate actors have attacked weaker nations. Lightly regulated social media platforms have enabled groups and individuals to influence the national and international narrative about critical issues, leaving only nonstate actors to regulate who speaks.

Issues such as reduced post-Western dominance, the inclusion of other nations' international relations perspectives, and the emergence of nonstate actors are significant factors in laying the foundation for a new understanding of nation-state interactions. This edited volume underlines that Anne Marie Slaughter's *The Chessboard & the Web* (2017) fills the void. Slaughter analyzes the "Web" that exists alongside the "Chessboard" (nation-states), thereby highlighting the interaction between these "factors" and examining how networks contribute to as well as impact national strategies that address global issues. Slaughter's perspective recognizes webs of connected networks, which are not bound by nation or border. She explains that networked power is "power with," not power over, thus suggesting that networks' interactivity make them viable and provides insight into how they exert power.

Slaughter's framework also differentiates organically grown networks based on shared interests from ones that can purposefully be designed to tackle global, shared-fate issues. Her description of resilience, tasks, scale, and innovation networks suggests ways that global networks can address, for example, environmental stewardship issues, while Chessboards keep focus on nationalistic interests. Her framework can explain the work of uncivil networks to help account for the unrest that does not necessarily rise to the level of nation-state incitement yet may require a nation-state response. Her "Both/And" strategy allows the Chessboard and the Web to develop different options to address similar issues.

The Chessboard/Web dichotomy also provides a better way to understand the complexities of addressing global data ethics. Linking the network influences of data scientists, technology developers, data platforms, cultural preferences, and business interests to network affiliations may reveal networks' strengths and cross-network dependencies. Most importantly, Slaughter's framework acknowledges nongovernmental organizations' work addressing issues like the pandemic while explaining how these same organizations gain or lose legitimacy based on their network's viability. Concerning privacy, the framework can help explain the origins and structure surrounding data platforms' ecosystem and provides insight into networks that develop power as nonstate actors. Her strategy can highlight how different nations balance the competing interests of innovation and privacy in response to different interest groups' relative influence. Network behavior can provide insight into whether new Internet decentralization strategies, thought to increase privacy protection, will be adopted by Chessboards or whether these strategies will succumb to interest-based network power.

This volume underlines *the critical role of the Chessboard*. Slaughter's strategies do not underestimate the critical need for Chessboards to understand and influence network strategies and guidelines, especially related to data privacy. Governments still have a critical role in influencing the ethicality of even a decentralized, distributed network by ensuring it is "open, inclusive, ethical and transparent" (Poblet, 2018). Slaughter's perspective explains that some solutions will be driven by networks, some by influential groups, some through international pressure on Chessboards. Slaughter's grand strategy suggests creating open order building methods that link society, government, and international systems versus attempting to maintain "hard" gatekeeping. Governments should practice sovereignty as a responsibility and not control.

Each of the chapters in Part I of this edited volume speaks to the concerns raised by Slaughter in her insightful and timely analysis. The comparative study in Chapter 1 focuses our attention on the risks to human rights of the rapid evolution of technology's reach in the PRC and the United States. The spread of "fake news," as explained in Chapter 2, makes us aware of the dangers that populism can pose in the EU despite the legal precedent set by the GDPR. Chapter 3 reaches deep inside the Iranian context to grapple with the harm to society that can be the result of arbitrary uses of technologies by the state to track individuals in a COVID-19 environment.

The second question asks how the relevance of personal data is changing our understanding of GIS 1.2, which Acharya and Buzan identify as a shift that gets underway during the first decade of the twenty-first century (p. 219), through the introduction of additional levels of analysis and a new ism in the discipline of international relations. Our digital lives are not separate from our lives. This truth ensures that the GIS continues to expand as more individuals are identifiable as participants in our society. As we allow or are forced to allow external entities (individuals and institutions) to identify our individuality and distribute information about our identities, they will influence the makeup of our communities' evolution.

The current neorealist state assumes that we live in a static system of zero-sum politics where whatever is gained by one is lost by the other. Yet, the real physical world is far more dynamic than that presumed realism or our forefather's political reality. Inclusionism is rooted in the thermodynamic phenomenon of entropy. This is the truth that randomness or the degree of disorder will always expand in a system over time. As a concept introduced in the international relations literature in this edited volume, inclusionism asserts that individuals are at their best when they identify with a community; likewise, communities are only at their best when they identify all their individuals.

The seemingly never-ending quest to appropriate the disorderly is our political and business community's causality. In that regard, the method with which we identify our system's growth is via the identification of our most micro-representations of self. Perhaps micro or even nano is an inadequately large term for us as humanity. As we endeavor to place a data point on the very particles of our existence or the overall sum of our community of particles, we will identify the meta definition of our personhood.

Personal data is metadata that derives from living and nonliving individuals. It can be identified as information originating from an individual transacting with other individuals or institutions. This is true regardless of the possession or primary control of the information. All data is a derivative of personal data.

Contrary to how popular media might engage personal data as a privacy issue or a derivative of the ideological movement of individualism, our data is not a function of our complete independence from our communities: rather, our data is our ticket into those communities. Consider that one's mother's name is required in the United States for a child's certificate of live birth and a birth certificate; the mother's name is that child's personal data. Still, it is also the mother's name and, as a result, her personal data. In this Information Age, the evidence of our lives is required to be affirmed by those who were identifiable before us to certify our existence. It is also a measure to tie our individual being to our communities' being.

As we expand our lens from our micro identities to the macro identity of ecosystems, we should consider the evolution of human rights post-Second World War through the COVID-19 pandemic to ask ourselves: what rights are our communities owed? A necessary evolution to neorealism's advocacy for the structure of individuals as bureaucracies is the need to derive structure from the agency of individuals: that is inclusionism. To be plain, individuals lead, not the system. For instance, the debate on whether to wear a mask or not is one to be considered by global leaders inclined to incentivize or even demand the rights of the many nodes of the community over the individual's human rights. In the same line of thought, just leaders would empower freedoms of speech while not allowing a cry of fire in an enclosed public space to go without criminal consequences. Global leaders must answer the question if citizens have the right to experience a community wearing masks during a pandemic or not. In the COVID-19 context, we witnessed regions with more homogeneous cultural participants stifling the spread of the novel coronavirus while the most diverse regions of the planet argue over agency to decide how they participate in the mutual work of protecting the community. It is not an exaggeration to note that the diverse pockets of humanity fail to see all their neighbors as the same community.

This is not new. States that have a history of honoring human rights more than others have already endeavored to start "hacking digital ethics" (Belliger and Krieger, 2021) by distributing their digital human rights outside of their borders. Europe's General Data Protection Regulation (GDPR) is many things: the GDPR is also a deliberate effort to distribute rights via each one of Europe's citizens' travels. In this capacity, Europeans' personal data is being instrumentalized as it is a part of the makeup of many systems across the globe. This granular level of analysis is an opportunity to understand how an expanding society exists instead of the ways in which we would like society to exist as, per our legacy, the static system posited by neorealism. Acknowledgment of people by the data points transforms our thinking away from the images of nature, state, and system (Waltz, 1959).

The realities of a new millennium prompt this volume to question Waltz from the vantage point of what presently occurs in our postpandemic world. The end of the twentieth-century bridge to the early twenty-first century is in the changed nature of conflict—primarily from interstate to largely intrastate. A new ism is required that speaks to this revolution in globalization, which cuts into the hierarchical pyramid of power that defined the short twentieth century. This volume questions the nature of society as civil and global, particularly as the COVID-19 pandemic renders the majority increasingly marginalized and the chaos in most of the developing world is undesigned—despite human nature, which has the aspiration and motivation to design. Just as the international system continues to expand with more states than ever in the United Nations, Waltz's structural realism incessantly calls for the interstate system to contract. Neorealism in the twenty-first century focuses narrowly, exclusively on the PRC and the United States at the apex of the pyramid; yet, Russia is ever-present, notably in Syria, Ukraine, as well as spaces in its sphere of influence in Central Asia where the Great Game is still played. The impact of the COVID-19 pandemic calls for the distribution of more agency as democracy, experienced with a small "d," calls for the evolution of humanity. Contrary to the realist assertion, the evolution of humankind occurs through increasing agency in a world that is not dominated by the static nature of structure. In a postpandemic environment, there is recognition that older structures are stuck in space and time. Placemaking underlines the urgent calls by humanity in all corners of the globe to experience a sense of belonging despite borders that deny their inclusion in societies characterized by the "fear of small numbers" (Appadurai, 2006). These calls for agency to be nourished are the essence of "inclusionism," meaning that although structure continues to be relevant, its presence should not inhibit the expansion of agency, thereby anchoring exclusionary nationalism as the dominant experience of "the Other" (Kapuściński, 2008) in the twenty-first century.

The chapters in Part II of this edited volume contrast the response to COVID-19 by Taiwan, which Lee asserts delineates its democratic identity in contradistinction to that of the PRC, with the misuses of technologies by the tightly centralized CCP to heighten the surveillance of the Uyghurs in Xinjiang. The attempts by the citizens of Taiwan to expand their agency in the face of the rigidity of the power structure in the PRC is intricately interwoven with the uses and abuses of technologies and personal data in a pandemic-driven environment.

The third question this volume raises is, how do we expand the definition of inclusionism, introduced in the public discourse by James Felton Keith a decade ago and referenced in terms of GIS 1.2 by Mazzucelli in this volume, as the newest lens after environmental stewardship? Inclusionism is a new international relations paradigm, which recognizes what realism, in all its variants, denies: the lack of capacity in present structures to respond proactively to the challenges of this present time. Moreover, the inherent deficiencies of solutions that build on such inadequate structures can only lead to greater inequalities. In contradistinction, there are the kinetic, constitutive, and interactive relationships between human beings identified via personal data, which define a more integral type of agency to complement the innate relevance and responsibility of people, not only states, in the spread and, likewise, the mitigation, of the COVID-19 pandemic worldwide. Likewise, billions in our world increasingly confront the transnational nature of social protest, triggered, although less driven, by isolated experiences, that is, the murder of George Floyd, and animated more by the structural inequalities, the missed opportunities, and the systematic discrimination against the majority of the world's peoples by the market-driven, "instrumentarian power" (Zuboff, 2019) of a technologically determined minority elite.

Inclusionism is a code of equity that derives from the notion that value is like that of energy: it cannot be created or destroyed; it can change form. This is driven by the physiological truth of the First Law of Thermodynamics: energy can be changed from one form to another and yet, it cannot be destroyed. Throughout the modern era, this truth has compelled the scientific field of engineering to study the movement of matter and the friction that matter creates to witness energy proliferate. Humanity has engaged this from a mechanical, electrical, and chemical standpoint and continues to do so. Per value, it is like energy in that the movement of data and the transactions that data creates bear witness to a proliferation of value.

Matter	Friction	Energy
Data	Interaction	Value

In the context of economics and our interconnected society, which Acharya and Buzan identify as a shift that gets underway during the first decade of the twenty-first century (p. 219), it is high time that economists start to evaluate the proliferation of value in the way that engineers would energy. Our objective is to create real markets with participating entities empowered by their agency in the network society (Castells, 1996) through which a seemingly spiritual contract proliferates from our physical reality.

Inclusionism is the notion that:

1. People have an intrinsic value.
2. People only derive that value from interactions with each other.
3. People are owed some equity in the proliferation of value from those interactions.

The first notion is based on the idea that value exists as a real and tangible thing in the same vein as energy.

The second notion is based on the moments we exist in physical spaces with participants who possess their own agency. There is an immediate friction that we generate in reaction and relation to those participants. In that moment, we witness the proliferation of energy (or value). If we existed in an empty white space, we would have nothing to react to and that lack of movement of matter would render no energy and, therefore, no value. Such a place is impossible to create except in one's imagination.

The third notion is where we engage our interpersonal or even international relations ("ir," as defined by Acharya and Buzan) and consider how to distribute both agency and the subsequent equity to the participants who generate friction. Regardless of the percentage split in equity for our participation, it must be acknowledged that we, the people, per our interactions, are the transactors of the most micro entity of matter (in the form of data) and, therefore, witness value.

The question must be asked: what are we owed? When considering our economic measure of friction, we encourage the reader to consider a staple, like gross domestic product (GDP), a measurement of transactions within an ecosystem. Each transaction can be reduced to a unit of data or even the most micro unit of identification, personal data. In an expanding ecosystem of interaction, inclusionists rely on participant identification to distribute agency. Agency is specific to an individual's will.

Since agency is our priority, our system is inherently dynamic and presents an evolution to all static systems of interaction, transactions, and relations. This is as true for realism versus constructivism in the discipline of International Relations ("IR," as defined by Acharya and Buzan) or Communism versus Fascism in politics or Marxism versus classism in capital distribution. By distributing agency and asking the previously mentioned systems *What are we owed?* we are compelled to engage the policy through which we distribute ownership. Real agency in the space of physics or economics must come with tangible consequences for influence. In the Information Age, our ability to leverage personal data is the connective tissue for our community; we are now incentivized to distribute tangible equity per our ownership stake in the inevitable and uncharted expansion of our system.

The parallel to physics is omni-important here. Although physics has existed in some form since the fourth century AD, it was not until the middle of the nineteenth century that thermochemistry evolved into thermodynamics. It happened when James Prescott Joule used the scientific method to quantify *Joules* as a unit of energy. Interestingly, Joule was born in 1818 along with Karl Marx. Joule outlived Marx by six years until 1889 designing a system of energy whereas Marx's goal was to design a system that eliminated the differences in classes between his proletariat (have-nots) and the *bourgeoisie* (haves). Marx, arguably the most influential political economy philosopher of modern times, could not have known enough about the way the world or universe or multiverse works to consider a socioeconomic system that is rooted enough in our reality, in other words, one where Joules is more valuable than jewels in distributing ownership of productivity. Regarding the actual or perceived social injustices of exclusion, it is necessary to design a system where the incentives dilute the very real cultural gaps of inequality by creating a hack to the egalitarian ideal of equality. The academy in its relation to society persists in using the mythology of Marxism as the way to solve the problem of distributing agency in community. In the reality of his lifetime, Marx was not in a position to address distribution in a granular way. The objective here is to distribute equity through agency rather than constantly engaging the abstract notion of equality.

Inclusionism is not a nod to utopian egalitarianism just as it is not a nod to *laissez-faire* economics. As inclusionists, we are more curious about how to incentivize justice than with justice itself. If we make sure a person has a seat at the table, other participants seated there are incentivized adequately to ensure more of the risks derived from desperation on the part of those excluded from participation. Agency without ownership is empty. In the twenty-first century, our capability to distribute micro-ownership stakes is the ability to eliminate the systemic exclusion to which humanity bore witness during centuries past.

Inclusionism, in Part III, considers a new distribution of agency. Chapter 7 is a linchpin with its focus on gender and race in the story of Safecity in India, capturing stories of domestic violence against women as well as their harassment in public spaces during the pandemic. Crowd-mapped testimonies pioneered by the Safecity app are illuminated by Chapter 6's focus on the privacy-driven crisis of data misappropriation. Similarly, Chapter 8 charters the evolution of group voices challenging the military structure at the heart of the state (Aron, 2003) by addressing sexual violence among its ranks. Inclusionism expands group dialogue in the data space between government and society to explore the climate change and global pandemic nexus, thereby speaking to the deficiencies of liberalism with its emphasis on the individual.

Overview of Chapters

The thread running through the chapters highlights the inadequacy of current international relations models to account for the practical effects of information technology innovation, especially in situations where domestic and international strategies overlap. The chapters in this edited volume reflect the non-Western frame of inquiry with its use of constructivist emphasis on culture and identity, advanced by Acharya and Buzan, as well as their GIS 1.2 model of pluralism in which no one nation-state dominates, and the wider diffusion of wealth, power, and cultural authority exists. The chapters that follow also support Slaughter's (2018) recognition of simultaneous chessboard (nation-state) and web-networked activities, thereby illustrating how current global information technology requires nation-states formally to integrate domestic and international strategies to address emerging information technology interdependence. As a collection of chapters and yet specific in the local focus explored by each case, the volume's content urges a formal acknowledgment of nonstate actors' roles, social media influences, and "networked" solutions alongside legally supported chessboard strategies.

In Chapter 1, Brevard's comparison of China and the United States' individual rights policies regarding surveillance suggests that the effects gap between democratic and autocratic regimes has practically diminished. She notes that China's surveillance activities are incorporated into its legal structure and billed to achieve a successful trust between citizens. However, the United States' legal mandates have not kept pace with surveillance innovation and fail to reconcile the tension between the state's interest in providing security and the individual's interest in the protection of privacy. Each nation's legitimate interest in security is handled via chessboard mandates and shows, for the United States, that a lack of chessboard action results in reducing the impact of democracy-related privacy protection. The implications for inclusionism must be drawn looking ahead in the twenty-first century.

In Chapter 2, Ehmke's research on the emergence of "fake news" discusses both fabrications and misinformation tactics used during the COVID-19 pandemic. She explores the extent to which the legal and practical methods to regulate fake news highlight the difficulty of using prior chessboard "journalistic" and regulatory schemes to address network-based (social media) issues of influence. Here, the European Court of Human Rights' (ECtHR) Article 10 ECHR chessboard structure seems to lack the tools to incorporate new, networked-based influences. This volume asks the reader to consider the implications of this evolution for inclusionism in the early decades of the twenty-first century.

In Chapter 3, Cameron's research on Iran's government response to the pandemic creates knowledge about the intersection of many Iranian peoples' issues, including resource mismanagement and the government's international strategies. Her chapter notes that Iran's slow response to close its borders was motivated by a need to maintain relationships with China, as the country struggles under the weight of US sanctions. Personal data collection to track COVID-19 transmission required personal data use under circumstances that caused further burdens on citizens. These "chessboard-related" decisions, both those from the Iran government and the international community, harmed its citizens' health and safety. Even the government's attempts to quash negative social media reports seem to reflect a miscalculation of social media's network-based resilience. This chapter's analysis serves to prompt further research from the inside out to assess the relevance of inclusionism's tenets in the Iran case.

In Chapter 4, Lee's analysis of Taiwan's identity suggests that technology played a significant role in enhancing and enabling trust in the government response to the COVID-19 pandemic. In Taiwan, technology is embedded in culture and acts for and not against the chessboard. The nation's successful response to COVID-19 was in part due to its experience dealing with the SARS outbreak in 2003 and the subsequent building of "integrated technology, civic participation, and the vigilance of government and people." This chapter models Slaughter's framework description of the building of strategic domestic networks that address tasks, scale, and innovation issues. Even in the face of pressure from the Chinese government to limit Taiwan's international participation as a sovereign state, the Taipei government's domestic focus and semi-economic autonomy support its international community position. Given the asymmetric relationship between the PRC and Taiwan, this chapter represents a hard test case for inclusionism, which requires additional field research to explore.

In Chapter 5, Davis depicts Xinjiang's reeducation camps to make sense of the "genocide" of the Uyghurs. Her study notes that the Chinese Communist

Party's (CCP) handling of the conflict between itself and its autonomous regions is a "blended balance of foreign and domestic affairs," suggesting that chessboard and network strategies are integrated. Davis calls China an "enigmatic outsider" in the GIS 1.2 system because the country does not fit into the bipolar US–Russia scheme. However, this chapter notes that other "networks" of ethnic minority groups, such as the Tibetans living in similar conditions, could be the most significant actors in a constructivist analysis of a solution. The chapter also notes that since international organizations (IOs) and nongovernmental organizations (NGOs) are already spreading survivors' stories (using social media), their efforts may create a new opportunity for the NGOs to open space for the CCP to connect with the Uyghur people to end the genocide. This chapter reflects the inability of traditional nation-state categories to describe the role of myriad actors and networks influencing the Uyghurs situation in Xinjiang, supporting the need to blend domestic and international strategies. The relevance of inclusionism in this case begs to be explored in future research given the resonance of this case on the GIS 1.2 agenda, especially given the considerable limitations placed on Responsibility to Protect (R2P) in such contexts.

In Chapter 6, Adams' consideration of the data privacy regulatory framework for smartphones outlines the unevenness in US regulations with other countries, especially regarding the ways in which the EU has dealt with data privacy domestically, between, and among nation-states. Her study points out how the volume and type of data generated by smartphone devices impact privacy protection in the current compliance-based regulatory environment even though data scientists supported that environment by creating new privacy-protective designs. Using Slaughter's Chessboard & Web analysis, notably its definitions of node types in networks, Adams highlights the impact on privacy based on the current role and influence of data platforms mentioned by Slaughter, including the kind of "Supernode" network. Adams subsequently reviews the development of COVID-19 tracking apps to show the ways in which these same data platforms act like a nation-state, thereby influencing privacy protection well beyond their defined role. Moreover, her chapter illustrates how the proliferation of the design and evolution of smartphones, especially through apps, increases global agency in line with the notion of self-sovereign identity. Finally, Adams discusses how future privacy concerns may be addressed through non-platform-centric solutions that are capable of sustaining agency and engaging users to share privacy protection. Her analysis concludes by agreeing with Slaughter that traditional chessboard and network strategies, even in a decentralized environment, require chessboards to acknowledge network roles in their international strategy while strictly regulating future solutions. Adams' chapter resonates with the definition of inclusionism in this volume as its analysis urges further consideration of the lack of capacity in present structures to respond proactively to the data privacy challenges of the present time.

In Chapter 7, the analysis by Lea and D'Silva supports different networked approaches that exist in spaces where needs are not addressed by "chessboards." This is because certain group protections, though acknowledged as necessary, cannot thrive within existing networks. They propose using data-enabled dialogue that is collected to help "describe" the parameters of a problem and, according to Slaughter, decentralizes and democratizes the information. An ecosystem representing community networks is showcased that many other networks can support, like law enforcement, yet do not prioritize. Using the Safecity app to crowd-map sexual assault incidents uncovers place-based infrastructure and community-related safety issues. The crux of the networking process within the ecosystem is integrating ways to increase dialogue around sensitive issues. This case study provides examples of how the development and guarding of data within an ecosystem support its ability to influence "chessboard" structures to engage in how information is studied. The implications for inclusionism in the country whose billion plus population is most vulnerable to the COVID-19 pandemic in 2021 require further research as the context of sexual assault as well as domestic violence incidents rapidly evolves.

In Chapter 8, Garcia and Riley's review of the US Air Force Academy's efforts to eradicate sexual assault incidents provide insight into how closed ecosystems can use internal "chessboard" support and innovative data-gathering strategies to support in-group victims. Military academies are akin to college campuses; yet the chessboard hierarchy requires additional alignment. Garcia and Riley note that chessboard and group strategies do not always align. The need carefully to balance programming with the need to protect individual privacy is the greatest concern. Even though the Department of Defense (DOD) seeks to support increased reporting by victims of sexual assault, many cadets do not believe that their privacy can be protected. Moreover, the reporting and investigation systems include steps where consent to investigation might impact anonymity and leaked information would result in social ostracism. The EEA professorial team developed a Health Insurance Portability Accountability Act (HIPAA)-compliant survey instrument to ensure cadet privacy during the team's intervention and carved out an ecosystem that supported individual cadet's trust. The impressive results suggest that even internal "task" networks designed for a specific purpose can succeed where chessboard regulatory methods may not. These initial results form the basis for ongoing research that assesses the relevance of inclusionism within a relatively closed ecosystem in which the protection of data privacy is as much a community as an individual cadet concern.

References

Acharya, A., and Buzan, B. (2019) *The Making of Global International Relations: Origins and Evolution of IR at Its Centenary*. Cambridge: Cambridge University Press.

Appadurai, A. (2006) *Fear of Small Numbers: An Essay on the Geography of Anger*. Durham, NC: Duke University Press.

Aron, R. (2003) *Peace & War: A Theory of International Relations*. New York: Routledge.

Basrur, R., and Kliem, F. (2021) Covid-19 and international cooperation: IR paradigms at odds. *SN Social Sciences*, 1(1), pp. 1–10.

Belliger, A., and Krieger, D. (2021) *Hacking Digital Ethics*. London: Anthem Press.

Castells, M. (1996) *The Rise of the Network Society, the Information Age: Economy, Society and Culture Vol. I*. Cambridge, MA: Blackwell.

Darby, P., ed. (1997) *At the Edge of International Relations*. London: Continuum.

Ersoy, E. (2018). Conceptual cultivation and homegrown theorizing: The case of/for the concept of influence. *All Azimuth: A Journal of Foreign Policy and Peace*, 7(2), pp. 47–64.

Ho, M. (2018) "The Activist Legacy of Taiwan's Sunflower Movement," *Carnegie Endowment for International Peace*. Available at https://carnegieendowment.org/2018/08/02/activist-legacy-of-taiwan-s-sunflower-movement-pub-76966 (accessed April 26, 2021).

Hoffmann, S. (1960) *Contemporary Theory in International Relations*. Englewood Cliffs, NJ: Prentice Hall.

Kapuściński, R. (2008) *The Other*. London: Verso.

Lieber, R. J. (2000) *No Common Power*. London: Pearson Education.

Mazzucelli, C. (2020) *Inclusionism Exploring Levels of Analysis in Global Affairs*. Monroe Township, NJ, https://storymaps.arcgis.com/stories/39cea59687b6476a87d100f9e9a68d2e (accessed December 11, 2020).

Naimer, K., Brown, W., and Mishori, R. (2017) "MediCapt in the Democratic Republic of the Congo: The Design, Development, and Deployment of Mobile Technology to Document Forensic Evidence of Sexual Violence," in C. Mazzucelli and A. Visvizi (eds.), "Information and Communications Technologies in Mass Atrocities Research and Response," *Genocide Studies and Prevention*, vol. 11, no. 1, pp. 25–35.

Ochab, E. (2020) "The Fate of Uighur Muslims in China: From Re-education Camps to Forced Labor," *Forbes*. Available at https://www.forbes.com/sites/ewelinaochab/2020/04/04/the-fate-of-uighur-muslims-in-china-from-re-education-camps-to-forced-labor/?sh=64684ae32f73 (accessed May 25, 2021).

Paolini, A. (1997) "Globalization," in P. Darby (ed.), *At the Edge of International Relations*. London: Continuum, pp. 33–60.

Poblet, M. (2018) Distributed, privacy enhancing technologies in the 2017 Catlan referendum on independence: New tactics and models of participatory democracy. *First Monday*, 23(12). Retrieved on October 19, 2020. https://doi.org/10.5210/fm.v23i12.9402.

Preidt, R. (2021) "Climate Change May Have Helped COVID-19 Emerge," WebMD. Available at https://www.webmd.com/lung/news/20210205/climate-change-may-have-helped-covid19-emerge (accessed May 1, 2021).

Slaughter, A. M. (2018) *The Chessboard and the Web: Strategies of Connection in a Networked World*. New Haven, CT: Yale University Press.

Waltz, K. (1959) *Man, the State, and War*. New York: Columbia University Press.

Zakaria, F. (2009) *The Post-American World and the Rise of the Rest*. New York: Penguin Books.

Zuboff, S. (2019) *The Age of Surveillance Capitalism: The Fight for a Human Future at the New Frontier of Power*. New York: Public Affairs.

Part I

Chapter 1

INFORMATION TECHNOLOGY: NATIONAL SECURITY SAVIOR OR CIVIL RIGHTS DISASTER

Celeste Brevard

Introduction: Information Technology—Tool for State Security or a Civil Rights Concern?

According to Freedom House, global Internet freedom is in its ninth year of decline as of 2019. The United States is in its third year of decline and it was determined China had the worst Internet freedom abuses in the world. This declaration is a direct contradiction of the space that Sir Tim Berners-Lee—the inventor of the World Wide Web—thought he had created. Along with other early web developers and users, Sir Berners-Lee's goal of decentralization according to the World Wide Web Foundation (2020) was to create "freedom from indiscriminate censorship and surveillance." However, this has been replaced with a trend "toward illiberalism, exposing citizens to an unprecedented crackdown on their fundamental freedoms" (History of the World Wide Web, 2020). When the Internet was created, it was exported with the fundamental ideals of democracy. It would be a space where people could collaborate, inform, and connect. However, as Julie E. Cohen has made clear in her book *Between Truth and Power: The Legal Constructions of Informational Capitalism* neoliberal forces have morphed this changing technology and the laws meant to regulate it to align "with the efficiencies that powerful interests have identified and the rationalizations they advance to frame particular kinds of change as desirable" (Cohen, 2019, p. 4). Could this shift be the result of the ideas laid out in "A Declaration of the Independence of Cyberspace" in which John Perry Barlow, a cyberlibertarian and philosopher, states, "Your legal concepts of property, expression, identity, movement, and context do not apply to us. They are all based on matter, and there is no matter here?" (ibid., p. 238). Was it the September 11 attacks and the "age of terror" that created this dichotomy as sociology professor and director of the Surveillance

Studies Center David Lyon states in *Surveillance after September 11* or is it the change in global competition and the shift from conventional warfare to cyberspace with the Internet posing a threat to "the right of a state to govern itself without external interference," as James Andrew Lewis (2018), director of the Technology and Public Policy Program at the Center for Strategic and International Studies, suggests? Regardless of the cause, this trend's supporters are in favor of increased state security due to the role international terrorism still plays in the world. Critics warn of global civil rights implications if these shifts are not closely monitored. Each of these arguments is constructed within the parameters of the regime in which the technology is being utilized. This section examines the relationship between state-sponsored surveillance and corporate surveillance and its impact on democracy by conducting a comparative analysis of this relationship in China and the United States. These countries were chosen as they are the leading developers and exporters of information technology.

To examine the increased use of these technologies by two different regimes, a descriptive qualitative comparative analysis on the use of this technology just prior to September 11 to the present day was conducted. This research examined the development and deployment of United States and Chinese surveillance technology while also investigating the efficacy of the security programs. Most of the evidence is qualitative due to differences in data collection and their complex nature. As much of this information is provided by states or state organizations, most sources are secondary. The analysis conducted from these sources was done with the understanding they are not immune to corporate and political biases of the organizations that collect and present the information. This study was done to encourage future research on the implication of the exportation and utilization of this technology regardless of regime type on civil rights and to encourage the adoption of laws and policies dedicated to the restoration of the balance of power between civilians and corporations.

Technology, Security, and the New Environments They Create

Between the state and private sectors, collection and utilization of data have many names. Those most often used will be defined for a deeper understanding of their similarities. Information Capitalism or "the alignment of capitalism as a mode of production with informationalism as a mode of development" (Cohen, 2019, pp. 5–6). Information Power:

> The ability to leverage information to shape the perceptions, attitudes, and other elements that drive desired behaviors and the course of events. This includes the

ability to use information to affect the observations, perceptions, decisions, and behaviors of relevant actors; ability to protect and ensure the observations, perceptions, decisions, and behaviors of the Joint Force; and the ability to acquire, process, distribute, and employ data (information). (Department of Defense, 2018, p. viii)

Surveillance Capitalism: "A new economic order that claims human experience as free raw material for hidden commercial practices of extraction, prediction, and sales" (Zuboff, 2019, p. 10). Lastly, the Information Environment: "The aggregate of individuals, organizations, and systems that collect, process, disseminate, or act on information" (Department of Defense, 2016, p. 2). However, as the use of this data has one goal—influence and control on cognition and societal behaviors—these terms will be used interchangeably throughout the text. The connection between user-generated data and power over society's actions should be front of mind when hearing these terms.

As this research attempts to determine the role of regime type in the use of this technology, differences between these regime types should be made clear. The difference between authoritarian and democratic regimes has historically depended on the participation of the populace in political decisions and the electing of officials as well as the freedoms of the people within the territory. According to Juan Linz, the definition of democracy means individuals have

> legal freedom to formulate and advocate political alternatives with the concomitant rights to free association, free speech, and other basic freedoms of person; free and nonviolent competition among leaders with periodic validation of their claim to rule; inclusion of all effective political offices in the democratic process; and provision for the participation of all members of the political community, whatever their political preference. (Linz, 1978, p. 5)

While this definition of a democratic regime applies to this research, it needs to be noted that "free speech," "free association," and "other basic freedoms of person" are being interpreted as having a certain amount of privacy, self-determination, and cognitive liberty associated with them. As far back as the 1970s, a subcommittee on Constitutional Rights had been formed after the CIA began to focus on behavioral-modification research. This research was dedicated to understanding the "Chinese brainwashing techniques, reinterpreting them through the established frameworks of behavior modification" (Zuboff, 2019, p. 323). The research concluded, "'human material was changeable'—that one's personality, identity, awareness, and capacity for self-determining behavior could be crushed, eliminated, and replaced by external control" (ibid., p. 321). Senator Ervin stated in the subcommittee's 1974 report,

> When the founding fathers established our constitutional system of government, they based it on their fundamental belief in the sanctity of the individual [...] They understood that self-determination is the source of individuality, and individuality is the mainstay of freedom [...] Recently, however, technology has begun to develop new methods of behavior control capable of altering not just an individual's actions but his very personality and manner of thinking [...] [this] touches upon the most basic sources of individuality and the very core of personal freedom. (ibid., p. 324)

Privacy will be defined as it relates to the Fourth Amendment to the US Constitution. This amendment declares "The *right* of the people to be secure in their persons, houses, papers, and effects, against unreasonable searches and seizures, shall not be violated, and no warrants shall issue, but upon probable cause, supported by oath or affirmation, and particularly describing the place to be searched, and the persons or things to be seized" (U.S. Const. Art. 4). Barry Friedman and Orin Kerr, professors of law at NYU and George Washington University, respectively, in their "common interpretation" of this amendment admit that the technologies discussed above have made the interpretation of this amendment more complex and vital to the conversation of what constitutes a "search" and whether "cause" is even considered. In their collective analysis they ask whether the information given to Internet providers or other third parties if used by the government constitutes a "search." In terms of cause, they give the example of being searched at the airport. No one has been accused of doing something wrong and yet everyone knows upon entering they will be searched. They liken this to the collection of bulk data and potentially the use of biometric information gathered through surveillance technology (Freidman and Kerr 2020). They do not—in this interpretation—state whether any of these new questions presented by technology have answers concerning this amendment. Thus, the newly passed California Consumer Privacy Act (CCPA) or "AB 375" enforced as of January 1, 2020, and Europe's GDPR will act as the litmus test to what democracies feel constitutes the right to privacy in terms of data. As Heward-Mills and Turku (2020, p. 319) state in the Hastings International Comparative Law Review, "The right to privacy is a fundamental human right enshrined in the Universal Declaration of Human Rights, The European Convention on Human Rights, and the European Charter of Fundamental Rights." Therefore, these new legislative acts extend these to data protection in the following ways: "(1) limits on the collection of personal data; (2) transparency in collection and processing; (3) substantive rights for individuals subject to data collection; and (4) enforcement and accountability" (ibid., p. 321). Categories that align with the definition of democracy put forth by Juan Linz.

How to determine whether a democracy is under siege is a complicated subject that many books published after the US 2016 presidential election have been brave enough to undertake. While the goal of this analysis is not to determine whether the entire institution of democracy is at stake in the United States, defining how this technology is being used compared to China's authoritarian regime is an allusion to the threat the system is facing because of these newfound technologies and the means through which they are being deployed. Shoshana Zuboff illustrates in her book the relationship between social trust and civic engagement. She states, "In its absence the authority of shared values and mutual obligations slips away [...] Confusion uncertainty, and distrust enable power to fill the social void"(Zuboff, 2019, p. 383). She states that surveillance capitalism and the instrumentarian power of corporations fill the void (ibid.). I would add that the Department of Defense's focus on what they define as the "information environment" and "information power" and the efforts of the Chinese government to create a "Social Credit" system show that the state is also seeking to take advantage of this uncertainty without the publics' consent. They must, however, rely on these technologies to do so. As a prediction of this trend, Zuboff shows the percentage of Americans who said they had trust in the government "most or all the time" (ibid.). In 1985 this number was at 75 percent, in 2017 it was at 18 percent (ibid.). This analysis uses the inability of well-educated lawyers like Barry Friedman and Orin Kerr to determine whether the Fourth Amendment holds merit in the technological realm and the work of Juan Lintz, Steven Levitsky, and Daniel Ziblatt on what elements threaten a democracy to determine whether this technology is being used in a way the definition of democracy would denote. A modified version of the metrics created by Levitsky and Ziblatt (2018, pp. 21–22) based on Juan Lintz's work is applied to conduct this analysis. These will be applied to the government and corporations in the United States and China. They are as follows:

1. The rejection "in words or action" of democratic norms
2. The denial of the legitimacy of alternative choices
3. "Tolerates or encourages violence"
4. "Indicates a willingness to curtail the civil liberties of opponents including media"

The similarities and differences of the United States to China in these categories are the basis for the conclusion to the following hypothesis:

Hypothesis: While the type of political rule created vastly different types of information technology when the Internet was first created, the pressure international terrorism put on state security concerns and the use of surveillance capitalism by corporations have been compounded by the lack of transparency in their use. The result is that the gap between information technology in authoritarian and democratic governments has diminished over time.

One last concept must be clarified before this hypothesis can be fully examined, namely, that of an autocracy. An autocracy is typically defined as a system of government by one person with complete power and usually has either a dictator or monarchic figure in control. According to a study produced by the Center for European Studies at the University of Texas at Austin, China is classified as a one-party authoritarian regime where there is "generally an elected legislature where only one party is represented" (Wahman et al., 2013, pp. 19–34). While some have argued that China does not fall under the category of an authoritarian regime because of the popularity of the government, it is still commonly accepted that China is an authoritarian dictatorship, albeit a popular one. Due to this popularity, the type of autocracy this analysis uses for China is a "soft authoritarianism whereby collective well-being is more important than individual liberties and national development is more important than political rights" (Gueorguiev, 2019). Due to the nature of this regime, business practices and government in China are inextricably linked. Thus, while separate attention is paid to both corporations and the state in the case of the United States, China's situation is analyzed understanding that business and the government are not separated in the same way.

China's Increasing Surveillance and Its Impacts on the Marginalized

The implementation of the Belt and Road initiative has shifted the country's economic focus to technology and surveillance. This has resulted in these technologies increasing locally and internationally. China's thought process that cyberspace is a territory dominated by "Western" influence consumes the relationship between the government and technology. A piece in the *Global Times*, a state-run newspaper in China, "accused the United States of using the notion of an unrestricted Internet as a disguised imposition of its values on other cultures […] information imperialism" (Open Net Initiative, 2012). In China, large corporations work closely with the government to create "Safe Cities" and a "Social Credit System." While the reasons for these partnerships vary, massive amounts of personal data are being collected and used to establish a "rule of trust" instead of a "rule of law." These systems are targeted toward already marginalized populations. Furthermore, the technologies that are being created in China are being exported globally. Therefore, their proliferation could lead to a potential international human rights issue. This section looks at the connection of surveillance by the state and businesses in China to illustrate the consequences of a pervasive surveillance system on daily life when utilized by the government and corporations without regulation.

China's relationship with the "western" infrastructure under an authoritarian regime has meant that Internet content filtering is not a new tool for the government. This has often come under US scrutiny. Secretary of State Hillary Clinton in 2010 criticized the country for compromising the open flow of information. Some content is stopped at the router level, making it impossible for a computer's IP address from accessing information deemed inappropriate initially while also preventing that address from making similar requests for a certain amount of time. Other methods include blocking URL addresses and keywords from being visited or searched from within China (Chadwick and Howard, 2008, p. 324). Many identify this as the "Great Firewall of China." The *Global Times* supported these tactics by stating "countries disadvantaged by the unequal and undemocratic information flow have to protect their national interest and take steps toward this. This is essential for their political stability as well as normal conduct of economic and social life" (Open Net Initiative, 2012). The Chinese Foreign Ministry site also quoted Ma Zhou, a spokesperson for the government, who stated, "We urge the U.S. to respect facts and stop attacking China under the excuse of the so-called freedom of the Internet" (ibid.). While this statement is a clear indicator of the current Chinese government's views on the Internet, they have not always had as strict a position. In 1994 it was a portal to Western information and a tool for opening the economy. However, as its use increased in the country, it began to come under further restrictions, culminating in the establishment of the "Great Firewall" in 2000. This was combined with a project called the "Golden Shield" that worked with China's security forces to create a surveillance system driven by data. This system targeted citizen's records. The focus on China's "cyber sovereignty" has been further increased under President Xi Jinping. Now over 50,000 staff members of the government have been made responsible for this censorship. Companies that wish to access Chinese markets must respect the decision of the administration by creating backdoors into users' profiles as well as allowing the data gathered through products to be stored in China for easier access by the Chinese government (E. Chan, 2018). This censorship and surveillance have increased exponentially in provinces such as Xinjian where the Uyghur population is the most concentrated.

According to an article by the *Wall Street Journal*, "China's Central Asia frontier may be one of the most closely surveilled places on earth" (Chin et al., 2017). After the ethnic riots in 2009 in Erdaoqiao that resulted in several deaths, the mosque and religious shops were closed in the region. This was escalated by terrorist attacks in 2014 that China blames on militants in Xinjiang influenced by Islamic extremists abroad. These attacks, much like the terrorist attacks that took place on September 11, have resulted in increases in surveillance in the area and across the country. With improved technology and efforts toward enhancing systems put in place, a ubiquitous surveillance system has been created. ID cards must be swiped for routine transactions such as filling a car with gas or when going to the mall. Police now use handheld scanners to search the contents of smartphones for items like chat applications that use encryption. A plethora of cameras scan faces, retinas, and at times entire bodies. Cars are stopped when crossing regional borders. License plate cameras and location trackers placed in all commercial vehicles make spotting visitors easy. Chen Quanguo, the Xinjiang party chief appointed recently by Xi Jinping, has increased police presence and is responsible for the use of cameras capable of creating DNA sequencers, 3-D face images, and analyzing voice patterns. Companies such as China Telecom and Xiamen Meiya Pico Information have received contracts worth millions to increase surveillance in the region and improve the scanning devices used on smartphones (ibid.). The *Global Times* (2018) likens its use of surveillance technology in this region to "a similar trend […] in the US and Britain for the purpose of fighting terrorism." The piece claims, "About 95–98 percent of terrorist activities can be stifled in their nascent period" (ibid.). Operation "Xue Liang" or "Sharp Eyes" taken from the Communist phrase "the masses have sharp eyes" is not restricted to this region (Deneyer, 2018).

The anti-extradition bill protests in 2019 in Hong Kong show another minority targeted by these surveillance systems. Protests broke out as the Anti-Extradition Law Amendment Bill would have allowed local authorities to extradite fugitives that were wanted outside of Hong Kong. Citizens were afraid this legislation would hamper the region's independence and civil freedoms due to the ability to extradite citizens to mainland China (Caffrey, 2019). Hong Kong protesters faced digital surveillance from authorities. In Hong Kong protesters refused to use subway cards linked to their identities, and security cameras were either smashed or disrupted by laser pointers. Face masks were also worn to prevent detection (this took place before COVID-19). Protesters also stopped using credit cards or driving their cars to protests due to a fear of being recognized by license plate scanners (Ovide, 2020). The cooperation between Hong Kong police and mainland China as well as similar surveillance technology in both areas worried the protesters. This is not unwarranted as Hong Kong sends about 150 officials to China each year for training from police academies. However, it was still possible in Hong Kong for protesters to install VPNs on their devices and communicate through a secure messaging app called Telegram. Protesters were able to share information about how to avoid detection using pay-as-you-go sim cards and changing the number associated with the encrypted chat. Many warned against taking pictures during the protest so as not to be targeted on social media accounts (Mahtani, 2019). In a hearing conducted by the House of Representatives Subcommittee on Asia, the Pacific and Nonproliferation, in the United States, protesters were included with a representative from Human Rights Watch and a Uyghur who had been through the "re-education camps" in China (House of Representatives Subcommittee on Asia, the Pacific and Nonproliferation of the Committee on Foreign Affairs 2019). In the report, the House of Representatives spoke out against the "Orwellian Surveillance State" and the "digital authoritarianism" being used in China (ibid.). However, as is discussed in the following sections on the United States, the systems used to target these individuals are not vastly different than those being developed in the United States.

This technology is being used across China in various ways. Facial recognition is used to unlock resident apartments, by customers at bank ATMs, when users "beautify" themselves with phone applications, and at restaurants such as Kentucky Fried Chicken where a customer can purchase items through their "smile to pay" system (Deneyer, 2018). All of this is in an effort to create a "Social Credit System" and create a predictive crime system. China's system is said to be effective enough to scan the population of China in one second and the world's population in two. China had released information previously stating their goal was to have 570 million cameras in the country by this year. That would equate to one camera for every two citizens (T. Chan, 2018). The "Police Cloud," or Integrated Joint Operations Platform, also goes by the name "Sky Net." This system collects information such as whether someone's phone is off for an extended amount of time, if they use the backdoor or the front door, where people have been, who they have been associating with, delivery records, and medical histories. This information is shared across a number of platforms. It is aggregated with information pulled from government organizations, police data, and company data. This can include information from telecom companies, Internet blogs, and social media accounts. Some information is also purchased from third-party companies that give information such as search data on the Internet and purchases from e-commerce companies (Human Rights Watch, 2020). By using artificial intelligence, this program can also alert police to behaviors it deems as unusual, such as someone staying in a hotel they know to be a resident locally. It is also anticipated this system will be able to identify relationships authorities would not otherwise recognize. Specific groups are made priorities, such as those that have been involved with crimes, drugs, and those who have mental health issues or who "tend to cause disturbances" (ibid.). This system and its predictive capabilities are limited at the moment for several reasons. These include but are not limited to incomplete information, inconsistent information, and the skills of those meant to utilize the system. Once these are improved, however, the surveillance possibilities are endless as few laws require the police to obtain court orders to conduct this surveillance they deem necessary. Instead, these practices are being incorporated into China's legal system and are being used to create a "rule of trust."

In June 2017, The Intelligence Law was passed by the National People's Congress. This "makes explicit what has long been done in practice" (Canadian Security Intelligence, 2018). There are also State Security Laws and Cybersecurity Laws incorporated into the system that allows massive amounts of information to be collected and stored within the Chinese territory (Human Rights Watch, 2020). The social credit system is pushing the country away from the claims of "governing the country in accordance with the law" and forming instead a "rule of trust" whose definition is frequently changing and directly undermines the "rule of law" (Chen et al., 2018, pp. 3–6). The Chinese government's use of "trust" enables them to justify intrusive technologies like those described above and the discrimination against those deemed as "trust-breakers" such as those in the Xingjian province categorized as such because of their ethnic or religious connections to those the government deems troublesome. While the Chinese Social Credit System does not yet give the citizens a universal score, companies such as Ant Financials' Sesame Credit use cloud systems and machine learning to give users a score. As Broussard illustrates in her book, artificial intelligence and machine learning "doesn't mean the machine has a brain made out of metal. It means that the machine has become more accurate at performing a single, specific task according to a specific metric that a person has defined, this kind of learning does not imply intelligence" (Broussard, 2018, p. 99). Therefore, the parameters being used to make these determinations must also be put under scrutiny. The Chinese government is also using the system to further aggregate credit information collected across platforms into a "National Credit Information Sharing Platform" (Chen et al., 2018, pp. 12–17). This system includes departments designed to serve the people such as tax, police, civil affairs, environment treasury, finance, customs agencies, and so on totaling 37 ministries. This system is to distribute both rewards and sanctions to those the government decides are keeping the trust or breaking it, respectively (ibid., pp. 3–6). Those in the Xinjiang province are not the only ones being micro-targeted by such systems.

The uses of these technologies are permeating cities abroad as well. This can be seen in the creation of Huawei's "Safe City." Huawei, a Chinese company, is a major factor in this global adoption of technologies. It offers cheaper products that US companies like Apple and Google make with very similar capabilities. They also export goods such as cameras and monitors. China's Belt and Road Initiative has made this global exchange of goods a priority. Over 197 cooperation documents were signed with 137 countries and 30 international organizations in October 2019. The trade between January and September with these countries totaled approximately 950 billion US dollars and its "non-financial direct investment in these countries topped 10 billion dollars" (Xinhuanet, 2019). Huawei in its 2018 end-of-year report wrote, "Our cloud business needs to further develop its AI capabilities and hone its competitive edge in enterprise services. It needs to establish a stronger presence in e-government, automotive ICT components, and safe city domains, and maintain high-speed growth with healthy gross margins" (Huawei Investment & Holding Co. Ltd. 2019, p. 6). It describes a "Safe City" as using ICT technologies such as AI, cloud computing, the Internet of things, and big data. To understand the ubiquitous nature of this technology, Google's CEO until 2011 Eric Schmidt's description of the Internet of things is the most applicable. He stated, "The internet will disappear. There will be so many IP addresses [...] so many devices, sensors, things that you are wearing, things that you are interacting with that you won't even sense it. It will be a part of the presence all the time" (Zuboff, 2019, p. 199). The creation of this system enables bulk data interception through Information Communication Technology (ICT) and monitoring abilities through the Internet, wireless networks, cell phones, and computers. Huawei's report mentions having exported these technologies to over 700 cities in 100 countries. These regions include places like Brazil, Mexico, Serbia, South Africa, Turkey, Spain, and Singapore (ibid.). Other companies, such as Cloudwalk, are following closely behind with the *Global Times* reporting exportation of facial recognition to Zimbabwe in 2018 as part of the Belt and Road initiative (Jie, 2018). Therefore, China's use of surveillance technology is not only becoming ubiquitous in the region but is proving internationally relevant through its Belt and Road initiatives and focus on making technology a connecting factor between countries.

As the counterexample to the United States, it is clear that the parameters put in place to determine if democratic processes are being followed do not apply to China. There are no limits or transparency in the data collection process. The rights of individuals regarding the use of their data do not appear to be relevant. No alternative choices can be made as to how users' interactions with technology are monitored. A simple Internet search that is deemed inappropriate could gain an individual negative marks on their "social credit" score. Taking the backdoor instead of the front out of the house could result in being classified by authorities as someone to be watched by the predictive crime system. Minority groups are especially impacted. This takes place in the form of "re-education camps" and the classification of opponents to the government such as the Hong Kong protestors as subversives. These categorizations can hurt individuals' chances of getting a loan or leaving the country. Such labels could also result in direct violence due to the cultural tension between different ethnic groups.

The following section evaluates similar cases of surveillance in the United States. It focuses on the substantial shift that occurred in how surveillance was used from pre-9/11 to post-9/11. By using the same parameters of how data should be protected in a democracy and focusing on the metrics previously laid out, the section analyzes the use of this technology in the United States to determine if our democracy is strong enough with enough systems in place to prevent Orwellian tendencies to become a norm in America as they have in China.

State of Emergency and the New Normal-State Control

September 11 prompted an unprecedented crackdown on surveillance in the United States. The state felt it needed to pivot to protect its populace. Thus, the Patriot Act was passed a mere six weeks after the event on October 26, 2001. The legislation was over 300 pages in length and, therefore, was not read in its entirety by representatives. Therefore, it is unsurprising that this shift in legal framework had some unintended consequences. Trying to track decentralized terrorist organizations meant that the Fourth Amendment and civilian privacy concerns took a backseat to the collection of information (McAdams, 2005). The Patriot Act along with the Terrorist Screening Program not only led to the collection of information on foreigners in the United States, but these programs also increased the warrantless collection of personal information of the citizenry.

David Lyon describes the quick 180-degree shift from a consumer focus to security in his book *Surveillance after September 11th*. The Federal Trade Commission before the attacks had already realized that the self-regulation of technological companies was not going to be sufficient for protecting consumer rights. One year before the attacks, the majority of the FTC commissioners recommended a change to the laws that would regulate privacy. In a report, they concluded, "Because self-regulatory initiatives to date fall short of broad-based implementation of self-regulatory programs the Commission has concluded that such efforts alone cannot ensure that the online marketplace as a whole will follow the standards adopted by industry leaders" (Zuboff, 2019, p. 118). They called for "'clear and conspicuous' notice of information practices; consumer choice over how personal information is used; access to all personal information including rights to correct or delete; and enhanced security of personal information" (ibid.). This focus on protecting consumer rights faded after 9/11. Peter Swire, the chief counsel for privacy in the Clinton Administration and a member of the Review Group on Intelligence and Communication Technologies under Obama, said, "With the attacks of September 11, 2001 everything changed. The new focus was overwhelmingly on security rather than privacy" (ibid., pp. 118–19). Lyon also explains how the speed at which this act was passed left little room for debate. He attributes the emotion evoked from the nature of the attack to the lack of scrutiny of the bill by those passing it into law. Due to the lack of understanding by representatives of its complexities, it was unrealistic to expect the citizenry to realize its reach. Thus, he states, "Not only is a culture of suspicion emerging, but a culture of secrecy is also emerging alongside it" (Lyon, 2003, p. 52). As previously mentioned, this has become detrimental to civil participation due to a lack of trust in the government.

The nature of the information collected also made it difficult to uphold previous privacy promises. Emails and Call Detail Records (CDRs) were supposed to be collected and analyzed at an individual level only if something suspicious was deciphered (ibid.). In 2002, 440,606 terabytes of emails were collected (McAdams 2020)—a number that is impossible to justify as warranting inspection based on probable cause. Much like the airport analogy put forth by Barry Friedman and Orin Kerr when analyzing the Fourth Amendment, people were being searched without regard to probable cause. There are critics and supporters regarding Edward Snowden's leaks related to the collection of information in bulk. Regardless of public opinion of the messenger, the Second Circuit Court of Appeals ruled in May 2015 that the practices that Snowden exposed were not supported by the Patriot Act. Despite previous presidents such as Bush and Obama referencing Section 215 as justification for the collection of American phone calls en masse, the judges reviewing the case concluded, "Statues to which the government points have never been interpreted to authorize anything approaching the breadth of sweeping surveillance at issue here" (Friedersdorf, 2015). They also stated that many members of Congress and none of the public had an understanding of this program that leads to a lack of debate on a "momentous decision that [...] defies any limiting principle" (ibid.). While it is clear liberties were taken by the state in the aftermath of September 11 it was only through a leak from a contract employee at the NSA that the information being tracked was revealed, and able to be debated. Due to this development, imperfect but substantial attempts such as the USA Freedom Act, which was passed in 2015 to limit the collection of bulk data, were created (Franklin, 2019). This act did not do nearly as much as promised in terms of reestablishing civil liberties breached by the Patriot Act despite President Obama's reassurances. As late as June 2018 it was reported that the NSA admitted to "technical irregularities" that led to CDRs being collected they did not have the legal authority to obtain (ibid.). David Lyon and the Privacy and Civil Liberties Oversight Board argue that collecting data in this way is not an effective means to combat terrorism in any case. Section 215 of the Patriot Act and Section 702 of the Foreign Intelligence Surveillance Act were created to allow the international communication of citizens to be monitored as "foreign intelligence." However, they have only been associated with identifying one terrorist suspect (ibid.). Furthermore, David Lyon explains in his book that the amount of information the government had was never the issue. It was the nature of their analysis. He goes as far as to say, "The most vital terrorist communication may be missed (al-Qaeda groups use, but are not dependent on, the internet) the increased volume of data may simply slow the response by producing a glut. Targeted security [...] would deny opportunities for terrorist network activity without infringing on civil rights as present methods do" (Lyon, 2003, p. 121). Thus, this collection of data is considered overreaching by the judges on the Second Circuit Court of Appeals and ineffective by scholars. Snowden also faces legal backlash should he return to the United States despite these developments. Effective or not, the precedent that the Patriot Act created combined with the progress that has been made in surveillance and information technology collection means that the potential extent of what the government is surveilling is extensive. Not only does the government now have the incentive to create systems of surveillance, the actual infrastructure of the Internet and therefore information technology runs on a system that can easily be commandeered by a central power.

As mentioned above, the events that shook the world on September 11 have not yet been eliminated, and nefarious actors have begun using online tactics allowing further justification of monitoring the cyber realm. The "Information Operations Roadmap" released by the US Department of Defense in 2003 shows that the "U.S. and its regional allies intend on taking the war on terrorism to the internet, using a variety of means ranging from taking down 'illegal content' through to using the internet as a mean to 'deter, deny and destroy terrorist groups" (Chadwick and Howard, 2008, p. 333). Thus, the filtering content tactics that have been used by countries like China but have not been widely utilized in democratic countries like the United States historically may be exercised under the effort to stop threats "before they are fully formed" (ibid.). These include actions by the NSA such as their "extra-legal tapping of domestic communications (including the internet) suggest, even open and democratic societies are undertaking covert internet surveillance (ibid., p. 334). This can be seen in NSA's project PRISM through which the agency gained access to the systems of Google, Facebook, Apple, and other Internet companies. Search history, email contents, and live chats were accessible despite the denial of knowledge of such a program by these companies' CEOs (GreenWald and MacAskill, 2013). In 2018, the Department of Defense released an off-cycle report on the *Joint Concept for Operating in the Information Environment*. In it, they state that "information" is being added to the *Doctrine of the Armed Forces of the United States*, as the seventh Joint Function (Department of Defense, 2018, p. iii). They also outline how they plan to apply this tool. They state, "The Joint Force applies informational power to achieve three ends: Change or maintain the observations, perceptions, attitudes, and other elements that drive desired behaviors of relevant actors. Protect and ensure the observations, perceptions, attitudes, decisions, and behaviors of the Joint Force, its allies, and its partners. Acquire, process, distribute, and employ data to enhance combat power" (ibid., p. viii). This shows an expanded focus on this area since the release of their 2016 report in which the information environment and information power were identified. With the decentralized structure of modern-day terrorist organizations and the legacy of the Patriot Act, it is unclear the limits of who will be targeted by these tactics, especially considering the emphasis on "maintaining domestic order" in the report (ibid, p. vii). Thus, the parameters set out by the Patriot Act have not been effectively counteracted by the Freedom Act and are being exploited further by the state because of the changing landscape of warfare to an online platform. Thus, the technology researched as early as the 1970s regarding behavior modification is now the determined focus of the Department of Defense. The increased surveillance is also being utilized by US corporations for profit. The interconnectedness of these two entities' use of surveillance in the United States is examined in the following section.

Corporations' and State's Aligned Interest in Information Technologies

The US government and corporations have worked together in the past on projects like the atomic bomb and satellite technology (Nesbit, 2017). The skeleton of what would become the Internet (ARPAnet) was also created by the Defense Department. Thus, it is not surprising that the events of 9/11 were amplified by the opportunistic nature of capitalism. The desire to assert control over the Internet post-9/11 means that corporations were also able to take advantage of the "new normal" that had taken hold of the information privacy infrastructure. Although 9/11 was not the beginning of corporations and governments working together, it was the catalyst for citizen acceptance. The state sold users on the idea that privacy may not be necessary in a world where their protection depended on it being invaded and they would be taught to enjoy the convenience of corporation's predictive controls.

The CIA and the NSA knew in the 1990s that intelligence and supercomputing may mean that their work may be moving outside the sphere of the government system. This was compounded by the lack of funding they were receiving and the immense wealth Silicon Valley was accumulating at the time. Thus, the private sector and the intelligence community (IC) came together to create the Massive Digital Data Systems (MDDS) Project. Computer scientists at leading universities such as Stanford, MIT, Caltech, and Harvard were recruited and given a white paper brief that told them what these institutions were looking to achieve and could later be expanded by the private sector if their projects were successful. The 1993 MDDS white paper stated that the IC is "taking a proactive role in stimulating research in the efficient management of massive databases and ensuring that IC requirements can be incorporated or adapted into commercial products" (ibid.). Millions of dollars were directed through the National Science Foundation (NSF) so that the most successful projects could be used to create the type of companies attracting investment in Silicon Valley. Some successful companies that were created through this program include Qualcomm, Symantec, and Netscape. Other projects researched areas like fiber optics that are essential to AccuWeather, Verizon, and the major Internet provider for a large part of the United States like AT&T. The NSF, as of 2017, still provides 90 percent of federal funding to universities for computer-based research. One such project labeled "birds of a feather" was aimed at sorting digital information on users such as their online queries in order of importance, type, and so on, thus allowing specific communities to be tracked by their common interests and essentially tracking groups' digital fingerprints. The goal was to be able to identify terrorists and criminals. Two such grants funded by the NSA and CIA were given to Larry Page and Sergey Brin, Google's cofounders. One grant funded by NSF and the Defense Advanced Research Projects Agency (DARPA) was awarded to create a "digital library," which would turn the information on the Internet into easily searchable material. The other grant had the objective of "query optimization of very complex queries that are described using the 'query flocks' approach" (ibid.), in other words, implementing the "birds of a feather" project.

Google's CEO Eric Schmidt in 2009 said, "If you have something that you don't want anyone to know, maybe you shouldn't be doing it in the first place" (Lee, 2014, p. 401). This sentiment combined with projects such as Dragonfly and Maven has left many Google employees feeling the removal of the statement "Do no evil" from the preamble of their code of conduct. Before the revision, this phrase appeared multiple times throughout the document. Now it is only mentioned once in the 6,313-word piece in the sentence encouraging employees to speak up if they see something they don't feel is right (Cuthbertson, 2018). Ross LaJeunesse was appointed to specifically protect human rights in China after announcing in January 2010 that Gmail accounts of Chinese Human Rights activists had been breached, which prompted them to stop censoring searches in China (which they had been doing since January 2006 when Google.cn was founded). Google secretly reengaged in catering to the Chinese authoritarian regime by covertly taking on a project named Dragonfly in 2017 (Su, 2019). In protest 1,400 employees signed an internal letter in response to the lack of transparency concerning plans to work with China. While they ended the project in 2019, they have not committed to ensuring such a search engine is not created by them again for the Chinese market. Furthermore, Google created an AI Center in Beijing in December 2017 despite LaJeunesse's protests reminding Google that business in China is inextricably linked with the government. During this same period, Google's cloud computing section was working on Project Maven. The goal of the project for the Pentagon was to provide computer vision technology for drones (Tiku, 2020). Despite Google's encouragement to employees to say something if they felt their ethics were misdirected, some dozen resigned after 3,100 of Google's employees signed an open letter asking the company to stop the project in 2018. Many feared Google users' personal data would be combined with military surveillance to help achieve targeted killings (Cuthbertson, 2018). Google has 1.5 billion active users globally through Gmail alone. That does not include the information they collect through their mobile stores (Elias and Petrova, 2019). While Google did decide not to renew the contract because of the dissent it received, it did not do so before many lost their jobs. There is also nothing preventing another company from taking the place of Google and using the data they have collected on users in the same way. Ross LaJeunesse lost his position in April of this year (Tiku, 2020).

Google is not the only company working closely with the US and Chinese governments. China's big data industry has been growing exponentially in the last six years. It grew from an 8.4 billion yuan market in 2014 to 57.8 billion yuan in 2020 (Wong, 2020). It is also the world's most populous country. Therefore, it is a prime market for upcoming and established technology companies. Microsoft has been in China since 1992. The company helped create the government's computer systems, including a version of Windows that complies with China's censorship controls. Along with Google, Cisco, and Yahoo, Microsoft also helped build the Great Firewall of China (Bass and Banjo, 2020). Government contracts can bring in substantial sums of money for these companies. This is why Microsoft and Amazon fought just this year for the Pentagon's Joint Enterprise Defense Infrastructure (JEDI) project worth 10 billion dollars. Microsoft was awarded the project and is now tasked with designing cloud services such as artificial intelligence processing, machine learning, storage, and the ability to process "mission critical workloads" (Lyons, 2020). How these systems will be created and whether they will use user data is not clear at this point. Microsoft is also working with the government to produce the Integrated Visual Augmentation System (IVAS) HoloLens, an augmented reality headset for combat that will track soldier's data such as their location and heart rate to increase efficiency. A base in Austin, Texas, named the Futures Command base, is set up to allow small and large tech companies alike to bring their technology to the battlefield (Haselton, 2019).

Misuse of User Data and Its Consequences

The above actions of technology corporations illustrate the power of the companies domestically and globally as well as the relationship they have with various governments. As can be seen, user information is a tool. User agreements—the legal documents meant to regulate the wielding of this tool—are often long, blanketed statements that must be accepted before access is given to technology. However, these contracts are only between the user and the company and can be changed at the discretion of the company. If the user does not wish to stop using the products, they have to accept the new policies. Unsurprisingly, "it has been observed that data subject [users] often do not read complex data protection policies, and in any case, given the fact that access to services and goods on the market of the information society relies on a few number of monopolistic providers, data subject would not have a real free choice" (Contissa, 2017, p. 115). Google replaced over 60 different privacy policies across Google products in March 2012 (Lee, 2014, p. 50). In the announcement of this new policy, they admitted to data mining user information across platforms. Whether the user is on YouTube, an Android phone, or Gmail, what is being searched or discussed on the platforms is now used to "tailor your search results" (ibid). While this may be convenient for some, "search data can reveal particularly sensitive information about you, including facts about your location, interests, age, sexual orientation, religion, health concerns, and more" (ibid.). These new policies do not allow users to opt out either. They must be accepted and if the user has enough technological literacy to know where to look, they may go to their settings and filter through the pages of information the company automatically collects and change the settings. On Google's Privacy Policy page, it states, "We also collect information about the interaction of your apps, browsers, and devices with our services, including IP addresses, crash reports, system activity, and the date, time, and referrer URL of your request." This takes place even when users are not logged into a Google account.

This type of data is gathered by a plethora of companies. According to Giuseppe Contissa in *Information Technology for the Law*,

> [A]n algorithm processes a slew of statistics and comes up with a probability that a certain person might be a bad hire, a risky borrower, a terrorist, or a miserable teacher. The probability is distilled into a score, which can turn someone's life upside down. And yet when the person fights back "suggestive" countervailing evidence simply won't cut it. The case must be ironclad. The human victims [...] are held to a far higher standard of evidence than the algorithms themselves. (Contissa, 2017, pp. 109–10)

While Google or Microsoft user profiles are not yet integrated with these systems, companies frequently view potential hires' social media presence and if your profile is private, employers may wonder what you have to hide. Thus, these structures begin to resemble the "Social Credit System" in China, with those who play along getting rewarded and those that do not getting punished. Furthermore, when agreeing to privacy policies the user is assuming the company will protect their information or at least limit its use to the company's internal projects. Therefore, should the company have a data breach, it is up to the company to determine what information has been accessed and how to rectify the situation. Users may never discover that their information has been used in a way they did not agree to at all.

One prominent example of this blatant misuse of user information can be seen in the collection and utilization of it by Clearview AI, a company that was able to invent and distribute their services, without any input from the public or legislators. The company's operations were revealed by the *New York Times* in 2016. It was released that they had scraped Facebook, Venmo, Twitter, LinkedIn, Instagram, and other such sites for photos despite the user agreements on each of these sites. The tool they created was a search engine much like Google or Bing. But instead of information as a subject, you could upload a photo and be given the digital history of the person whose face was analyzed by the system. This information was then turned into a surveillance tool that was sold to local police. When the *New York Times* article was published, it was estimated 600 law enforcement agencies had started using the product. This technology has allowed for some cases to be solved in record time but has also led to incorrect detainment of those misidentified by the system. This tool was developed by the company and sold directly to the police (Hill, 2020a). This means the information collected on users was utilized by both the company and by the police without any input from civil society or government organizations. It was only after the *New York Times* article that the companies whose systems were scraped were aware of the breach. Even then, the cases filed by these companies were on behalf of themselves and the misuse of *their* data. This software caught the ACLU's attention in Michigan as Robin Julian-Borchak Williams was detained for 30 hours by Detroit police for a theft he did not commit based on the software. His case was dismissed but "without prejudice." This means he can be tried again, despite the fact it was proven he was not the man in the video despite the software's determination (Hill, 2020b). This reliance on software shows the cultural "assumption of fairness or objectivity" when decisions are made by computer algorithms. It occurs so often that it has a dedicated term to describe the phenomena. "Data fundamentalism, namely the tendency to believe that the correlation assessed by the algorithm implies causality, and that the analysis carried out with data mining techniques on large sets of data always provides an objective view of reality" (ibid.). This occurs even with the fact that these "systems can be vulnerable to a variety of problems that can result in systematically faulty and biased determinations" (ibid.). This is because humans are flawed and have built-in biases and they are responsible for the creation of these systems. The National Institute of Standards and Technology illustrated in a study produced in December 2019 that "incorrect associations of two subjects" by facial recognition systems were "2 and 5 times higher in women than men." They also found false positives or incorrect associations of one face with another were the worst in African Americans and Asian populations (Grother et al., 2019, pp. 2–8). These statistics apply to government databases like the FBI's Next Generation Identification System that use facial recognition algorithms based on their mugshots database (Deneyer, 2018). However, the case of Robin Williams in Michigan shows that even though Clearview AI's system has a more extensive database, the algorithms can still render incorrect results. The affiliates of the ACLU have declared distress with the expanse of this technology and the potential adoption of it by government agencies. This alarm is clearly not misplaced. Local police, the FBI, and ICE are now all using similar tools to gather information on people, track dissent, as well as solve crimes.

The FBI and local police used the exposure of Black Lives Matter protests on social media platforms to identify protest organizers and participants. In Cookeville, Tennessee, those involved were targeted at home and work and were brought in for questioning. The Department of Homeland Security has been monitoring the spread of this movement through social media since 2015. Immigration and Customs Enforcement has also used Facebook to track protests against immigration and gun-control policies. These were used to create a list of activists, journalists, Facebook group administrators, and lawyers that were then classified as deserving "greater scrutiny" at the US–Mexico border

(Funk, 2020). The government also has automated license plate readers, Stingray devices (which allow police to track cell phones and discover phone numbers of those in the vicinity), facial recognition, and drones with cameras (ibid.). They are not being used just to target protesters either. Police have been using algorithms to predict where crimes are likely to occur (Deneyer, 2020). These tools and applications alone mirror those used in China. However, the targeting by authorities of those exercising their right to peacefully protest is the proverbial straw that may break the back of our democracy.

Conclusion: China and the United States—Concurrent or Contrasting Realities?

Minorities being further disenfranchised, authorities monitoring civilians, companies profiting from government contracts, and micro-targeting based on user profiles are all common traits between the United States and China's use of surveillance technology. Both the United States and China are exporting their technologies, and both are continuing to innovate products that incorporate data mining through big data found on the ubiquitous Internet of things. Is the result a trend toward authoritarian tendencies in the United States? This study makes a case for this argument in the affirmative.

The hypothesis at the beginning of this chapter predicted the divide between what constitutes civil liberties in a democratic and authoritarian regime was diminishing with the proliferation of this new technology. The limits on the collection of personal data, rights for individuals subject to data collection, the ability to hold entities accountable, and the transparency in the process were set as parameters for this determination. These factors were to be combined with the modified metrics from Ziblatt and Levitsky to determine whether the US democracy was being negatively influenced by these technologies. Questions raised about applications of this technology regarding the Fourth Amendment were answered in the cases showing a targeting of protesters in both countries. Limiting their ability to exercise their right to free speech and peaceful assembly goes against the determined democratic norms. The lack of alternative choices to privacy policies goes against the second metric. The creation of Clearview AI without public or government input, the use of commercial data brokers by law enforcement without user consent, and the possible use of user data to develop government projects like Google's Maven for the Pentagon or Microsoft's JEDI are just a few illustrations of a lack of transparency in the process. Violence both direct and indirect can be seen because of these technologies. Only a few examples were given such as the risk to women through the "Girls Around Me" application, Latinas, survivors of sexual abuse, and those targeted by authorities in the United States and

China such as the Uyghurs, Hong Kong protestors, and Black Lives Matter protestors. Other examples were given of technology created for one purpose, such as targeted advertising, and used in another like influencing election results. All of this clearly shows the "willingness to curtail the civil liberties of opponents" and the citizenry as a whole. This does not, however, mean that the United States must continue on this path.

The United States is still for all intents and purposes a democracy backed by the rule of law. The "rule of truth" has not yet been widely applied as it has in China. However, the book *Information Technology for the Law* that was published in 2017 states, "the law is just starting to look at the issues raised by the combination of data mining techniques and algorithmic decision-making process" (Contissa, 2017, p. 109). Companies and the US government have been creating such systems since the 1970s; therefore, one must wonder how much longer the law will take to catch up with these programs if it ever will. Europe's GDPR, California's Consumer Privacy Act, and Illinois' Biometric Information Privacy Act are all steps in the right direction. Yet, the same year the Consumer Privacy Act was passed, Proposition 25 was proposed in California. This proposition would have replaced cash bail with an algorithm that would determine whether the accused should be released before trial. This also came after SB 10 was passed in conjunction with SB 36 in 2018 and 2017, respectively. These were all aimed at creating a system to mitigate the bias of algorithmic systems as a result of a report from the American Psychological Association. This showed throughout the country nine out of ten pretrial detention agencies use such a system along with 28 states using them for parole decisions and 20 states for sentencing (Johnson, 2020). While these made external audits a means to combat this bias, who is determining what is bias and fair is not clear, nor was it further outlined in Proposition 25. In terms of the GDPR legislation, consent and purposes of data use, the use of pseudonymization of data, and transparency are all topics outlined by the legislation. However, it has already been determined the legislation focused on these areas has significant flaws. The uses of data in ways that prove valuable are not usually known when the data is collected. Yet this is when the GDPR determined purposes of data collection should be made known. It has also been shown "that the adoption of technical measures for pseudonymisaiton [*sic*] may not provide [...] privacy nor fairness" (Contissa, 2017, pp. 115–16). Lastly, imperative terms such as transparency lack an agreed-upon definition (ibid). Thus, it would seem the rule of law is not current enough or comprehensive enough to truly protect citizens from the authoritarian tendencies of information technology as it is currently structured. Furthermore, as has been shown, data is an economic driver. Consequently, politicians wishing to get elected may not wish to unsettle a thriving economy as it could hurt their chances of reelection.

Corporations are also relentless about lobbying to ensure their main source of income online is protected. It is, therefore, up to the people to ensure these concerns are a focus of future legislators.

The purpose of this analysis was to appropriately alarm the masses by showing the similarities of China and the United States concerning information technology. There are many more instances of misuse of data, cooperation of US companies with China and the US government while using user data in ways they are unaware of. So many books and sections of libraries have been dedicated to them. Corporations and states have been made aware of the many forms of information power and surveillance capitalism, but the masses are still largely in the dark. It is the duty of the state, legislators, civil society, journalists, and organizations to ensure the use of information technology does not continue down a path that will lead to an authoritarian use-case. It is hoped this analysis will be part of a larger effort to continue to research, report, and change the use of information technology until systems are put in place that truly protects users from unwarranted surveillance. Commissions should be created at the state and local level with experts from various fields such as lawyers, engineers, and civil rights organizations to create legislation that allows users to opt in to these pervasive information systems instead of opt out. Efforts should be made to build on existing legislation to ensure this technology is used in a way that aligns with the democratic values the United States and the Internet were founded on. The fact that this technology has permeated almost every aspect of society means that this shift will not take place overnight. Instead, the efforts will be akin to the turning of a large boat. In the United States, it is up to the people, not one authority, to determine the direction of society. Therefore, provided those at the helm in the United States make the effort, the ship should eventually arrive at a more democratic destination.

References

Bass, D., and Banjo, S., 2020. Bloomberg.com, viewed December 12, 2020. Available at https://www.bloomberg.com/news/articles/2020-08-03/microsoft-s-long-history-in-china-complicates-potential-tiktok-deal.

Broussard, M., 2018. *Artificial Unintelligence: How Computers Misunderstand the World*. Cambridge, MA: MIT Press. Available from: ProQuest Ebook Central (May 12, 2021) (accessed December 15, 2020).

Caffrey, C., 2019. 2019 Hong Kong Anti-Extradition Bill Protests, viewed December 15, 2020. Available at http://search.ebscohost.com.proxy.library.nyu.edu/login.aspx?direct=true&db=ers&AN=\140435609&site=eds-live.

Canadian Security Intelligence. Government of Canada, May 17, 2018. https://www.canada.ca/en/security-intelligence-service/corporate/publications/china-and-the-age-of-strategic-rivalry/chinas-intelligence-law-and-the-countrys-future-intelligence-competitions.html.

Chadwick, A., and Howard, P. N. (eds.) 2008. *Routledge Handbook of Internet Politics*. London: Taylor & Francis Group. Available from: ProQuest Ebook Central (May 12, 2021).

Chan, E., The Great Firewall of China. Bloomberg.com, viewed December 2, 2020, https://www.bloomberg.com/quicktake/great-firewall-of-china.

Chan, T. F., 2018. 16 Parts of China Are Now Using Skynet, the Facial Recognition Tech That Can Scan the Country's Entire Population in a Second. *Business Insider Australia*, viewed December 12, 2020. Available at https://www.businessinsider.com.au/china-facial-recognition-technology-works-in-one-second-2018-3.

Chen, Y.-J., Lin, C.-F., and Liu, H.-W., 2018. "Rule of Trust: The Power and Perils of China's Social Credit Megaproject," *Columbia Journal of Asian Law*, 32(1), pp. 1–36, viewed May 12, 2021. Available at http://search.ebscohost.com.proxy.library.nyu.edu/login.aspx?direct=true&db=edshol&AN=edshol.hein.journals.colas32.4&site=eds-live.

Chin, J., Bürge, C., and Marchi, G., 2017. Twelve Days in Xinjiang: How China's Surveillance State Overwhelms Daily Life. *Wall Street Journal*, viewed December 5, 2020. Available at https://www.wsj.com/articles/twelve-days-in-xinjiang-how-chinas-surveillance-state-overwhelms-daily-life-1513700355.

Cohen, J. E., 2019. *Between Truth and Power: The Legal Constructions of Informational Capitalism*. Oxford: Oxford University Press USA—OSO. Available from: ProQuest Ebook Central (May 12, 2021).

Contissa, G., 2017. Information Technology for the Law, G. Giappichelli, Turin. Available from: ProQuest Ebook Central (May 12, 2021).

Cuthbertson, A., 2018. Google Just Quietly Removed References to "Don't Be Evil" from Its Code of Conduct. *The Independent*, viewed December 11. Available at https://www.independent.co.uk/life-style/gadgets-and-tech/news/google-dont-be-evil-code-conduct-removed-alphabet-a8361276.html.

Deneyer, S., 2018. China's Watchful Eye. *Washington Post*, viewed December 10, 2020. Available at https://www.washingtonpost.com/news/world/wp/2018/01/07/feature/in-china-facial-recognition-is-sharp-end-of-a-drive-for-total-surveillance.

Department of Defense, 2016. *Strategy For Operations in the Information Environment* (pp. 2–15, Rep.). Washington, DC: Department of Defense.

———, 2018. *Joint Concept for Operating in the Information Environment (JCOIE)* (Rep.). Washington, DC: Department of Defense.

Elias, J., and Petrova, M., 2019. Google's Rocky Path to Email Domination, viewed on January 21, 2021. Available at https://www.cnbc.com/2019/10/26/gmail-dominates-consumer-email-with-1point5-billion-users.html.

Franklin, S. B., 2019. Fulfilling the Promise of the USA Freedom Act: Time to Truly End Bulk Collection of Americans' Calling Records. *Just Security*, viewed January 20, 2021. Available at https://www.justsecurity.org/63399/fulfilling-the-promise-of-the-usa-freedom-act-time-to-truly-end-bulk-collection-of-americans-calling-records/.

Freedom House, Press Release: Freedom on the Net 2019 Reveals Crisis on Popular Platforms. *Freedom House*, viewed on January 15, 2021. Available at https://freedomhouse.org/report/freedom-on-the-net/2019/the-crisis-of-social-media/press-release.

Freidman, B., and Kerr, O., The Fourth Amendment. *Interpretation: The Fourth Amendment | The National Constitution Center*, viewed January 20, 2021. Available at https://constitutioncenter.org/interactive-constitution/interpretation/amendment-iv/interps/121.

Friedersdorf, C., 2015. A Federal Appeals Court Vindicates Edward Snowden's Leak of NSA Secrets. *The Atlantic*, viewed January 15, 2021. Available at https://www.theatlantic.com/politics/archive/2015/05/the-vindication-of-edward-snowden/392741/.

Funk, A., 2020. How Domestic Spying Tools Undermine Racial Justice Protests. *Freedom House*, viewed on January 11, 2021. Available at https://freedomhouse.org/article/how-domestic-spying-tools-undermine-racial-justice-protests.

Global Times. 2018. Surveillance Tech Grows in Xinjiang, Necessary to Counter Terrorism, viewed on January 11, 2021. Available at https://www.globaltimes.cn/content/1109176.shtml.

Greenwald, G., and MacAskill, E., 2013. NSA Prism Program Taps in to User Data of Apple, Google and Others. *The Guardian*, viewed on January 12, 2021. Available at https://www.theguardian.com/world/2013/jun/06/us-tech-giants-nsa-data.

Grother, P., Mei N., and Kayee H., 2019. Rep. *Face Recognition Vendor Test (FRVT) Part 3: Demographic Effects*. Department of Commerce.

Gueorguiev, D., 2019. Analysis | Mike Bloomberg Said China Isn't a Dictatorship. Is He Right? *Washington Post*, viewed January 10, 2021. Available at https://www.washingtonpost.com/politics/2019/12/04/michael-bloomberg-said-china-isnt-dictatorship-is-he-right/.

Haselton, T., 2019. How the Army Plans to Use Microsoft's High-tech HoloLens Goggles on the Battlefield. *CNBC*, viewed January 20, 2021. Available at https://www.cnbc.com/2019/04/06/microsoft-hololens-2-army-plans-to-customize-as-ivas.html.

Heward-Mills, D., and Turku, H. 2020. "California and the European Union Take the Lead in Data Protection," *Hastings International and Comparative Law Review*, 43(2), pp. 319–38.

Hill, K., 2020a. The Secretive Company That Might End Privacy as We Know It. *New York Times*, viewed January 10, 2021. Available at https://www.nytimes.com/2020/01/18/technology/clearview-privacy-facial-recognition.html.

———, 2020b. Wrongfully Accused by an Algorithm. *New York Times*, viewed January 10, 2021. Available at https://www.nytimes.com/2020/06/24/technology/facial-recognition-arrest.html.

H.R. Rep. No. Hearing before the Subcommittee on Asia, the Pacific and Nonproliferation of the Committee on Foreign Affairs House of Representatives One Hundred Sixteenth Congress-Authoritarianism with Chinese Characteristics: Political and Religious Human Rights Challenges in China. 2019.

Human Rights Watch, 2020. China: Police "Big Data" Systems Violate Privacy, Target Dissent. *Human Rights Watch*, viewed December 20, 2020. Available at https://www.hrw.org/news/2017/11/19/china-police-big-data-systems-violate-privacy-target-dissent.

Huawei Investment and Holding Co. Ltd. 2019. Annual Report.

Jie, S., 2018. China Exports Facial ID Technology to Zimbabwe. *Global Times*, viewed on January 15, 2021. Available at https://www.globaltimes.cn/content/1097747.shtml.

Johnson, K., 2020. California's Prop 25 Would Replace Cash Bail with Algorithms, but Questions around Fairness and Transparency Remain. *VentureBeat*, viewed on December 21, 2021. Available at https://venturebeat.com/2020/11/03/the-unavoidable-glaring-cproblem-with-californias-prop-25-to-replace-cash-bail-with-an-algorithm/.

Lee, N., 2014. *Facebook Nation: Total Information Awareness*, New York: Springer. Available from: ProQuest Ebook Central.

Levitsky, S., and Ziblatt, D., 2018. *How Democracies Die*. New York: Broadway Books.

Lewis, J., 2018. Cognitive Effect and State Conflict in Cyberspace. *Cognitive Effect and State Conflict in Cyberspace | Center for Strategic and International Studies*, viewed on January 20, 2021. Available at https://www.csis.org/analysis/cognitive-effect-and-state-conflict-cyberspace.

Linz, J. J. 1978. *The Breakdown of Democratic Regimes: Crisis, Breakdown, and Reequilibration*. Baltimore, MD: Johns Hopkins University Press.

Lyon, David. 2003. *Surveillance after September 11*. Malden, MA: Polity Press in association with Blackwell Pub. Inc..

Lyons, K., 2020. The Pentagon Says Microsoft Should still Get Its $10B JEDI Contract Following an Investigation. *The Verge*, viewed on January 20, 2021. Available at https://www.theverge.com/2020/9/4/21423312/pentagon-microsoft-jedi-amazon-trump-defense-contract-cloud-bezos.

Mahtani, S., 2019. Masks, Cash and Apps: How Hong Kong's Protesters Find Ways to Outwit the Surveillance State. *Washington Post*, viewed on January 20, 2021. Available at https://www.washingtonpost.com/world/asia_pacific/masks-cash-and-apps-how-hong-kongs-protesters-find-ways-to-outwit-the-surveillance-state/2019/06/15/8229169c-8ea0-11e9-b6f4-033356502dce_story.html.

McAdams, A. J. 2005. "Internet Surveillance after September 11: Is the United States Becoming Great Britain?," *Comparative Politics–New York*, pp. 479–98.

Nesbit, J., 2017. Google's True Origin Partly Lies in CIA and NSA Research Grants for Mass Surveillance. *Quartz*, viewed on January 20, 2021. Available at https://qz.com/1145669/googles-true-origin-partly-lies-in-cia-and-nsa-research-grants-for-mass-surveillance/.

Open Net Initiative, 2012. China. *China | OpenNet Initiative*, viewed January 20, 2021. Available at https://opennet.net/research/profiles/china-including-hong-kong.

Ovide, S., 2020. The Real Dangers of Surveillance. *New York Times*, viewed on January 20, 2021. Available at https://www.nytimes.com/2020/06/12/technology/surveillance-protests-hong-kong.html.

Service, C. S. I., 2018. Government of Canada, viewed December 12, 2020. Available at https://www.canada.ca/en/security-intelligence-service/corporate/publications/china-and-the-age-of-strategic-rivalry/chinas-intelligence-law-and-the-countrys-future-intelligence-competitions.html.

Su, J., 2019. Confirmed: Google Terminated Project Dragonfly, Its Censored Chinese Search Engine. *Forbes*, viewed January 15, 2021. Available at https://www.forbes.com/sites/jeanbaptiste/2019/07/19/confirmed-google-terminated-project-dragonfly-its-censored-chinese-search-engine/?sh=4279a61a7e84+%5BAccessed+May+10%2C+2021%5D.

Tiku, N., 2020. A Top Google Exec Pushed the Company to Commit to Human Rights. Then Google Pushed Him Out, He Says. *Washington Post*. Available at https://www.washingtonpost.com/technology/2020/01/02/top-google-exec-pushed-company-commit-human-rights-then-google-pushed-him-out-he-says/ (accessed May 12, 2021).

Wahman, M., Teorell, J., and Hadenius, A. 2013. "Authoritarian Regime Types Revisited: Updated Data in Comparative Perspective," *Contemporary Politics*, 19(1), pp. 19–34.

Wong, S., 2020. China: Big Data Market Size 2014–2020. *Statista*, viewed January 20, 2021. Available at www.statista.com/statistics/796500/china-big-data-market-size/.

World Wide Web Foundation, History of the Web. *World Wide Web Foundation*. Available at https://webfoundation.org/about/vision/history-of-the-web/?gclid=EAIaIQobChMI1LeZqfn16wIVCtvACh0HOgfEEAAYASAAEgKPtfD_BwE (accessed May 12, 2021).

Xinhuanet. 2019. China Signs 197 B&R Cooperation Documents with 137 Countries, 30 int'l Organizations. *Xinhua*, viewed January 20, 2021. Available at http://www.xinhuanet.com/english/2019-11/15/c_138558369.htm.

Zuboff, Shoshana. 2019. *The Age of Surveillance Capitalism: The Fight for a Human Future at the New Frontier of Power*. New York: PublicAffairs.

Chapter 2

IS THIS CHAPTER "FAKE NEWS"?: EXPLORING THE POSSIBILITIES OF REGULATING ONLINE DISINFORMATION WHILE PRESERVING THE RIGHT TO FREEDOM OF EXPRESSION IN EUROPE

Sophia Ehmke

Introduction

Just think what Goebbels could have done with Facebook.

With such provocative statements and his observation that *"freedom of speech"* can never translate into a right to *"freedom of reach,"* Comedian Sasha Baron Cohen's (2019) recent speech at the ADL's International Leadership Conference reignited the heated debate as to how to deal with fake news online: How much should be done? And leaving moral considerations aside, how much can actually be done?

Claims of fake news dominated major national elections on a global scale, notably the 2016 US Presidential Elections and the UK Vote to leave the European Union ("Brexit") (Alcott and Gentzkow, 2017, p. 211; Rose, 2017, pp. 555–56; Humprecht, 2019, p. 1973). Recent studies found that 47 percent of adults are getting their news from social media (Reuters Institute, 2020). These findings illustrate the worrying potential of fake news online. Fabricated information has always existed (Katsirea, 2018, p. 160); however, the concerning novelty is the tendency of such news to spread globally at an extraordinary pace (Alemanno, 2018, p. 1). Fake news spread "significantly faster, farther, deeper and more broadly through social networks than does true news" and it takes true stories about six times as long as false stories to reach people (Vosoughi et al., 2018).

Some, predominantly US, scholars, operating under the "marketplace of ideas" theory, have argued that instead of restricting speech the proper strategy would be more speech (Timmer, 2017, pp. 703–4)—flooding people with actual news so that eventually, when presented with both, they are able to "sort out truth from falsehood" (Kerr, 2019, p. 494). Keeping in line with such metaphor we should however recognize that sometimes markets simply fail. Indeed, with research and reporting requirements and the need for editors and fact checkers, true news stories take longer and are much more expensive to create. In contrast, the "creative process" behind fake news takes only "one person with a little imagination and a working computer" to create content within minutes (Andorfer, 2018, p. 1423). Psychological factors such as our cognitive bias when processing information, our tendency to be more open to stories that are in line with our preconceived views or engage our emotions, and often our unwillingness or lack of time to extensively research both sides of a story further undermine this theory (McIntyre, 2018).

Fake news is a social problem that poses several threats to democracy. Through "shaping and manipulation" of beliefs and thus behavior the authenticity and freedom of the electoral process is at risk. Fake news might trick people into voting differently than they would have and ultimately risk the capacity to translate the will of the people into government representation. This might entail further consequences as to the protection of minorities, adherence to basic human rights standards, and government accountability (Venice Commission, 2019, p. 10). Moreover, in the long run, it threatens the public's ability to trust the information we are receiving, which may translate into a generation of people who are disengaged ("reality apathy") (Stover, 2018, p. 285). They may not participate in democracy. They may not vote at all. What is more, there have been "more immediately dangerous consequences stemming from 'fake news'," such as an armed man storming a Washington, DC, pizzeria. A widely shared fabricated article had claimed that children were held hostage at that restaurant as part of a child sex slave ring operated by the Clintons (Butler, 2018, p. 419). A few weeks after *"pizzagate,"* the Pakistani Minister of Defense Khawaja Asif threatened nuclear retaliation against Israel, reacting to a fake news story that claimed that his Israeli counterpart had officially announced to initiate a nuclear attack on Pakistan should they send ground troops to Syria (*Duped by fake news*, 2016). If the Spanish-American War was driven by fake news (Kashatus, 2018), is it so outrageous to think that another war could be too?

Faced with this "market failure" and these perceived threats, governments around the world are searching to find an adequate solution to fake news. However, such attempts have proven to be highly controversial in light of the "other side of the coin"—that is, the misuse of the concept of fake news as a tool to crack down on political dissent and unpopular views as is often employed by regimes with authoritarian hues (Katsirea, 2018, p. 160). This confronts lawmakers with questions such as what is fake news to begin with and what the law can actually do to address the problem considering the fundamental freedom of expression and linked concerns of possible democratic costs and effectiveness (Francis, 2018, p. 101), leaving the complex question as to what in the end poses the greater risk to democracy: Fake news or the measures to control it?

With a view to the potential consequences of nonregulation (e.g., for upcoming important elections in Germany and France), and the complexity of this task, this chapter aims to answer the question as to what extent can fake news be regulated while preserving the fundamental right to freedom of expression in Europe. To answer the research question above, both primary and secondary sources will be used in order to inform a classical doctrinal analysis. The chapter is divided into three substantive sections. Section I provides an introductory discussion of the term fake news and its meaning and sets out the working definition. Section II outlines the European Court of Human Rights' (*hereafter* ECtHR) practice when assessing the legitimacy of interference with freedom of expression under Art. 10(2) of the European Convention on Human Rights (*hereafter* ECHR), explaining the inherent balancing exercise. To this end, this section will also analyze possible limitation arguments in light of Art. 17 ECHR's prohibition of abuse of rights. Finally, Section III discusses two novel approaches to justify limiting freedom of expression: treating fake news as commercial speech and extending the "duties and responsibilities" of journalists.

Jurisdictional Choices

In examining the (im)possibilities of regulating online disinformation while preserving the right to freedom of expression, the territorial scope of this work is focused on Europe. This decision was made as the European continent is unique in its strong regulatory urge toward fake news. Countries such as Germany, France, Hungary, and Russia introduced laws to tackle online disinformation, and the European Commission has put forward its EU-wide Code of Conduct for online platforms. To the best of this author's knowledge there is no other centralized effort to set out rules for the identification and removal of fake news. The chosen territorial focus explains why the case law of the ECtHR as the highest judicial authority for fundamental rights in Europe forms the main basis for this chapter. Ultimately, it is this Court that determines the legal framework applicable to untruthful expression. However, in its endeavor to protect the democratic order the Court is fed by practices and ideas that are influenced by various actors: As fake news is a global phenomenon that all legal systems struggle with, standards can be drawn from different national and institutional jurisdictions even outside of Europe. Moreover, as a consequence of the ECtHR's significant backlog, the Court may very well adjudicate a case more than a decade after it was filed. It is then barred from referring to the newest technological and legal developments as the case was brought under very different realities. Thus, analyzing how national courts are construing freedom of expression standards in light of current developments is of value.

Fake News—What Is It and Where Do We Stand?

"Defining 'fake news' would appear simple at face value" (Sugow, 2019, p. 26). Considering the English meaning of both words it seems easy to conclude—as one of the first academic definition attempts did—that fake news is simply news articles that are factually "false and could mislead the reader" (Alcott and Gentzkow, 2017, p. 212). However, the concept goes far beyond this simple understanding as false information, as it contains complex considerations as to the type of content, the motivations behind it, and its method of dissemination. In the growing body of literature from academics and nonprofit organizations there is considerable controversy over at least two of those: (1) whether fake news should only refer to complete fabrications or whether it should also refer to other "misinformation tactics"; and (2) whether the concept should only include false content that is produced intentionally (Moretto Ribeiro and Ortellado, 2018, p. 71).

As to the former, numerous types of problematic content have been discussed, which indicates that fake news can include complete fabrication, satire or parody, misleading information, content impersonating genuine sources, "click-bait" (false connections when headlines do not relate to the content), content shared with false context, manipulated content, bad journalism, and foreign interference in domestic politics (Tambini, 2017, p. 3; Wardle, 2017; Craufurd Smith, 2019, p. 57). No matter which one of these forms of fake news, they all ultimately deceive the public and thus an approach encompassing all of them could be envisaged. However, this would fail to acknowledge the varying levels of seriousness and ultimately threaten legitimate forms of speech. Especially satire and parody are highly desirable as an important part of political commentary and should not be treated the same as pure fabrication. In addition, such a classification approach is of little help for defining fake news since these different types may overlap in practice. An article may contain both satire and fabrication.

As to the second point of contest, it has been suggested that rather than engaging in classification of form and relying on levels of inaccuracy, one could focus on "design qualifications" and look at the motivations behind fake news (Sugow, 2019, p. 38). However, financial, political, or simply mischievous motivations behind content are often blurred together as well, again frustrating definition attempts. This is when academic debate shifted to the criterion of intent. But has this brought the much desired clarity? While the European Commission and the Venice Commission of the Council of Europe, for example, both recommended that the term "disinformation" be used rather than the highly politicized fake news, the former operates with an intent to deceive (European Commission, 2018, p. 1) while the latter chose an intent to cause harm (Venice Commission, 2019, p. 16).

The wide span of fake news and their multifaceted nature make the term so difficult to define. "It is nonetheless necessary for the law to clearly and narrowly define 'fake news' to prevent overregulation that could chill speech and to comply with the rule of law" (Francis, 2018, p. 102). Thus, for the purpose of this chapter fake news is defined as "verifiably false or misleading information that is created, presented and disseminated to intentionally deceive the public." It does thus not include bad journalism, satire, or parody, for example. It further excludes already illegal types of speech such as defamation, hate speech, and incitement to violence.

Freedom of Expression and Fake News

Freedom of expression is the primary concern for any legal intervention toward restriction of fake news, even where they are indirectly addressed through regulating actions of the private sector. Three rationales are usually given for protecting freedom of expression as a fundamental right. Firstly, freedom of expression is the "lifeblood" of democracy, facilitating informed political discussions. Secondly, it empowers "personal development" enabling autonomy and individuals to find out how they wish to live their lives. Thirdly, it allows scientific and factual claims to be critically tested (Craufurd Smith, 2019, p. 64). It is not immediately apparent how intentional publication of false information assists these three core objectives, and yet, some of the highest courts around the world have shown their strict protective stance in relation to freedom of expression. Both the United States and Canadian Supreme Courts rejected the general and broad proposition that false statements do not benefit from the protection of freedom of expression, purporting that even a deliberate outright lie can have value (*United States v. Alvarez*, 567 U.S. 709 (2012); *R v Zundel* [1992] 2 S.C.R. 731).

While the highest judicial authority for fundamental rights in Europe, the ECtHR, has also clarified its strict stance in relation to freedom of expression (*Handyside v United Kingdom*, ECtHR no. 5493/72 (1976) para. 49), it adopted a different methodology than, for example, the US Supreme Court, which uses a categorical approach when determining the scope of free speech. Instead, in its jurisprudence the European Court engages in a balancing of societal and personal interests, allowing the more important interests to prevail or by allowing both interests to "prevail to an appropriate extent" (Aramyan, 2015, p. 94). Article 10(1) ECHR confers freedom of expression as the freedom to "hold opinions and to receive and impart information and ideas without interference by public authority." All forms of expression are included, most notably orally and printed, but also various forms of behavior and activity (*Hashman and Harrup v United Kingdom*, ECtHR no. 25594/94 (1999) para. 28), and the ECtHR has explicitly ruled on multiple occasions that the Internet plays an unprecedented role in "enhancing the public's access to news and facilitating the sharing and dissemination of information" (*Times Newspaper Ltd v United Kingdom*, ECtHR nos. 30002/03 and 23676/03 (2009) para. 27). Operating within this set framework/balancing methodology the UK High Court, for example, held that in light of Article 17 ECHR (abuse of law doctrine) and Article 3 Protocol 1 ECHR (right to free elections), the right to freedom of expression within Article 10(1) ECHR does not protect preelection publication of information that the creator knows "to be false or does not believe it to be true" (*Woolas, R v The Speaker of the House of Commons* [2011] 2WRL 1362 (December 3, 2010), para. 106).

Whether this reasoning will be upheld by the ECtHR remains to be seen since the Court itself has not yet directly dealt with the question whether legislation banning fake news is compatible with Art.10(1) ECHR, even though there is a case pending (*Dareskizb Ltd v Armenia*, ECtHR no. 61737/08) that to date has not been adjudicated. This case concerns a decree that imposed a "ban on publication or dissemination by mass media outlets of obviously false or destabilizing information on State or internal issues" during a state of emergency. It should be noted that this case was brought under very different realities and thus the law in question was not targeted at online disinformation. To the best of the author's knowledge, there are no newer cases concerning fake news laws currently pending. However, in the recent *Brzenziński v Poland* judgment (ECtHR no. 47542/07 (2019) para. 35) the Court, for the first time and on its own volition, used the term fake news. Neither the applicant nor the Polish government had made use of the term in their submissions, owing to the fact that it was not a fake news case per se (but rather a defamation case concerning the applicant's right to freedom of expression as a politician at election time) and that it had originated in 2007, well before the era of fake news. This choice is thus interesting as it suggests that the Court used this case as an opportunity to signal its acknowledgment of the existence and scale of the problem of (online) disinformation and its preparedness to address it.

So far the Court has made some relevant comments in other cases indirectly addressing the issue of fake news. In *Salov v Ukraine* (ECtHR no. 65518/01 (2005)) the Court considered the situation of an individual distributing false information (a forged copy of a newspaper incorrectly proclaiming the death of a presidential candidate) that was not produced or published by him, ultimately finding that Article 10(1) ECHR does "not prohibit the discussion or dissemination of information received even if it is strongly suspected that this information might not be truthful. To suggest otherwise would deprive persons of the right to express their views and opinions about statements made in the mass media" (para. 113). This case is relevant to the public's sharing of fake news, especially in the context of social media, as it clarifies that this behavior cannot be punished by law. While this case does not have any direct impact on the legal position of those creating the fake news and releasing it "into the wild," let alone of social media platforms, it can, however, provide at least some authority as the Court clearly confirmed that "providing voters with true information in the course of an [election] campaign" was a legitimate ground to restrict freedom of expression (para. 110).

Already in its early case law, the Court introduced a distinction between factual allegations and value judgments, the latter being susceptible to a stricter standard of review under freedom of expression (*Lingens v Austria*, ECtHR no. 9815/82 (1986)). This distinction seems to indicate that a false statement of fact is particularly harmful and should thus be treated differently than other content. In recent judgments, the Court seems to further have acknowledged the impact and dangers of the Internet and especially social media platforms in this connection. It thus stressed that problematic speech "can be disseminated like never before, worldwide, in a matter of seconds, and sometimes remain[s] persistently available online" (*Delfi v Estonia*, ECtHR no. 64569/09 (2015), para. 110) and that this situation has a bearing on striking the balance between conflicting rights (*Barford v Denmark*, ECtHR no. 11508/85 (1989), para. 28).

With these statements in mind, it needs to be analyzed whether the actual application of the current legal framework for limiting the right to freedom of expression allows for adequate responses to the fake news problem. The ECtHR has two weapons in its arsenal that it uses to tackle problematic speech: the assessment of the legitimacy of interference with freedom of expression under Article 10(2) ECHR and, more radically, assessment under Art.17 ECHR's "abuse clause" that prohibits any activity "aimed at the destruction of any of the rights and freedoms set forth [in the Convention] or at their limitation to a greater extent than is provided for in the Convention." Along these lines, the following subsections will next briefly explore the degree to which freedom of expression can be restricted in order to prevent fake news.

The Balancing Exercise: Limiting Freedom of Expression under Art. 10(2) ECHR

Article 10(2) ECHR sets out three conditions that any legal "condition, restriction or penalty" on the exercise of freedom of expression must fulfil. They must be "prescribed by law," aimed at one or more of the exhaustively listed legitimate interests, and be "necessary in a democratic society."

"Prescribed by law"

Whether interference is "prescribed by law" depends on a threefold test, encompassing matters of construction and clarity. Firstly, the measure in question must have some basis in domestic law. Generally, this will not constitute any problems. Then the quality of the law will be tested: The law must be accessible—that is, it must be published; and lastly, the third requirement flowing from the expression of "prescribed by law" is foreseeability. The law in question must be "formulated with sufficient precision to enable the citizen to regulate his conduct" (*Rekvényi v Hungary*, ECtHR no. 25390/94 (1999), para. 34). He must be able to foresee the consequences of his actions. Therefore, the definitional struggle that was discussed extensively in Section I is highly relevant for any law's ability to address fake news. The 2020 OSCE and UN Joint Declaration on freedom of expression considered terms such as fake news or "non-objective information," which do not go beyond the content in question's false character to be too general and unacceptably vague (para. 1(a)(iii)(3)). Not only can what is "false" change over time with the emergence of new facts, but such definitions would also lead to a varied understanding of the legislation, in essence making the judicial/administrative official in question the determiner of what subjectively, for him, constitutes illegal speech. However, this does not mean that all is lost, but merely that very careful fine-tuning of definitions ("*Fingerspitzengefühl*") is required. The ECtHR itself has long recognized that "attaining absolute precision in the framing of laws" is impossible (*Müller and Others v Switzerland*, ECtHR no. 10737/84 (1988), para. 29) and that the need to "avoid excessive rigidity and to keep up with changing circumstances means that many laws are inevitably couched in terms which, to a greater or lesser extent, are vague" (*Markt Intern Verlag GmbH and Klaus Beermann v Germany*, ECtHR no. 10572/83 (1989), para. 30).

Thus, to be "sufficiently precise," any definition adopted by law must include other qualities such as form (by, for example, focusing on content disguised as news reports and official government statements) and more importantly requirements for intent or knowledge. As included in the working definition of this chapter, an intent to deceive is certainly narrower in scope, limiting the application of fake news laws to blameworthy instances. This conclusion is in line with the ECtHR's findings in *Salov v Ukraine* (ECtHR no. 65518/01 2005), in which the Court accepted Article 127 of the Ukrainian Criminal Code to be sufficiently precise. This provision prohibits the interference with the exercise of electoral rights and election results through, among others, deceit (paras. 41&109). While the "prescribed by law" condition thus provides room for fake news laws, the impossibility to make use of broad, open-ended definitions means that they will not be able to catch every type, let alone piece, of fake news.

"Legitimate aim"

The second condition of Article 10(2) ECHR stipulates that interferences with the right to freedom of expression must only be introduced for certain *legitimate aims*. These justifications are set out in an exhaustive list, the ones with the most potential for fake news laws being: interests of national security, the protection of health and morals (especially for COVID-19-related fake news), and the protection of reputation and rights of others. The scope of these aims is wide and the Court normally accepts the Government's explanation that the challenged rule protects one of these aims (Rainey et al., 2014, p. 314).

On face value, deception does not engage with any legally recognized rights of others. However, "rights of others" is not limited to those rights and freedoms explicitly spelled out in and protected under the Convention and the Court has, for example, rather easily accepted that providing others (the voters) with true information in the course of an election campaign amounts to such a legitimate aim (*Salov v Ukraine*, ECtHR no. 65518/01 (2005), para. 110). Additionally, content deliberately spreading a false narrative, which was created by foreign powers to interfere with national elections, could permit legal intervention for national security objectives (McIntyre, 2018, p. 106). However, such restrictions of free expression would only hold up in the most exceptional circumstances: They can only be considered as "legitimate" if their "genuine purpose and demonstrable effect" is to protect the existence of a country from "expression intended to incite imminent violence" (ARTICLE 19, 1996, principles 2(a)&6). The Court explained its very strict approach in *Klass and Others v Germany* (ECtHR no. 5029/71 (1978)) where it warned that restrictions imposed on freedom of expression in the name of national security pose a danger of "undermining or even destroying democracy on the ground of defending it" (para. 49). One of the few examples where such an aim convinced the Court was for legal measures preventing and punishing the disclosure of sensitive military secrets (*Hadjianastassiou v Greece*, ECtHR no. 12945/87 (1992)).

Throughout the current global COVID-19 pandemic, a novel type of fake news has developed, which would allow speech restriction for the legitimate objective of "protection of health." An alarming number of information is currently being published claiming that, for example, drinking bleach or prophylactically taking a high dose of the malarial drug Chloroquine would provide a cure (Hoffmann, 2020). In a case where information was restricted because it was deemed dangerous (by proposing therapeutic regimes that were not scientifically approved for the treatment of serious conditions such as cancer or high blood pressure), the ECtHR found the "protection of health" reasons provided by the French authorities to be legitimate (*Vérités santé partique SARL v France*, ECtHR no. 74766/01 (2005), part. 3). The "legitimate aim" condition too is thus not inhibitive of the law's ability to address fake news. The crux of the matter—the central issue—is the third criterion.

"Necessary in a democratic society"

The third condition, the "necessary in a democratic society" test, requires the Court to determine whether the interference corresponds to a "pressing social need," whether it was "proportionate to the legitimate aim pursued," and whether the reasons given by the national authorities to justify it are "relevant and sufficient" (*Sunday Times v United Kingdom (no.1)*, ECtHR no. 6538/74 (1979), para. 62; *Zana v Turkey*, ECtHR no. 18954/91 (1997), para. 51). The principle of proportionality especially goes to the foundation of the Court's balancing exercise and the Court held that "every formality, condition, restriction and penalty imposed must be proportionate to the legitimate aim pursued" (*Handyside v United Kingdom*, ECtHR no. 5493/72 (1976), para. 49). As a starting point, the scope of the "margin of appreciation" that State Parties enjoy when deciding whether restriction of the right to freedom of expression is acceptable in the given circumstance depends on the type of speech that is targeted (is the expression political, commercial, or artistic in nature?). States have the littlest room for maneuver when it comes to restriction of political speech or debate of questions of public interest (*Lingens v Austria*, ECtHR no. 9815/82 (1986), para. 42) since the toleration of individual viewpoints is most essential for an effective pluralist democracy. Apart from the exception of scientifically disproven medical claims or advertising pieces, States enacting fake news laws operate within a very tight frame of acceptability. Once the nature of the expression and thus the relevant margin is established, multiple factors have to be taken into account when reviewing proportionality. To name but a few, whether a fake news law survives will depend on:

(1) *The proven value of the targeted expression and the required mental element of its creator*: The Court has created a distinction between information (facts) and opinions (value judgments). In most cases, a requirement to prove the truth of a value judgment is impossible to fulfil and would thus be disproportionate (*Jerusalem v Austria*, ECtHR no. 26958/95 (2001), para. 42). However, when restricting factual publications, proportionality is observed when there is proof "that the description of events given in the articles was totally untrue" (*Dalban v Romania*, ECtHR no. 28114/95 (1999), para. 50). In *Salov v Ukraine* (ECtHR no. 65518/01 (2005)) another criteria for the interference's disproportionality was the fact that the national court failed to prove that the accused was intentionally trying to deceive the public and to sabotage the election (para. 113);

(2) *The medium the expression was communicated in, the audience it was able to reach, and thus the possible degree of impact of the content*: The Court found a restriction to be disproportionate where the accused only held eight paper copies of the fake newspaper and had only talked about it with few persons. He had not shared any of it via a platform capable to reach masses and thus the impact of his actions was "minor" (para. 114);

(3) *Any special "duties and responsibilities" that might apply to the author* (to be discussed below);

(4) *The context in which the expression is prohibited and related temporal limits*: A case in point is the limitation of deliberations in the context of elections—which in themselves are an essential tool enabling the freedom of expression of the citizens. In *Bowman v United Kingdom* (ECtHR no. 24839/94 (1998)), the ECtHR upheld restrictive measures applied up to six weeks prior to an election, stressing that placing "certain restrictions of a type which would not normally be acceptable on freedom of expression, in order to secure the 'free expression' of the opinion of the people in the choice of the legislature" may thus "be considered necessary in the period preceding and during an election" (paras. 43–45). In line with these cases, the French Constitutional Council, for example, held that the French fake news legislation was proportionate since its application was limited to the three months' campaign period preceding general elections (Conseil Constitutionnel, *Décision n°2018-773*, 20 décembre 2018, paras. 19–26);

(5) *The way how the law is translated into restrictions on specific content*: A finding of proportionality will be favored where fake news laws foresee restrictions only after judicial review (expedited orders) and not automatically, for example, after a complaint to a social media platform (Craufurd Smith, 2019, pp. 73–74);

(6) *The nature and severity of penalties imposed*: Fake news laws must generally refrain from making use of criminal sanctions, especially imprisonment, since such penalties may lead to individuals censoring themselves out of fear of prosecution (*Lewandowska-Malec v Poland*, ECtHR no. 39660/07 (2012), para. 70). Even financial sanctions may amount to a disproportionate interference where they are "excessive" in that they endanger the financial survival of the person who is ordered to pay them (*Tolstoy Miloslavsky v United Kingdom*, ECtHR no. 18139/91 (1995), para. 49).

In sum, under the current Article 10(2) ECHR framework, restriction of free expression in the name of fake news appears to be possible, although the scope of such laws will be severely limited. Only restrictions of undisputable false statements, which are backed with convincing evidence as to impact, distributed with the proven intent to deceive the public, and subject to individual and independent review and reasonable penalties, are likely to be deemed compatible with freedom of expression.

Article 17 ECHR's "Abuse of Rights" Doctrine

To overcome this limited capacity of the law to address fake news, rather than operating within the limits of Article 10 ECHR, it could be argued that fake news could instead constitute a categorical exception from the protection of freedom of expression. In such a case, Article 17 ECHR would altogether remove the use of Article 10(1) ECHR to claim protection for creating and disseminating false information (Zand, 2017, p. 225). Article 17 ECHR outlaws any activity "aimed at the destruction of any of the rights and freedoms" set out in the Convention. It is meant to prevent individuals from abusing the human rights contained in the Convention by relying on them to justify and further their totalitarian or extremist cause (*W.P. and Others v Poland*, ECtHR no. 42264/98 (2004)). Thus, where the right to freedom of expression is relied upon by applicants to justify publication and dissemination that infringes "the very spirit of the Convention and the essential values of democracy" the Court will have recourse to Article 17 ECHR in declaring their application manifestly ill-founded and thus inadmissible (*Vona v Hungary*, ECtHR no. 35943/10 (2013), para. 34).

In order for Article 17 ECHR to be applied, the aim of the content in question must be to "spread violence or hatred," to "encourage the use of violence," to "undermine the nation's democratic and pluralist political system," or to "pursue objectives that are racist or likely to destroy the rights and freedoms of others" (*Lehideux and Isorni v France*, ECtHR no. 24662/94 (1998) Concurring Opinion of Judge Jambrek, para. 2). In line with earlier discussions on the dangers posed by fake news to the democratic process, an argument could be made that such content is "aimed at undermining the nation's democratic political system." Yet, so far, the Court has reserved this more radical treatment to "negation or revision" of "a category of clearly established historical facts"—such as the Holocaust (*Chauvy and Others v France*, ECtHR no. 64915/01 (2004), para. 69). The denial, "in a biased and polemical manner, far from any scientific objectivity," of the systematic killing of Jews runs counter to "one of the basic ideas of the Convention, namely justice and peace and further reflects racial and religious discrimination" and incites racial hatred (*Honsik v Austria*, ECtHR no. 25062/94 (1995), 6). The Court has carefully contained this strict doctrine to "extreme cases" and has shown far greater tolerance even with regard to the denial of the 1915 genocide of the Armenian people in Turkey whose historical and legal qualifications are controversial (*Perinçek v Switzerland*, ECtHR no. 27510/98 (2015), para. 114).

This strict doctrine as well does not leave much room for the enactment of fake news laws. It is unlikely that such expression reaches the level of destructiveness in the way required by the Court. With the exception of those disinformation pieces relating to the denial of the Holocaust, fake news as a whole does not appear to "immediately and clearly" promote ideas contrary to the values of the Convention. Additionally, since the application of this "abuse" doctrine would carve out a categorical exception, it would significantly restrict the Court's ability to provide an independent, case-by-case proportionality review of States' fake news laws (Craufurd Smith, 2019, pp. 66–67). In conclusion, both of the Court's weapons to tackle fake news are blunt. Freedom of expression prevents generalized restrictions and allows for only a very narrow, piecemeal protection against fake news. Moreover, those few legal measures that are possible are questionable from a perspective of effectiveness.

"Thinking Outside the Box": Alternative Justifications for Regulation

Operating under a traditional approach to the current ECtHR's freedom of expression framework thus offers unsatisfactory conclusions for a problem that has arisen in an entirely new context of a very different communication and media landscape than when the Court developed its case law. Accordingly, there is a need to rethink the boundaries of this freedom. The Court's existing legal framework must be reconceptualized in order to allow for wider possibility for restrictions of fake news.

The hierarchy of expression: Fake news as commercial speech

One of these novel legal approaches builds on the fact that fake news is not actually "news." This view, that fake news is merely "false advertising in core political speech's clothing" (Riggins, 2017, p. 1336), enjoys some academic support. Indeed, fake news is often political in appearance yet commercial in their purpose, and to differentiate between appearance and de facto function is not a novelty in the field of law. If the ECtHR can thus be convinced that those who create and disseminate false information are not actually engaging in political discourse but rather "pursue a commercial enterprise where 'fake news' is a commercial commodity" then perhaps they can be regulated by law (Andorfer, 2018, p. 1425).

As briefly touched upon in earlier sections, the ECtHR does not protect all categories of expression to the same extent. The scope of the margin of appreciation afforded to States seeking to regulate speech and the connected level of scrutiny exercised by the Court are dependent on the type of speech that is targeted. While political speech is the most highly protected category of free speech (*Lingens v Austria*, ECtHR no. 9815/82 (1986), para. 42), commercial speech receives a much lower level of protection and thus leaves a wide margin of appreciation to States. In such cases the Court "must confine its review to the question whether the measures taken on the national level are justifiable in principle and proportionate" (*Markt Intern Verlag GmbH and Klaus Beermann v Germany*, ECtHR no. 10572/83 (1989), para. 33).

The Court has pointed out that commercial speech is typically economically motivated and has broadly defined "advertising" as "a means of discovering the characteristics of services and goods offered" to the public (*Krone Verlag GmbH & Co. KG (No.3) v Austria*, ECtHR no. 29069/97 (2003), para. 31). An argument along these lines is conceivable: In the same way that advertisers seek to persuade the public by creating a particular image of a product, the supplier of fabricated political information seeks to persuade voters that a candidate is either unworthy for office or indeed the best person for the job. As to the economic motivation, there is extensive empirical evidence showing how fake news distributors benefit financially. Fake news sites generally feature advertisements for a legitimate product imbedded into the articles, thus keeping the tills ringing with every click (Riggins, 2017, p. 1322). The *New York Times* published a research piece titled "Inside a Fake News Sausage Factory: This is all about Income," providing a detailed account of those in the fake news business. Foreign actors without any political agenda made up to $6,000 monthly revenue with pro-Trump stories that took mere minutes to fabricate (Higgins et al., 2016).

Thus, in light of this similarity to advertising, the margin of appreciation afforded to States when regulating fake news might be wider. After all, the Court stressed that advertising can be restricted if it is "untruthful or misleading" (*Krone Verlag GmbH & Co. KG (No.3) v Austria*, ECtHR no. 29069/97 (2003), para. 31). There is nothing in the Court's case law that would point to an immediate dismissal of this idea. To the contrary, in a case concerning the ban of a Raëlian poster campaign with a proselytizing objective the Court stated that even though there was no incitement to buy a particular product, this speech was "closer to commercial speech than to political speech *per se*" as its "aim was to draw people to the cause of the applicant and not to address matters of political debate." The State's margin of appreciation was therefore broader (*Mouvement Raëlian Suisse v Switzerland*, ECtHR no. 16354/06 (2012), para. 62). This newly created category of a "lower level," "quasi-commercial" speech could conceivably encompass fake news since they are not even providing a minority view on a controversial topic. They simply have no basis in reality and are thus not capable of addressing any debate in the public interest.

However, care must be exercised when translating this idea into law. The Court's strict approach to protecting free expression certainly impedes the conclusion that all fake news could automatically fall within this relaxed standard of review. Instead, a separate provision targeting only false information with a clear economic objective could be envisaged. Fake news, for such purpose, could be defined as verifiably false or misleading content intentionally drafted to mimic journalistic sources for the primary purpose of generating revenue. In these situations, States restricting free expression would then have more leeway as they would operate within the ambit of commercial speech. Whether such an approach would bring the longed-for solution to the fake news disease is questionable though, as the application of such provision would necessarily be preceded by a complex case-by-case (judicial) analysis of motive.

Extending "duties and responsibilities" of journalists

Another solution on how greater restriction of fake news through law could be aligned with the ECtHR's case law on free expression was brought forward by

Chloe Francis (2018). She asserts that there is room for further development of the limitations of the freedom with respect to online users "because of their heightened and unprecedented influence in cyberspace." Since the Court has imposed positive obligations on States to create a "favourable environment" for the exercise of freedom of expression, she argues that States have the ability to impose certain "duties and responsibilities" on online users, similar to those applying to journalists (p. 108). This is an intriguing idea which has, to the knowledge of the author, not yet received any further academic attention.

The fact that a person belongs to a particular category may provide for special treatment within the framework of freedom of expression. This is the case for journalists and editors, due to the essential function the press fulfils in a democratic society (*Haldimann and Others v Switzerland*, ECtHR no. 21830/09 (2015) para. 45; *Observer and Guardian v United Kingdom*, ECtHR no. 13585/88 (1991), para. 59). They exercise the important role of a "public watchdog," supplying the public with information and ideas on political affairs and all matters of public interest and ensuring that individuals and organizations in positions of power are held publicly accountable for their actions. This important function, for which they need to be free from any State influence, justifies the broad freedom that is awarded to the press (*Dalban v Romania*, ECtHR no. 28114/95 (1999), para. 49). However, this broad freedom is counterpoised by a requirement of professionalism and greater diligence in respect of factual information. The Court has repeatedly clarified that there are "duties and responsibilities" attached to the exercise of freedom of expression (*Haldimann and Others v Switzerland*, ECtHR no. 21830/09 (2015), para. 46) and that journalists must "act in good faith and on an accurate factual basis" to "provide 'reliable and precise' information in accordance with the ethics of journalism" (*Fressoz and Poire v France*, ECtHR no. 29183/95 (1999), para. 54). Therefore, Article 10 ECHR prevents journalists in traditional media from publishing fake news. This is a logic trade-off: If you receive more power to impart information and reach masses of people in order to further democratic debate, you should be forced to use that power in a responsible manner.

However, the fake news disease arose from significant changes in our "media ecosystem." The Internet and social media platforms have reformed the ways how content is disseminated: on a much larger scale and with fewer professional requirements. Traditional media is increasingly being replaced by individuals producing and distributing content outside any professional standard (Council of Europe, 2011, para. 5). While the Court extended the application of Article 10 ECHR and the "duties and responsibilities" principle to the audiovisual media (*Haldimann and Others v Switzerland*, ECtHR no. 21830/09 (2015), para. 45) and communication via the Internet (*Times Newspaper Ltd v United Kingdom*, ECtHR nos. 30002/03 and 23676/03

(2009); *Editorial Board of Pravoye Delo and Shtekel v Ukraine*, ECtHR no. 33014/05 (2011); *Ashby Donald and Others v France*, ECtHR no. 36769/05 (2013), para. 34), it has so far failed to directly comment on whether this special role of the traditional media also extends to other actors in this new media environment.

The Council of Europe Committee of Ministers (2000) has purposefully adopted a broad definition of "journalist" as "any natural or legal person who is regularly engaged in the collection and dissemination of information to the public via any means of mass communication," thus leaving room for certain actors such as bloggers to be regarded as journalists. However, this term can surely not be stretched to such an extent as to cover "everyone with a keyboard" (Francis, 2018, p. 107). Nevertheless, an argument can be made for all Internet users to be regarded as a distinct and influential category of people in this new media environment who should also be subject to certain "duties and responsibilities." Francis (2018) explains this approach with the fact that "the public nature and viral potential of online content places internet users and professional journalists on an equal footing in terms of ability, reach and influence" (p. 107). Therefore, those Internet users that create content covering news and current events should be under similar obligations as journalists in terms of "accuracy and reliability" (*Fressoz and Poire v France*, ECtHR no. 29183/95 (1999) para. 54) of the information they supply.

Even though the Court has never explicitly extended these specific "duties and responsibilities" to another category of nonprofessional individuals, it is this author's view that existing case law can be used in favor of this solution. In *Steel and Morris* (ECtHR no. 68416/01 (2005)) the Court held that the obligation to "act in good faith in order to provide accurate and reliable information" must also apply to "others who engage in public debate" (para. 90). In *Stoll* (ECtHR no. 69698/01 (2007)) and in *Haldimann* (ECtHR no. 21830/09 (2015)) the Court stressed that every person who exercises his freedom of expression "undertakes 'duties and responsibilities' the scope of which depends on his situation and the technical means he uses" (para. 102; para. 47), thus suggesting that the application of a heightened standard of "duties and responsibilities" may not necessarily be limited to journalists alone and that the chosen platform to distribute the content could be of importance in that regard. Perhaps the most important decision was delivered in *Fatullayev* (ECtHR no. 40984/07 (2010)). In this case it was not clear whether the statements posted on an Internet forum were placed by the applicant in his capacity as a journalist providing information to the public or whether they simply expressed his personal opinions as an ordinary citizen in the course of an Internet debate. The Court found that this distinction was irrelevant. What was important was that he did not remain anonymous and that his statements were publicly disseminated on a "freely accessible popular internet forum, a medium which in modern times has no less powerful an effect than the print media" (para. 95). The Court thus seems to have already indirectly applied such heightened due diligence standard in regard to factual information to an Internet user because of the highly influential nature of cyberspace.

In sum, it has been argued that there is more room for the limitation of freedom of expression, not only with respect to certain fake news with a primarily economic motivation but more generally in respect to online users who report on "news" because of their similarity to journalists in their power to reach and influence the public. With these findings, States can address fake news more broadly.

Conclusion

The goal of this chapter has been to examine to what extent fake news can be regulated while preserving the right to freedom of expression in Europe. As fake news threatens to undermine the free electoral process and thus the future of democracy, the question how to tackle the phenomenon of fake news has raised a myriad of discussions and initiatives hoping to deliver the winning shot in this fight. What some of these initiatives forget to sufficiently consider is the fundamental right to free expression that is at stake and the high protection that it is awarded by constitutional courts. A detailed discussion of the ECtHR's case law has shown that at first glance, only those restrictions of undisputable false statements, which are backed with convincing evidence as to impact, distributed with the proven intent to deceive the public, and are subject to individual and independent judicial review as well as reasonable penalties, appear to be compatible with freedom of expression under Article 10 ECHR. Faced with such findings it comes as little surprise that many worry that effective regulation of fake news may ultimately not be possible.

However, this chapter has argued that the ECtHR has so far failed to address the significant change in our media ecosystem. Traditional media outlets are increasingly replaced by individuals producing and distributing content outside any professional standard on a much larger scale. This realization leads to the inevitable conclusion that existing legal frameworks must be reconceptualized if we want to stay on top of these developments. There is room to redraw these narrow boundaries of freedom of expression with respect to online users who report on news and current events. As the public nature and viral potential of online content places Internet users and professional journalists on an equal footing in terms of ability, reach, and influence, an argument can be made that they should be under similar obligations as journalists in terms of their "duties and responsibilities" as to the "accuracy and reliability" of the information they supply. By no means is the author arguing for a carte blanche, a categorical exception for online fake news from the protection of Article 10 ECHR, but by realizing this kinship States could be granted a wider margin of appreciation when engaging in careful proportionality assessments to consider all individual and public interests.

It has thus been demonstrated that the law in Europe can address disinformation online while preserving the right to freedom of expression. The exact extent to which it can do so effectively (both directly and indirectly—by addressing fake news through regulating other technological, economic, and social processes) will ultimately depend on the concrete regulatory methods that governments put in place. While some possible regulatory modalities show high potential in this regard (e.g., imposing certain operational obligations on online platforms such as "bursting the bubble"; flagging, downranking, and correcting mechanisms; as well as targeting the wider cultural conception of fake news by promoting media literacy skills), there is a need for more research to be carried out. In order to enable us to fine-tune such legal measures and technological processes to achieve the most effective results at least costs in terms of freedom of expression; such efforts should involve all stakeholders with legislators and policy makers, heads of social media companies, software engineers, journalists, and researchers working together to be able to more accurately identify shortcomings and solutions thereto when it comes to, among others, technological capabilities (AI development, algorithmic accountability, and the identification of "bots"), the practicalities of proposed regulatory mechanisms (in terms of resources), and developing quick and transparent harmonized procedures and effective oversight mechanisms. As a last observation, given the nature and the cross-border dimension of the problem of fake news, there appears to be the need for a solution at a centralized (European Union) level in order to ensure efficacy and justice.

References

Alcott, H., and Gentzkow, M. (2017). Social Media and Fake News in the 2016 Election. *Journal of Economic Perspectives*, 31(2), pp. 211–36.

Alemanno, A. (2018). Editorial: How to Counter Fake News? A Taxonomy of Anti-fake News Approaches. *European Journal of Risk Regulation*, 9, pp. 1–5.

Andorfer, A. (2018). Spreading like Wildfire: Solutions for Abating the Fake News Problem on Social Media via Technology Controls and Government Regulation. *Hastings Law Journal*, 69(5), pp. 1409–32.

Aramyan, A. (2015). Freedom of Expression and Its Limitations: Certain Theoretical and Practical Aspects. *21st Century*, 2, pp. 89–101.

ARTICLE 19 (1996). The Johannesburg Principles on National Security, Freedom of Expression and Access to information. The International Centre against Censorship, London. Available at https://www.article19.org/wp-content/uploads/2018/02/joburg principles.pdf. (accessed June 1, 2020).

Butler, B. (2018). Protecting the Democratic Role of the Press: A Legal Solution to Fake News. *Washington University Law Review*, 96(2), pp. 419–40.

Cohen, S. B. (2019). *Keynote Address at ADL's 2019 Never Is Now Summit on Anti-Semitism and Hate*. ADL. Available at https://www.adl.org/news/article/sacha-baron-cohens-keynote-address-at-adls-2019-never-is-now-summit-on-anti-semitism (accessed May 11, 2021).

Council of Europe (2000). Recommendation No. R(2000)7 of the Committee of Ministers to member states on the right of journalists not to disclose their sources of information.

——— (2011). Recommendation CM/Rec(2011)7 of the Committee of Ministers to member states on a new notion of media.

Craufurd Smith, R. (2019). Fake News, French Law and Democratic Legitimacy: Lessons for the United Kingdom? *Journal of Media Law*, 11(1), pp. 52–81.

European Commission (2018). Action Plan against Disinformation, JOIN (2018) 36 final.

European Commission for Democracy Through Law (Venice Commission) (2019). Joint Report of the Venice Commission and the Directorate of Information Society and Action against Crime of the Directorate General of Human Rights and Rule of Law (DGI) on Digital Technologies and Elections. Opinion NO. 925/2018, CDL-AD(2019)016. Available at https://www.venice.coe.int/webforms/documents/default.aspx?pdffile=CDL-AD(2019)016-e (accessed May 28, 2020).

Francis, C. (2018). Trial of Truth: Law and Fake News. *Edinburgh Student Law Review*, 3(3), pp. 100–13.

Higgins, A., McIntyre, M., and Dance, G. J. X. (2016). Inside a Fake News Sausage Factory: This Is All about Income. *New York Times*, November 25. Available at https://www.nytimes.com/ 2016/11/25/world/europe/fake-news-donald-trump-hillary-clinton-georgia.html (accessed May 28, 2020).

Hoffmann, C. (2020). Mit Knoblauch gegen Corona. *Tageschau*, March 29 (online). (*In German*). Available at https://www.tagesschau.de/faktenfinder/fakenews-corona-afrika-101.html (accessed June 1, 2020).

Humprecht, E. (2019). Where "Fake News" Flourishes: A Comparison across Four Western Democracies. *Information, Communication & Society*, 22(13), pp. 1973–88.

Kashatus, W. (2018). This Was a Real "Fake News" Story—And It Landed Us in War. *History News Network of the Columbian College of Arts & Science*, George Washington University. Available at https://historynewsnetwork.org/article/168374 (accessed May 12, 2021).

Katsirea, I. (2018). "Fake News": Reconsidering the Value of Untruthful Expression in the Face of Regulatory Uncertainty. *Journal of Media Law*, 10(2), pp. 159–88.

Kerr, R. L. (2019). From Holmes to Zuckerberg: Keeping Marketplace-of-Ideas Theory Viable in the Age of Algorithms. *Communication Law and Policy*, 24(4), pp. 477–512.

McIntyre, L. (2018). *Post-Truth*. Cambridge, MA: MIT Press.

Moretto Ribeiro, M., and Ortellado, P. (2018). Fake News: What It Is and How to Deal with It. *Sur–International Journal on Human Rights*, 27, pp. 69–82.

OSCE (2020). *Joint Declaration on Freedom of and Elections in the Digital Age*. Available at https://www.osce.org/representative-on-freedom-of-media/451150?download=true (accessed June 1, 2020).

Rainey, B., Wicks, E., and Ovey, C. (2014). *Jacobs, White & Ovey: The European Convention on Human Rights*, 6th ed. Oxford: Oxford University Press.
Reuters Institute (2020). *Digital News Report: Interactive*. Available at www.digitalnewsreport.org/interactive (accessed December 16, 2021).
Riggins, J. A. (2017). Law Student Unleashes Bombshell Allegation You Won't Believe: Fake News Commercial Speech. *Wake Forest Law Review*, 52(5), pp. 1313–38.
Rose, J. (2017). Brexit, Trump, and Post-Truth Politics. *Public Integrity*, 19(6), pp. 555–58.
Stover, D. (2018). Garlin Gilchrist: Fighting Fake News and the Information Apocalypse. *Bulletin of the Atomic Scientists*, 74(4), pp. 283–88.
Sugow, A. (2019). The Right to Be Wrong: Examining the (Im)Possibilities of Regulating Fake News While Preserving the Freedom of Expression in Kenya. *Strathmore Law Review*, 4, pp. 19–46.
Tambini, D. (2017). *Fake News: Public Policy Responses*. Media Policy Brief 20. London: Media Policy Project, London School of Economics and Political Science. Available at https://core.ac.uk/download/pdf/80787497.pdf (accessed May 29, 2020).
Timmer, J. (2017). Fighting Falsity: Fake News, Facebook, and the First Amendment. *Cardozo Arts & Entertainment Law Journal*, 35(3), pp. 669–706.
Vosoughi, S., Roy, D., and Aral, S. (2018). The Spread of True and False News Online. *Science*, 359(6380), pp. 1146–51.
Wardle, C. (2017). *Fake News. It's complicated*. First Draft, February 16. Available at https://firstdraftnews.org/latest/fake-news-complicated/ (accessed May 12, 2021).
Yahoo (2016). Duped by Fake News, Pakistan Minister Makes Nuke Threat to Israel. *Yahoo*, December 26. Available at https://news.yahoo.com/duped-fake-news-pakistan-minister-makes-nuke-threat-074808075.html (accessed May 12, 2021).
Zand, J. (2017). The Concept of Democracy and the European Convention on Human Rights. *University of Baltimore Journal of International Law*, 5(2), pp. 195–228.

Cases

Ashby Donald and Others v France, ECtHR no. 36769/08 (2013)
Barford v Denmark, ECtHR no.11508/85 (1989)
Bowman v United Kingdom, ECtHR no. 24839/94 (1998)
Brzeziński v Poland, ECtHR no. 47542/07 (2019)
Chauvy and Others v France, ECtHR no. 64915/01 (2004)
Conseil Constitutionnel, Décision n°2018-773, 20 décembre 2018
Dalban v Romania, ECtHR no. 28114/95 (1999)
Dareskizb Ltd v Armenia, ECtHR no. 61737/08 (pending)
Delfi v Estonia, ECtHR no. 64569/09 (2015)
Editorial Board of Pravoye Delo and Shtekel v Ukraine, ECtHR no. 33014/05 (2011)
Fatullayev v Azerbaijan, ECtHR no. 40984/07 (2010)
Fressoz and Poire v France, ECtHR no. 29183/95 (1999)
Hadjianastassiou v Greece, ECtHR no.12945/87 (1992)
Haldimann and Others v Switzerland, ECtHR no. 21830/09 (2015)
Handyside v United Kingdom, ECtHR no. 5493/72 (1976)
Hashman and Harrup v United Kingdom, ECtHR no. 25594/94 (1999)
Honsik v Austria (adm.), ECtHR no. 25062/94 (1995)
Jerusalem v Austria, ECtHR no. 26958/95 (2001)

Klass and Others v Germany, ECtHR no. 5029/71 (1978)
Krone Verlag GmbH & Co. KG (No.3) v Austria, ECtHR no. 39069/97 (2003)
Lehideux and Isorni v France, ECtHR no. 24662/94 (1998)
Lewandowska-Malec v Poland, ECtHR no. 39660/07 (2012)
Lingens v Austria, ECtHR no. 9815/82 (1986)
Markt Intern Verlag GmbH and Klaus Beermann v Germany, ECtHR no.10572/83 (1989)
Mouvement Raëlian Suisse v Switzerland, ECtHR no.16354/06 (2012)
Müller and Others v Switzerland, ECtHR no.10737/84 (1988)
Observer and Guardian v United Kingdom, ECtHR no.13585/88 (1991)
Perinçek v Switzerland, ECtHR no. 27510/08 (2015)
R v Zundel [1992] 2 S.C.R. 731
Rekvényi v Hungary, ECtHR no. 25390/94 (1999)
Salov v Ukraine, ECtHR no. 65518/01 (2005)
Steel and Morris v United Kingdom, ECtHR no. 68416/01 (2005)
Stoll v Switzerland, ECtHR no. 69698/01 (2007)
Sunday Times v United Kingdom (no.1), ECtHR no. 6538/74 (1979)
Times Newspaper Ltd v United Kingdom, ECtHR nos. 30002/03 and 23676/03 (2009)
Tolstoy Miloslavsky v United Kingdom, ECtHR no.18139/91 (1995)
United States v. Alvarez, 567 U.S. 709 (2012)
Vérités santé partique SARL v France (adm.), ECtHR no. 74766/01 (2005)
Vona v Hungary, ECtHR no. 35943/10 (2013)
W.P. and Others v Poland, ECtHR no. 42264/98 (2004)
Woolas, R v The Speaker of the House of Commons [2011] 2WRL 1362 (3 December 2010)
Zana v Turkey, ECtHR no. 18954/91 (1997)

Chapter 3

GEOPOLITICS, PERSONAL DATA COLLECTION, AND GLOBALIZATION: IRAN'S RESPONSE TO COVID-19

Megan Cameron

Introduction

In this chapter, the spread of the COVID-19 pandemic and subsequent state responses are analyzed through multiple perspectives. Iran is one of the countries hardest hit by the pandemic. The number of positive cases in the country has risen to staggering proportions compared to the number of cases in other Middle Eastern nations. Prior to the onset of the pandemic, the socio-economic conditions in Iran were already dire owing to the ongoing US campaign of sanctions and international pressure. These issues have been further exacerbated by the coronavirus pandemic, resulting in a lack of access to the most basic necessities and severe humanitarian concerns. The spread of the COVID-19 pandemic in Iran, and around the world, and the subsequent failures of governments to adequately contain the virus demonstrate faults in the existing global order. In particular, the past year has shown how the disjointed and fragmented system of geopolitics and human relationships, established after the Second World War, is limited when it comes to addressing complex issues that are truly global in nature. As American foreign policy analyst and lawyer Anne-Marie Slaughter noted, we are often taught to see the world as a chessboard, where actors craft and implement strategies that are designed to promote their nation's interests. By focusing on the military and diplomatic prowess of our individual, sovereign nations, however, we fail to recognize how citizens around the world are individually impacted by policy decisions (Slaughter, 2017, pp. 5–7). We also fail to establish meaningful connections and global processes for addressing crises like the COVID-19 pandemic.

Authors Danah Zohar and Ian Marshall similarly argue that the current global framework we operate within is inadequate. According to Zohar and Marshall, the original theories and laws of physical reality, made popular by figures such as Isaac Newton, Adam Smith, and Thomas Hobbes, stressed mechanistic physics. Mechanistic physics emphasized the existence of a vast gap between human beings and the physical world. These figures also pushed for frameworks that emphasized isolated and interchangeable parts. During the Enlightenment and for centuries afterward, these framings helped promote economic growth and technological innovation, including through the Industrial Revolution. However, these frameworks do not integrate factors such as human consciousness, societal issues, and politics, which can help to bridge the gap between human beings and the physical world (Zohar and Marshall, 1995, pp. 25–29). This chapter concludes by arguing that we need to revisit the isolated and disjointed global structure that we currently operate in, in order to better address future global crises at scale. We need to recognize that competition between states undermines the promotion of citizen well-being around the globe. It also undermines the overall influence of nation-states, as it encourages the evasion rather than the creation of dense relationships and connections (Slaughter, 2017, pp. 7–9). We must establish a new framework for managing global relations and foreign policy, which focuses on fostering connections across the globe and which seeks to establish a shared, singular reality that recognizes and thrives off varied social and political factors (Zohar and Marshall, 1995, pp. 29–33). This framework must account for racial and ethnic differences, socioeconomic divides, widening ideologies, recurring governance challenges, and the continuous and often harmful interactions between human beings and their natural environments (Saunders, 2005). In accounting for all these variables, this framework will establish a mechanism for understanding how one change in a singular region can have global ramifications and how global actors can take advantage of connections to address issues of global importance. Should another pandemic arise, or another major global crisis, leaders—and citizens—of the world will be better equipped to respond, demonstrate resilience, and survive.

Understanding the COVID-19 Situation in Iran

The coronavirus was first detected in Iran in February 2020 when the government publicly announced two individuals had died from COVID-19 in the conservative city of Qom ("Coronavirus: Iran," February 19, 2020), which is about two hours away from Tehran (Wright, 2020). The city is known for being home to Shiite seminaries that are run by leading ayatollahs. Its *Fatima Masumeh* shrine brings together pilgrims from around the globe (ibid.).

Preliminary reports suggested that the virus was brought to the country by a merchant who traveled to Wuhan, China, and then to Qom (ibid.). Within eight days of the first reported death from COVID-19, the virus had spread rapidly across the country to 24 of Iran's 31 provinces (ibid.).

Despite warnings from public health experts and governments around the world, the Iranian government was slow to respond to the onset of the pandemic and failed to implement prevention measures in a timely manner (ibid.). Officials in Qom even encouraged pilgrims to continue their visits to the site, stating, "We consider this holy shrine to be a place of healing. That means people should come here to heal from spiritual and physical diseases" ("Iran Cleric," 2020). Cases in countries ranging from Azerbaijan to Canada to Pakistan and Lebanon have been traced back to Iran. Many of these cases were directly tied to individuals who had visited Qom (Wright, 2020).

Initially, the government also refused to institute quarantines for infected patients. Deputy health minister Iraj Haririchi stated this was because quarantines are emblematic of the long-gone pre–First World War era, in which diseases such as the plague and cholera were prominent. Further, as reports of the virus rapidly spreading through China emerged, the Iranian government also made no efforts to curtail travel between the two countries. Some speculate that this is because Iran wanted to maintain positive diplomatic relations with China. Finally, when Iran's government imposed travel restrictions between Iran and China on January 31, 2020 ("ویروس کرونا ؟," 2020), Bahram Parsaei, a ranking member of parliament from Shiraz, noted that some Iranian airlines continued to engage in business as usual. These airlines also helped transport passengers traveling to China from other countries. Parsaei noted that even Turkey, whose economy heavily relies on Chinese tourism, cancelled flights between the two countries (ابهام در, 2020). Meanwhile, Iran's Mahan Air continued to offer flights between Tehran and Beijing until February 23. Politics also influenced how the government responded to the onset of the COVID-19 pandemic. On February 11, the country recognized the anniversary of Iran's Revolution. On February 21, the country held its parliamentary elections. The government had already expressed concerns that there would be low voter turnout at the polls due to ongoing political turmoil. Of note, in November 2019, the government violently put down nationwide protests staged against a state-instituted spike in fuel prices (Behravesh, 2020a). It also mistakenly shot down a passenger plane with 176 people onboard in January 2020 (ibid.). As a result, experts suggested that the government did not want to acknowledge the pandemic fearing this action would reduce participation in anniversary celebrations as well as parliamentary elections. Although Iran saw overall low voter turnout in the election, millions of people turned up, which could have contributed to increased transmission as well. The Iranian government's response to the spread of the virus was also heavily influenced by the country's bitter relationship with the United States. After the election, Iran's Supreme Leader Ayatollah Ali Khamenei claimed Iran's enemies were blowing the threat of the virus out of proportion to prevent voters from participating in the election. Former US Secretary of State Mike Pompeo responded by stating Iran was misleading its people and the world about "vital details" on the spread of the virus (Daragahi, 2020).

Over the past year, evidence has emerged suggesting that the Iranian government was well aware of the outbreak as it was happening. Despite this knowledge, the government failed to inform the public and act in a responsible manner (Behravesh, 2020b. Many public health experts speculated about why the government chose first to acknowledge the outbreak of the virus in the country based on the two confirmed deaths in Qom rather than confirmed infections. Experts suggested that by the time the government made the announcement, the virus must have spread rapidly across the country. The government knowing this still decided to act slowly (ibid.). The government's decision to bow to religious pressure and refuse to institute quarantines in Qom also allowed seminarians, clerics, and politicians moving between the city and Tehran to spread the disease widely (Daragahi, 2020). Additionally, on February 15, four days before the country officially recognized its first case of the coronavirus, reports suggest that Iran's Supreme Leader held a meeting with a group of religious eulogists. Yet, his security detail did not allow any of the eulogists to approach Khamenei and kiss his hand. This was uncharacteristic, leading some experts to suggest these measures were instituted to protect the Supreme Leader from the virus, which the government knew was circulating widely (Behravesh, 2020b).

Most recent figures suggest that Iran is a country of 83 million people (CIA World Factbook, 2021). Thus far, the country has seen approximately 1.52 million cases of the coronavirus and 58,945 deaths. Although around 1.3 million people have recovered from the virus in Iran, the country emerged as a global epicenter for the pandemic (Worldometer, 2021). The consequences of the pandemic have been profound. The virus has upended the country's society and economy, overwhelming hospitals and impacting access to necessities. In addition, the pandemic has called into question the government's motivations and ability to safeguard Iranians and support the Iranian society during its time of need.

The Socioeconomic Context in Iran Pre-COVID-19

It is important to examine the socioeconomic environment before coronavirus to understand how the Iranian government has responded to the outbreak of

COVID-19 and why the pandemic has had such a devastating impact on the country.

In 2018, when the United States withdrew from the 2015 Iran nuclear deal, then American President Donald Trump imposed a series of sanctions on Iran (Marx, 2020). The United States stated it was pursuing a campaign of "maximum pressure" on Iran in order to cut the Middle Eastern nation off from the world financial system and trade and bend the Iranian government to its will (ibid.). As a result of the sanctions, Iran's oil experts were reduced to shambles, which severely damaged the country's economy. On October 8, 2020, US Secretary of State Mike Pompeo announced the United States would sanction 18 prominent Iranian banks. This resulted in a sharp decline in Iran's currency and sent ripple waves across the country's economy (Marx, 2020). In addition, the United States under the Trump Administration unilaterally moved to reimpose UN-led sanctions against Iran despite protest from other global world leaders (Williams and De Luce, 2020). The Trump Administration blamed Iran's high COVID-19 numbers on the government's inadequacy and corruption. As explained above, the Iranian government was slow to act in response to the outbreak. However, the sanctions regime that the United States imposed on Iran has severely undermined the country's economy, thereby creating the conditions for the COVID-19 outbreak to become even more devastating. Since the sanctions effectively excluded Iran from the international banking system, the country was unable to obtain the critical medical supplies needed to treat COVID-19 patients (Mousavian, 2020). The United States has not sanctioned food and medicine. However, the transportation that Iran relies on to receive food and medicinal supplies in the country has been sanctioned by the United States (Keshavarz, 2020). According to data collected by Bourse & Bazaar, when the Trump Administration implemented sanctions against Iran, there was a simultaneous decline in imports of medical supplies from the European Union to Iran. This suggests that the Islamic Republic could not afford to import the critical supplies or that EU-based businesses were hesitant to conduct business with Iran due to the ongoing sanctions (Batmanghelidj, 2020).

As a result of the sanctions, Iran has also been unable to use its monetary reserves, which are trapped in international banks subject to US sanctions (Keshavarz, 2020). This is one of the reasons the government was also unable to implement economic and social programs to help offset the impacts of the coronavirus. Iran's Foreign Minister Javad Zarif tweeted that the United States had gone from imposing "economic terrorism" to "medical terror" on the country. Zarif pressed the international community to stop supporting "war crimes" by obeying "illegal and immoral" sanctions (Lederer, 2020). In 2020, numerous political leaders, diplomats, civil society organizations, and other experts pushed the Trump Administration to loosen the sanctions against Iran so that the country could effectively combat the virus. Such calls came from individuals, including former Democratic presidential candidates Elizabeth Warren and Bernie Sanders (Mousavian, 2020), United Nations Human Rights Chief Michele Bachelet (Daragahi, 2020), as well as *The New York Times* (Mousavian, 2020). Many of these individuals, organizations, and the media expressed concerns that a failure to address the spread of the virus in Iran could result in larger outbreaks in neighboring countries, including Afghanistan, Iraq, and Pakistan, each of which already has a fragile healthcare system (Daragahi, 2020).

However, several entities in the United States, including a series of right-wing think tanks in Washington, DC, lobbied the Trump Administration to tighten the sanctions and escalate military offensives against the country. Other experts operating in the same ideological circles believed that expanding the sanctions against Iran during this time of crisis would force the country to come back to the negotiating table on key issues such as nuclear weapons (Mousavian, 2020). Most recently, newly elected US President Joe Biden shared that he would not lift the ongoing sanctions on Iran until the country committed to halting uranium enrichment (McDonald, 2021). As a result, for the foreseeable future, Iran continues to fight the COVID-19 pandemic while also battling ongoing assaults to the economic fabric of the nation. This could prove disastrous. Amirhossein Takian and his colleagues at Tehran University of Medical Sciences, writing in a March letter in *The Lancet*, state that "all aspects of prevention, diagnosis, and treatment are directly and indirectly hampered, and the country is falling short in combating the crisis" (Stone, 2020).

This situation demonstrates how global actors currently still view the foreign policy arena as a chessboard, where one's enemy must be supplanted at all costs. This approach clearly, however, undermines the overall well-being of citizens around the globe. In addition, the US belief that its sanctions would have a limited impact on other nations, such as Iran's neighbors, is emblematic of the outdated frameworks previously discussed, which fail to recognize the connected nature of nation-states today.

Government Response to the COVID-19 Pandemic

As previously explained, the Iranian government's initial response to the spread of the COVID-19 pandemic was lackluster. In addition, both religious ideology and regime politics significantly influenced and undermined government efforts to respond to the virus. This section discusses some of the ways in which the Iranian government has responded to the coronavirus pandemic.

In February 2020, as the consequences of the pandemic began to become more apparent, Iran's President Hassan Rouhani established a "national headquarters for fighting the coronavirus" (Bastani, 2020). However, the headquarters continued to resist establishing organized quarantine measures with Deputy Health Minister Jaririchi claiming that even China's quarantine efforts had not proven beneficial (معاون وزیر, 2020). Under the direction of Ayatollah Khamenei, the Iranian military led by the Revolutionary Guards formed Imam Reza Base, helped spearhead the country's efforts to combat the pandemic. Under the leadership of General Mohammad Bagheri, the chief of staff of the Armed Forces, the military unit set forth a slate of preventive measures the Iranian government could adopt. These included creating a national monitoring program that could trace infections, using the military to facilitate 1,000 mobile and stationary clinics for screening and examining cases, and launching a nationwide campaign to "de-crowd stores, streets, and roads" (Nourmohammadian, 2020). Despite the fact that this March 2020 proposal reflected some of the best practices amplified by global public health experts at the time, military officers and government officials ignored the recommendations fearing the economic consequences of a nationwide shutdown and refusing to institute quarantines (2020, در کرونا).

In late February and early March, the government introduced new measures to halt the spread of the coronavirus. These included closing schools, malls, markets, and key religious locations as well as banning large gatherings, including cultural and religious events ("Coronavirus: Iranians," 2020). On March 25, President Rouhani instituted a partial lockdown across the country, which mandated that businesses and government offices close for two weeks, and prohibited travel between cities. However, in early April, the government devised a gradual reopening plan for businesses that were considered low or average risk for transmission of the virus to mitigate economic fallout. In late April, Iran reopened its international borders to stimulate regional trade. Mosques and schools were reopened in mid-May followed shortly after by all major businesses and religious sites. Figures from May and June suggest that these efforts helped industries to recover. However, critics also noted the rapid reopening plan contributed significantly to a rise in cases, thereby creating a "second wave" of COVID-19 infections (Wintour, 2020). As a result, the government instituted new restrictions, which mandated face masks in indoor and outdoor spaces and fined violators. The restrictions also saw schools, universities, restaurants, cafes, cultural centers, and beauty salons in Tehran close. Despite efforts to quell the spread of the virus, the country entered a "third wave" of COVID-19 in the fall (Eqbal and Rasmussen, 2020).

Although Iran is generally considered to have one of the best medical and public health infrastructures in the Middle East, the country's healthcare system was not well-equipped for the outbreak of COVID-19. The country has suffered through shortages of personal protective equipment and ventilators, which are critical to treating COVID-19 patients (Cunningham, 2020). A few charities and nongovernmental organizations such as Relief International and Moms Against Poverty have sent a limited number of medical supplies to the country. However, the ongoing spate of US sanctions, which penalize non-US companies for conducting business with Iran, have also impacted the country's ability to access relief. The European Union as well as nations such as Russia, China, Japan, Uzbekistan, Kuwait, Turkey, and the United Arab Emirates have provided unconditional aid to Iran (Daragahi, 2020). Further, the WHO country office has received over $80 million to support procurement of critical medical and laboratory equipment to combat the virus in Iran (World Health Organization, 2020). After sending personnel to Iran, the World Health Organization established that Iran's immediate priorities should be early detection, isolation and treatment, implementing effective contact tracing mechanisms, and creating a system of communications management given the vast spread of misinformation around the virus. The international organization delivered shipments of resources including masks, face shields, gloves, show covers, and other supplies to the country. The WHO also delivered shipments of medicines to enable Iran to participate in the Solidarity clinical trial, which is one of the world's largest ongoing studies working to identify effective treatments to the virus (World Health Organization).

In February 2020, the US Department of State offered Iran humanitarian assistance and medical supplies. However, Ayatollah Khamenei rejected the offer in March claiming the United States created the virus and as a result the Western nation could not be trusted (Khameini.IR, 2020). This reflects ongoing distrust, which has been reinforced by the continuous implementation of a chessboard approach to foreign policy and foreign relations.

Despite the fact that Iran is bearing the brunt of the COVID-19 pandemic, the Iranian government has also hindered Western relief organizations from operating in the country. The day after Iran rejected the American offer of aid, the Iranian government rescinded the permission it had given Doctors Without Borders to establish a 50-bed field hospital for COVID-19 patients in Isfahan, a major city located south of Tehran (Stone, 2020). The decision came after misinformation had spread online that the Doctors Without Borders team had arrived in Iran to steal information about the genomes of COVID-19 viruses spreading across the country (ibid.). The Iranian government has also accrued criticism for donating one million masks to China in early February, despite medical supply shortages in Iran (Yücesoy, 2020).

Over the course of the pandemic, the government has also introduced some measures to offset the impact of the COVID-19 pandemic on its citizens. These include a moratorium on tax payments to the government for a period of three months, subsidized loans to affected businesses and vulnerable households, cash transfers to vulnerable households (KPMG, 2020), and temporary penalty waivers for Iranians with nonperforming loans (International Monetary Fund). The government has also expanded funding to the healthcare sector, which amounts to 2 percent of the country's GDP. It also provided additional support to the unemployment insurance fund using 0.3 percent of the GDP. A portion of this funding is likely to come from Sukuk bonds, the National Development Fund (ibid.), and privatization proceeds (International Monetary Fund). These efforts represent over 10 percent of GDP in COVID-19 relief and recovery measures.

In April, the government also launched its largest ever initial public offering by selling shares in 18 companies, including its 12 percent share of the Social Welfare Fund (SHASTA), the largest public company. These efforts were intended to generate income for the government, as it continues to struggle with the sanctions' regime and economic fallout of the COVID-19 pandemic (International Monetary Fund). The Central Bank of Iran also announced it had injected $1.5 billion into the foreign exchange market in March to stabilize the country's currency (Central Bank of Iran, 2020). It followed this up with another $1 billion injection in July. In September, the Central Bank announced it would allocate 1 percent of the country's sovereign wealth fund to stabilize the stock market (International Monetary Fund). Further, the Central Bank also rolled out contactless payments and increased limits for bank transactions in order to reduce transmission of the virus via banknotes and debit cards (Contactless Payment, 2020).

Further, the government has offered 75 trillion tomans of loans with a preferential rate of 12 percent to impacted businesses that have not laid off employees with a return period of two years for service and production businesses. The government also provided 6 trillion tomans of credit to businesses (KPMG, 2020).

Thus far, government response efforts to the pandemic have been significantly influenced by online misinformation and disinformation. According to the Atlantic Council, opposition operatives in Iran have faked documents and audio records to exaggerate the pandemic and damage public trust (Daragahi, 2020). Misleading information online has also directly harmed Iranians. Reports indicate that over 700 Iranians have died after drinking ethanol to immunize themselves against the virus (*Iran: Over*, 2020). The government and prominent Iranian leaders have also been responsible for disseminating misinformation about the virus. As previously noted, Ayatollah Khamenei has claimed that the United States manufactured the coronavirus, stating that it is "specifically built for Iran using the genetic data of Iranians" (Takeyh, 2020).

General Hussein Salami, the head of the Islamic Revolutionary Guard Corps, also brandished a device called *Mustaan*, which he claimed could detect the coronavirus (ibid.). Experts have expressed concerns that such misinformation and disinformation could impact Iran's efforts to vaccinate its people. Iran launched a human trial of the Iranian COVID-19 vaccine at the end of 2020 (*Iran Begins*, 2020). Iran has also been in negotiations to acquire doses of Pfizer's vaccine and is working with COVAX and China to acquire more (Radio Free Europe/Radio Liberty, 2020). However, in January 2021, Ayatollah Khamenei banned the government from importing COVID-19 vaccines from the United States and the UK stating the Western powers were "untrustworthy" (Hafezi, 2021). Prior to the pandemic, the WHO Country Office did not have a communications officer position. However, today, there are six individuals working with the Ministry of Health to combat the spread of misinformation and augment trust in health publications (World Health Organization, 2020).

Government Data Collection on COVID-19 in Iran

Monitoring the spread of COVID-19 in Iran as well as evaluating government and international efforts to curtail the virus has been challenging. The government has been accused of vastly underreporting COVID-19 figures. When the coronavirus first hit Iran in February 2020, Iran's deputy health minister Iraj Haririchi told reporters that the country had "almost stabilized" the spread of the virus, thereby rejecting reports that 50 people had already died from the virus. Haririchi stated that he would resign "if the numbers are even half or a quarter of this," sharing that Iran had only 61 confirmed cases at the time, with 12 deaths (*Health Ministry*, February 24, 2020). Shortly after, the deputy minister confirmed that he had contracted COVID-19. As previously explained, experts are skeptical about the government's timeline for recognizing the virus and its concerns about how the fear concerning the COVID-19 pandemic could impact participation in parliamentary elections. Official figures from around February 2020 suggested that Iran had a COVID-19 mortality rate between 8 and 18 percent. In comparison, China, where the virus originated, had a 3 percent COVID-19 mortality rate. Other countries have had far lower mortality rates. Similarly, in late February 2020, the Iranian government shared that there were 388 confirmed cases of the coronavirus in the country as well as 34 deaths. However, many experts criticized these figures and accused the government of underreporting the number of cases and deaths. A team of Canadian epidemiologists, for example, crafted a mathematical model that suggested with a 95 percent confidence rate that Iran had over 18,000 cases of the virus at the time. The model was based on

Iran's official death toll and COVID-19's infection and mortality rates worldwide, shifts in COVID-19 in other countries that were linked to Iran, flight data, and travel patterns. Their estimates were published on medRxiv, which features preliminary research that has not yet been peer-reviewed (Tuite et al., 2020). Over the past year, the unreliable nature of official Iranian government data on the spread of the coronavirus has become apparent. One Iranian official admitted on television in late April that the health ministry and the National Security Council had directed him not to report the real number of coronavirus cases (Nili, 2020). Last April, Iran's own parliament even recognized that the death toll in the country could be at least twice what it had been reporting and the number of cases could be ten times higher (Associated Press, 2020). Simultaneously, a spokesman for Iran's armed focus has noted that 3,600 Iranians have been arrested for "spreading rumors on coronavirus," including those pertaining to official figures related to the spread of the virus (Radio Free Europe/Radio Liberty). This demonstrates how the Iranian government has repressed information during the age of COVID-19 and sought to advance its own carefully crafted narrative. It also reveals the weak scientific evidence-based structures the country has instituted. Several experts have criticized the government's dissemination and use of unreliable data as a major contributing factor to Iran's second and third waves of the pandemic. Facing looming signs of an economic downfall, President Rouhani began to relax COVID-19 restrictions in April 2020 (Yücesoy, 2020). Mosques in 132 towns were reopened for worship (Tasim News, n.d.). As Iran entered its third wave of the pandemic in October, an official of Iran's Medical Council shared that government underreporting of COVID deaths was significant and that the number of deaths could be four times higher than the official number. The official warned that suppression of data created the illusion that the pandemic was under control, thereby encouraging individuals to shirk restrictions and be less vigilant about virus prevention (Sinaee, 2020).

As the country became one of the global epicenters of the virus, the spread of COVID-19 has been unique in that it has impacted an uncharacteristic number of political and government figures. These include Iran's Vice President Masoumeh Ebtekar, two members of President Hassan Rouhani's cabinet, including the chairman of the Committee on National Security and Foreign Policy, and a senior cleric who served as Iran's ambassador to the Vatican. Despite these high-profile cases, the government has still failed to provide adequate transparency and accountability around how the virus has spread throughout the country to its people and the world (Wright, 2020). Many experts suggest the government's decision to suppress the data is also political, as Iran does not want to appear vulnerable in the face of its enemies, such as the United States. Given the global nature of this virus and the interdependent structures of modern financial, trade, travel, and other industries, the suppression of data poses a great risk to Iranians and the world at large. However, because nations continue to approach crises in a chessboard manner, they are primarily considered with the well-being of their own citizens and fail to recognize the ripple effects their actions can have on the well-being of citizens around the world.

A lack of transparency around COVID-19 data also influences global efforts to combat the virus.

Shortly after the onset of the pandemic, the Center for Systems Science and Engineering at John Hopkins University developed a COVID-19 Dashboard. The website maps data on the number of COVID-19 infections, recoveries, and deaths around the world (John Hopkins University of Medicine, 2020). However, the published data is derived from governmental sources. In the case of countries like Iran, where underreporting of COVID-19 figures is common, the data is not entirely reliable. This directly impacts international understanding of the crisis in Iran and other parts of the world. Following the COVID-19 pandemic, global actors will seek to use these shared data structures to prepare for future emergencies. Incomplete data sets will undermine these efforts and negatively impact future response efforts at large, not just for Iranians.

The Use of Personal Data Collection Mechanisms to Monitor the Spread of COVID-19 in Iran

As noted above, the collection of data is critical to understanding how the coronavirus spreads across a country and impacts its people. After the National Headquarters to Combat the Coronavirus was established in February 2020, this organization has created numerous avenues for Iranians voluntarily to participate in self-assessments, receive medical assistance, and obtain risk notifications. These websites and applications also disseminate prevention and statistical information (Gesley, 2020). Thus far, the Iranian government has responded positively toward the data it has gleaned from citizens' electronic and telephone self-assessments, in-person medical reviews, and COVID-19 tests. As of April 2020, the deputy minister of Health and Medical Education shared that through these avenues, it has obtained access to the COVID-19-related data of over 70 million Iranians out of the 84 million person-population (ibid.). However, as discussed in the previous section, there is little transparency around the true nature of the spread of the virus in the country.

The applications and websites the government has used to obtain access to data on COVID-19 in the country include:

1. **The AC19 App:** In March 2020, the Iranian Ministry of Health and Medical Education prompted users across the country via text message to download the Application for Combatting Coronavirus app (also known as the AC19 app). The app enables users to participate in a COVID-19 self-assessment test, which, once completed, recommends that individuals with mild symptoms self-quarantine. In addition, the app allows individuals to obtain medical assistance virtually, thus reducing the transmission of the virus by individuals visiting hospitals. The app was developed by the Tehran Headquarters for Combating Corona, the Ministry of Health and Medical Education, and the Information and Communications Technology (ICT) (ibid.). It is an Android app. As of January 2021, the Android operating system holds over 90 percent of the operating system market share in Iran (StatCounter, 2021). The AC19 app requests that users provide permission to access their location and asks for personal data including the user's phone number, name, address, gender, and weight. The app also asks about the medical symptoms of users, their family members, and social connections. The Application has stirred some controversy around privacy protections in Iran, as users from older Android phones are not prompted to provide consent for the app to access their personal data. In addition, a London-based security researcher has revealed that the app collects precise location data, including Wi-Fi and mobile-based data, GPS-based data, and live device movements. This raised concerns that the app is a form of spyware or malware. The Islamic Republic News Agency has refuted these claims (Gesley, 2020).
2. **The Salamat Website:** In response to criticisms related to the AC19 app, the Ministry of Health and Medical Education began requiring that all developers must comply with the guidelines of the National Headquarters for Combating Corona and register with the Ministry of Health before operating. The Ministry also stated that in cases where individuals' COVID-19 assessments reflect a higher probability of infection, these apps must direct these individuals to the Salamat.gov.ir website where the government carries out a unified method for medical response and registration rather than collect any of these individuals' personally identifiable information. Simultaneously, the Ministry of Health began encouraging citizens to register with the Salamat.gov.ir website and complete self-assessments online. Individuals must share their National Identity Codes, date of birth, and answer questions regarding their COVID-19 medical symptoms as well as the symptoms of their family members and social contacts to complete the self-assessment on the website. Individuals who demonstrate a high risk of infection are directed to nearby hospitals or health centers and are contacted by a dedicated health provider over the phone (ibid.).

3. **The Mask App and Website:** Mask is a contact tracing Application that was designed by volunteer technical experts from Sharif, Amirkabir, and Shahid Beheshti Universities for the Ministry of Health and Medical Education. The app shares an infection risk map based on aggregate data obtained from the Ministry of Health and Medical Education. It also offers a live contact/infection risk notification service. Users do not need to share personal information to use the app. However, if users want to participate in the self-assessment test or receive infection risk notifications, they must provide the app their phone number and authorize access to location data via their device. The app specifies that user phone numbers are used to alert individuals who have been in the proximity of others who have tested positive for COVID-19 within the last two weeks. The developers also specify that the contact and infection risk notification services are based on data users voluntarily share. The data is anonymized and collected via locating tracking, Bluetooth, GPS, and QR code (ibid.).
4. **Website for Coronavirus Self-Assessment, Information, and Registration:** Created by the Deputy of Research and Technology of the Ministry of Health and Medical Education, this website features educational information on the coronavirus, an infection risk map, and numerous self-assessment tests. One of these tests requires users to share their phone number (ibid.).

    Privacy Concerns: Although access to granular information is helpful in the context of public education and awareness around COVID-19, numerous experts have raised concerns that the dissemination of this information without safeguards also constitutes a threat to an individual's right to privacy and data protection. The Ministry of Health has published its privacy policy, which outlines that the Ministry safeguards individual privacy and personal data in compliance with the 2017 Decree of the Supreme Administrative Council Concerning the Charter on Citizens' Rights in the Administrative Systems, to bolster trust that user data will not be mismanaged (ibid.).

To date, Iran has not introduced any laws or mechanisms that would enable the government to access personal user data in an unauthorized manner to evaluate the spread of COVID-19 (ibid.). In addition, although Iran has not introduced comprehensive privacy legislation that is designed to protect personal user data, the right to privacy and data protection has been enshrined in numerous pieces of legislation as well as in the constitution. These laws create a reasonable expectation of privacy for individuals in both the physical and virtual spaces. The legislation covers personal documents, mail, phones, computers, telephone conversations, and data that is transferred in a private manner in the digital environment that could be linked to an individual, such as personally identifiable information, like a person's name, address, and bank accounts. As a result, access to and investigation of this information or materials containing this information are typically prohibited unless an individual has provided "informed, express, and written consent" (ibid.). Any legal requests or investigations for access to user data must have a clear scope and are subject to a series of requirements. These include consideration of the individual's dignity, transparency, anonymization, and aggregation to the extent required by the law, a clear statement explaining why access to the data is needed, and a scope that ensures access to data is limited to only that which is needed to achieve the stated purpose (ibid.).

To date, Iranian courts have responded to cyber violations based on the remedies defined in applicable laws or regulations. Depending on the law, this can include punitive damages, imprisonment, sanctions on the violator's bank accounts, and other measures. Crimes committed in cyberspace are considered within the jurisdiction of the Special Cyber Crime Court and the Iranian Cyber Police, which is also known as FATA (ibid.). Currently, Iran is also considering reform bills that would establish oversight measures for cyberspace violations (ibid.).

In addition to legal measures, the Maher Center in Iran has been tasked with receiving and responding to cyberspace complaints, informing impacted individuals that their private data has been compromised, and delivering appropriate notifications to the highest authority of the violating governmental entity (ibid.).

Proposing Greater Reliance on Personal Data

Given the limitations related to government collection and transmission of COVID-19 data in Iran, and the concerns around government collection of personal user data during contact tracing efforts, we must consider alternative avenues for data collection related to the coronavirus.

During the pandemic, social media has proven to be a valuable method for citizens to sidestep government censorship and suppression efforts and share accurate information in a timely manner. Over the past few months, numerous doctors, nurses, and medical staff members have taken to platforms such as Twitter to share harrowing stories about their experiences working on COVID-19 cases. These anecdotes have provided critical, on-the-ground information about the coronavirus situation in Iran to both domestic and international spectators.

In response, the Iranian government has contacted many social media platforms and demanded that such content be removed. Similarly, some individuals who hold prominent public positions have been asked to recant their positions publicly. Typically, social media platforms publish transparency reports that outline the scope and scale of government requests for content restrictions they receive from different countries. However, Twitter does not publish data on requests from the Iranian government (Twitter, 2020). This is a serious freedom of expression concern and must be rectified, especially given the critical role accurate information plays for public awareness and education during the pandemic.

It is also important to recognize the limitations of social media as a mechanism for data collection on COVID-19-related issues. While social media is valuable for sharing anecdotes that can reveal key insights about on-the-ground occurrences, it is not a reliable mechanism for collecting aggregate data on the spread of cases as well as on recoveries and deaths. In addition, during the pandemic, the amount of COVID-19-related misinformation and disinformation has grown significantly. Despite platform efforts to address these harmful forms of content, misleading information continues to circulate, especially in languages other than English. As a result, any information shared on social media about the pandemic must be verified before being used for official purposes (Pazzanese, 2020).

Analysis

As discussed in this chapter, the COVID-19 pandemic has significantly impacted the social, economic, and political fabric of Iran. Despite some government efforts to support its people and boost its economy, the country continues to suffer. In part, this is due to the ongoing US-led sanction regimes, which have damaged the country's financial flows and stability.

While the situation in Iran is dire, many other countries around the world are similarly suffering. To date, estimates indicate that the coronavirus could decrease global economic growth to an annualized rate of −4.5 percent to −6.0 percent in 2021. Major advanced economies, which make up 60 percent of global economic activity, are projected to operate below their potential output level through at least 2024. Around the world, unemployment has soared. Poverty is on the rise. As a result, it is in every nation's interest to combat the spread of the pandemic and transition back to "normal" as soon as possible (World Social Report, 2020).

However, the coronavirus situation in Iran has demonstrated how geopolitics can influence government pandemic response efforts negatively. Although the government has launched numerous methods to source data from citizens, the administration has demonstrated it is unreliable in communicating this data transparently. This lack of transparency and accountability around official coronavirus statistics has muddled global efforts to track and monitor the spread of the virus. The lack of access to clear data also makes it difficult to inform global and local response and aid efforts. Further, it negatively influences domestic efforts around public awareness and education. As previously noted, the opaque nature of data collection and sharing in Iran is politically motivated and likely designed to deter any notions in the international arena that the country is vulnerable or weak.

Social media can provide an alternative avenue for collecting data about on-the-ground occurrences in real time. However, as explained, social media is limited in that it is subject to misinformation and is not useful for calculating aggregate statistics.

The current approach to COVID-19 response and related data collection is deeply rooted in theories and frameworks of international relations and societal management that view different states and communities as isolated from, and typically in competition with, one another. As discussed, these theories fail to recognize the value of connected communities, and therefore they fail to develop robust mechanisms that can underpin these communities so that they can thrive. In a world that is increasingly globalizing, whether it be through economic flows, travel, or culture, outdated frameworks that seek to promote competition and isolation are no longer feasible.

The nature of data collection during the pandemic has demonstrated the need for us to revisit the frameworks with which we govern international and societal relations. Globalization has made actors around the world interdependent. But, without adequate recognition and support for these networks, the mechanisms that facilitate globalization, including shared data collection, are fragile. Going forward, domestic experts in Iran must reconsider how they can collect data on the local COVID-19 situation to enable more informed and reliable domestic and international policymaking. Experts in other countries should similarly engage in such reflections. For this to happen, experts must critically reexamine globalization and its associated frameworks, especially as they relate to public health structures. One way of doing this is to establish stronger national, regional, and global linkages around epidemiology-related reporting. Such structures can generate greater transparency and accountability as well as create checks and balances to ensure more reliable data. They will also allow for global actors to collectively respond better to future crises, which will consequently promote the well-being of citizens around the world.

Conclusion

For the past several centuries, nation-states have approached international and societal relations with the aim of promoting their own sovereign nations' interests and strengthening their own influence in the international arena. Since then, however, the world has globalized immensely. One nation's success can trickle down and promote advantages in another country. Similarly, one crisis, such as the outbreak of a pandemic, in one country can rapidly spread across the globe and kill millions. We need to stop approaching international and societal relations using outdated frameworks that prioritize isolationism and competition and fail to recognize the interconnected nature of today's worlds. Going forward, we must invest more in building and strengthening global interconnections between actors, particularly in the public health space, so that when future crises emerge, global actors can respond comprehensively and in collaboration with one another. Such a response will promote the well-being of the whole, rather than the part, and will reflect a major shift in international and societal relations.

References

Associated Press (2020, April 15). *Iran Parliamentary Report Says Official COVID-19 Death Toll Should Be Doubted.* CBC. https://www.cbc.ca/news/world/iran-report-coronavirus-1.553278 7 (accessed April 26, 2021)..

Bastani, H. (2020, March 10). تشکیل 'شورای پشتیبانی از تصمیمات ستاد ملی مبارزه با کرونا' [Formation of "Council for Supporting the Decisions of the National Anti-Corona Headquarters"]. *BBC.* https://www.bbc.com/persian/iran-features-51815296.

Batmanghelidj, E. (2020, March 20). *New European Limits on Medical Gear Exports Put Iranians at Risk.* Bourse and Bazaar. https://www.bourseandbazaar.com/articles/2020/3/20/new-european-limits-on-medical-gear-exports-put-iranians-at-risk.

Behravesh, B. (2020a, January 30). Were Iran's Gasoline Protests a "Controlled Explosion"? [Maysam]. *Inside Arabia.* https://insidearabia.com/were-irans-gasoline-protests-a-con trolled-explosion/.

——— (2020b, March 24). The Untold Story of How Iran Botched the Coronavirus Pandemic. *Foreign Policy.* https://foreignpolicy.com/2020/03/24/how-iran-botched-coronavirus-pandemic-response/.

Central Bank of Iran (2020). عرضه بیش از یک و نیم میلیارد دلار ارز در اسفند ۹۸ در بازار ثانویه [Supply of More Than One and a Half Billion Dollars of Foreign Exchange in March 1998 in the Secondary Market]. Central Bank of Iran. https:// cbi.ir/ showi tem/ 19981.aspx.

CIA World Factbook (2021). *Iran.* CIA World Factbook. https://www.cia.gov/the-world-factbook/countries/iran/#people-and-society.

Contactless Payment Tool to Cut Viral Transmission in Iran (2020, March 8). Financial Tribune. https://urldefense.proofpoint.com/v2/url?u=https-3A__financialtribune.com_articles_business-2Dand-2Dmarkets_102489_contactless-2Dpayment-2Dtool-2Dto-2Dcut-2Dviral-2Dtransmission-2Din-2Diran&d=DwMGaQ&c=G8CoXqdZ57E1EOn2t2CVrg&r=Qm7HmwEg-dr1FS2f4Is8aU5mmw5ce47r7aK3kxtf8ww&m=Pis_NiUMzPoFelR1M5IB-M9EE95ifo5zyY3_R3gfv0Q&s=yhWwsptXkMBYG0eq-R97up4hEK1Pf-zszmY_4UcN3Dg&e=.

Coronavirus: Iran Reports Two Suspected Fatal Cases at Qom Hospital (2020, February 19). *BBC*. https://www.bbc.com/news/world-middle-east-51563039.

Cunningham, E. (2020, March 29). As Coronavirus Cases Explode in Iran, U.S. Sanctions Hinder Its Access to Drugs and Medical Equipment. *Washington Post*. https://www.washingtonpost.com/world/middle_east/as-coronavirus-cases-explode-in-iran-us-sanctions-hinder-its-access-to-drugs-and-medical-equipment/2020/03/28/0656a196-6aba-11ea-b199-3a9799c54512_story.html.

Daragahi, B. (2020, April 2). *Separating Fact from Fiction and Fate: Assessing Iran's Response to COVID-19*. Atlantic Council. https://www.atlanticcouncil.org/blogs/iransource/separating-fact-from-fiction-and-fate-assessing-irans-response-to-covid-19/.

Eqbal, A., and Rasmussen, S. E. (2020, November 19). Iran Resorts to Its Strictest Lockdown Yet to Stem Covid-19. *Wall Street Journal*. https://www.wsj.com/articles/iran-resorts-to-its-strictest-lockdown-yet-to-stem-covid-19-11605806250.

Gesley, J. (2020, June). *Regulating Electronic Means to Fight the Spread of COVID-19*. The Law Library of Congress. https://www.loc.gov/law/help/coronavirus-apps/coronavirus-apps.pdf.

Hafezi, P. (2021, January 8). *Iran Leader Bans Import of U.S., UK COVID-19 Vaccines, Demands Sanctions End*. Reuters. https://www.reuters.com/article/us-health-coronavirus-iran-vaccines-idINKBN29D0YL.

Health Ministry: Coronavirus Death Toll Reaches 12 in Iran (2020, February 24). Press TV. https://www.abc.net.au/news/2020-02-24/iran-coronavirus-death-toll-12-fears-new-stage-global-spread/11996396.

International Monetary Fund (n.d.). *Policy Responses to COVID-19*. International Monetary Fund. https://www.imf.org/en/Topics/imf-and-covid19/Policy-Responses-to-COVID-19#I.

Iran Begins First Human Trial of Locally Made Virus Vaccine (2020, December 29). Arab News. https://www.arabnews.com/node/1784406/middle-east.

Iran Cleric Encourages Visitors to Qom Religious Sites, Despite Coronavirus Fears (2020, February 27). *Middle East Monitor*. https://www.middleeastmonitor.com/20200227-iran-cleric-encourages-visitors-to-qom-religious-sites-despite-coronavirus-fears/.

Iran: Over 700 Dead after Drinking Alcohol to Cure Coronavirus (2020, April 27). Al Jazeera. https://www.aljazeera.com/news/2020/4/27/iran-over-700-dead-after-drinking-alcohol-to-cure-coronavirus.

John Hopkins University of Medicine (2020). *COVID-19 Dashboard by the Center for Systems Science and Engineering (CSSE) at Johns Hopkins University*. John Hopkins University of Medicine Coronavirus Resource Center. https://coronavirus.jhu.edu/map.html.

Keshavarz, A. (2020, June 4). *Iran's COVID-19 Response and U.S. Policy*. Hoover Institution. https://www.hoover.org/research/irans-covid-19-response-and-us-policy.

Khameini.IR. (2020, March 22). *Why Does Imam Khamenei Say the US Offer to Help Iran Fight the Coronavirus Is Strange?* Khameini.IR. https://english.khamenei.ir/news/7449/Why-does-Imam-Khamenei-say-the-US-offer-to-help-Iran-fight-the.

KPMG (2020, April 29). *Iran: Government and Institution Measures in Response to COVID-19.* KPMG. https://home.kpmg/xx/en/home/insights/2020/04/iran-government-and-institution-measures-in-response-to-covid.html.

Lederer, E. M. (2020, March 12). *Iran Accuses US of "Economic Terrorism," Urges Sanctions End.* Associated Press. https://apnews.com/article/89d855a0ff8a68fce55dff128c8a90ef.

Marx, W. (2020, September 19). *U.S.-Iran Relations at a Crucial Crossroad as Nuclear Deal Hangs on Election Outcome.* NBC News. https://www.nbcnews.com/news/world/iran-nuclear-deal-future-n1240457.

McDonald, C. (2021, February 7). *Biden Says U.S. Won't Lift Sanctions until Iran Halts Uranium Enrichment.* https://www.cbsnews.com/news/biden-interview-iran-sanctions-nuclear-agreement/. https://www.cbsnews.com/news/biden-interview-iran-sanctions-nuclear-agreement/.

Mousavian, S. H. (2020, May 8). Sanctions Make Iran's Coronavirus Crisis more Deadly. *Al Jazeera.* https://www.aljazeera.com/opinions/2020/5/8/sanctions-make-irans-coronavirus-crisis-more-deadly.

Nili, H. [@HadiNili]. (2020, April 26). *here's another Iran official admitting that there're strict orders from Natl Security Council & Health Ministry to not release the actual data about #coronavirus outbreak in Iran. doesn't make you look smarter if just simply tag this as "under-reporting."* [Tweet]. Twitter. https://twitter.com/HadiNili/status/1254430712301793283.

Nourmohammadian, M. R. (2020, April). سرلشکر باقری: روند خلوت کردن شهرها در ۴۲ ساعت آینده سازماندهی می‌شود [Major General Bagheri: The Process of Secluding the Cities Will Be Organized in the Next 24 Hours]. Iranian Students' News Agency. https://www.isna.ir/news/98122317596/%D8%B3%D8%B1%D9%84%D8%B4%DA%A9%D8%B1-%D8%A8%D8%A7%D9%82%D8%B1%DB%8C-%D8%B1%D9%88%D9%86%D8%AF-%D8%AE%D9%84%D9%88%D8%AA-%DA%A9%D8%B1%D8%AF%D9%86-%D8%B4%D9%87%D8%B1%D9%87%D8%A7-%D8%AF%D8%B1-%DB%B2%DB%B4-%D8%B3%D8%A7%D8%B9%D8%AA-%D8%A2%DB%8C%D9%86%D8%AF%D9%87-%D8%B3%D8%A7%D8%B2%D9%85%D8%A7%D9%86%D8%AF%D9%87%DB%8C.

Pazzanese, C. (2020, May 8). *Battling the "Pandemic of Misinformation."* Harvard Gazette. https://news.harvard.edu/gazette/story/2020/05/social-media-used-to-spread-create-covid-19-falsehoods/.

Radio Free Europe/Radio Liberty. (2020, December 28). *Iran to Get 150,000 Doses of Pfizer Vaccines from "Philanthropists" in U.S.* Radio Free Europe/Radio Liberty. https://www.rferl.org/a/iran-vaccines-philanthropists-america/31023015.html.

Saunders, H. H. (2005). *Politics Is about Relationship: A Blueprint for the Citizens' Century.* Springer, New York.

Sinaee, M. (2020, October 25). *Covid Deaths in Iran Could Be Four Times Higher Than Official Numbers.* Iran International. https://iranintl.com/en/iran/covid-deaths-iran-could-be-four-times-higher-official-numbers.

Slaughter, A.-M. (2017). *The Chessboard and the Web: Strategies of Connection in a Networked World.* New Haven, CT: Yale University Press.

StatCounter (2021, March). *Mobile Operating System Market Share Islamic Republic Of Iran.* StatCounter. https://gs.statcounter.com/os-market-share/mobile/iran.

Stone, R. (2020, March 29). Iran Confronts Coronavirus amid a "Battle between Science and Conspiracy Theories." *Science Magazine*. https://www.sciencemag.org/news/2020/03/iran-confronts-coronavirus-amid-battle-between-science-and-conspiracy-theories.

Takeyh, R. (2020, May 7). *Iran's Perplexing Pandemic Response*. Council on Foreign Relations. https://www.cfr.org/in-brief/irans-perplexing-pandemic-response.

Tasim News (n.d.). وضعیت سفید ۱۳۲ شهرستان بلحاظ کاهش شیوع کرونا + اسامی شهرها [White Status of 132 Cities in Terms of Reducing the Prevalence of Corona +City Names]. Tasim News. https://www.tasnimnews.com/fa/news/1399/02/14/2256165/%D9%88%D8%B6%D8%B9%DB%8C%D8%AA-%D8%B3%D9%81%DB%8C%D8%AF-132-%D8%B4%D9%87%D8%B1%D8%B3%D8%AA%D8%A7%D9%86-%D8%A8%D9%87-%D9%84%D8%AD%D8%A7%D8%B8-%DA%A9%D8%A7%D9%87%D8%B4-%D8%B4%DB%8C%D9%88%D8%B9-%DA%A9%D8%B1%D9%88%D9%86%D8%A7-%D8%A7%D8%B3%D8%A7%D9%85%DB%8C-%D8%B4%D9%87%D8%B1%D9%87%D8%A7.

Tuite, A. R., Bogoch, I. I., Sherbo, R., Watts, A., Fisman, D., and Khan, K. (2020). Estimation of COVID-2019 Burden and Potential for International Dissemination of Infection from Iran. *medRxiv*.

Twitter (2020). *Removal Requests: Legal Demands*. Twitter Transparency. https://transparency.twitter.com/en/reports/removal-requests.html#2020-jan-jun.

Williams, A., and De Luce, D. (2020, September 21). *Trump Administration at Odds with Allies over Reimposing U.N. Sanctions on Iran*. NBC News. https://www.nbcnews.com/politics/national-security/trump-administration-odds-allies-over-reimposing-u-n-sanctions-iran-n1240653.

Wintour, P. (2020, April 13). Iran's President Has Left Nation Open to Second Covid-19 Wave—Critics. *Guardian*. https://www.theguardian.com/world/2020/apr/13/irans-president-has-left-nation-open-to-second-covid-19-wave-critics.

World Health Organization (n.d.). *"Solidarity" Clinical Trial for COVID-19 Treatments*. World Health Organization. https://www.who.int/emergencies/diseases/novel-coronavirus-2019/global-research-on-novel-coronavirus-2019-ncov/solidarity-clinical-trial-for-covid-19-treatments.

——— (2020, December 23). *In Middle East COVID-19 Hotspot Iran, WHO Walks the Talk*. World Health Organization News Room. https://www.who.int/news-room/feature-stories/detail/in-middle-east-covid-19-hotspot-iran-who-walks-the-talk.

Worldometer (2021, April 13). *Iran Coronavirus Cases*. Worldometer. https://www.worldometers.info/coronavirus/country/iran/.

World Social Report (2020). *Inequality in a Rapidly Changing World*. New York: United Nations Department of Economic and Social Affairs.

Wright, R. (2020, February 28). How Iran Became a New Epicenter of the Coronavirus Outbreak. *New Yorker*. https://www.newyorker.com/news/our-columnists/how-iran-became-a-new-epicenter-of-the-coronavirus-outbreak.

Yücesoy, V. (2020, May 29). *Iran's Coronavirus Response: A Lesson in What Not to Do*. Bulletin of the Atomic Scientists. https://thebulletin.org/2020/05/irans-coronavirus-response-a-lesson-in-what-not-to-do/.

Zohar, D., and Marshall, I. (1995). *The Quantum Society: Mind, Physics, and a New Social Vision*. HarperCollins: New York.

ابهام در مورد ادامه پرواز مسافران از چین به ایران [Ambiguity about the Continuation of Passenger Flights from China to Iran]. (2020, April 15). Radio Farda. https://www.radiofarda.com/a/iran-china-flight-conitnues/30416201.html.

کرونا در ایران؛ روحانی: چیزی به نام قرنطینه نداریم، نه امروز و نه در ایام عید [Corona in Iran; Rouhani: We Do Not Have Anything Called Quarantine, Neither Today Nor during Eid]. (2020, March 15). *BBC*. https://www.bbc.com/persian/iran-51894795.

معاون وزیر بهداشت: قرنطینه برای قبل از جنگ جهانی اول است!/ ممکن است مردم به مسافرت بروند [Deputy Minister of Health: Quarantine Is before the First World War! / People May Travel! The Deputy Minister of Health, Treatment]. (2020, March 26). Aftab News. https://aftabnews.ir/fa/news/638326/%D9%85%D8%B9%D8%A7%D9%88%D9%86-%D9%88%D8%B2%DB%8C%D8%B1-%D8%A8%D9%87%D8%AF%D8%A7%D8%B4%D8%AA%E2%80%8C-%D9%82%D8%B1%D9%86%D8%B7%DB%8C%D9%86%D9%87-%D8%A8%D8%B1%D8%A7%DB%8C-%D9%82%D8%A8%D9%84-%D8%A7%D8%B2-%D8%AC%D9%86%DA%AF-%D8%AC%D9%87%D8%A7%D9%86%DB%8C-%D8%A7%D9%88%D9%84-%D8%A7%D8%B3%D8%AA-%D9%85%D9%85%DA%A9%D9%86-%D8%A7%D8%B3%D8%AA-%D9%85%D8%B1%D8%AF%D9%85-%D8%A8%D9%87-%D9%85%D8%B3%D8%A7%D9%81%D8%B1%D8%AA-%D8%A8%D8%B1%D9%88%D9%86%D8%AF.

ویروس کرونا؛ 'کلیه پروازهای رفت و برگشت ایران به چین موقتا متوقف می‌شود [Coronavirus; "All Return Flights from Iran to China Will Be Temporarily Suspended"]. (2020, February). *BBC*. https://www.bbc.com/persian/iran-51323544.

Part II

Chapter 4

TAIWAN'S RESPONSE TO THE COVID-19 PANDEMIC: A SOCIAL CONSTRUCTIVIST ANALYSIS OF IDENTITY DIFFERENTIATION WITH THE PEOPLE'S REPUBLIC OF CHINA

Jasmine C. Lee

The world's two superpowers, the United States of America and the People's Republic of China, have entered into an all-round race from technology development, economic power, and military capacity to ideological confrontation. The tension between the United States and China has also focused global attention on the importance of cross-relations. Traditionally, the Cross-Strait Conflict is viewed through the prism of realism or liberalism. According to the balance of power, realists consider China (the status quo hegemonic power) and Taiwan (the anti–status quo rising power) as two strategic competitors that are expected to compete. Conflict is unavoidable and ultimately occurs in the Taiwan Strait. The realist paradigm shows its utility in explaining the increase in defense expenditure of China and Taiwan (Glaser et al., 2020). However, realism cannot explain why after the 1958 Taiwan Strait Crisis, a major military conflict between Taiwan and China has yet to erupt. Instead, Cross-Strait economic and cultural cooperation has increased, especially during the eight years of Ma Ying-jeou Administration (2008–16). The liberal school, on the other hand, believes that cooperation in the economic and social arenas would eventually spill over into the political realm of unification; yet liberalism also failed to predict the path of Cross-Strait Relations. The continued integration—primarily in the areas of "low politics," including economic, cultural, and societal integration between China and Taiwan during the Ma Administration—has not made the two sides come any closer to a visible and realistic road map of political integration, not to mention unification.

Recent discourses suggest that Cross-Strait Relations have increasingly evolved into a conflict of identity (Li and Zhang, 2016). Accordingly, social constructivism (in shorthand: constructivism) better serves to view Cross-Strait Relations and understand the consolidation of Taiwanese identity, which is the major factor for Taiwan to resist unification with China. Traditional IR theories focus on the distribution of material power whereas constructivism rejects such a one-sided view and argues that the most important aspect of international relations is social. Constructivists are concerned with human consciousness and knowledge and treat ideas as structural factors that influence how actors interpret the world. In constructivist theory, norms and ideas shape interests as interests shape the actions of individuals and nation-states. Norms and ideas can change people's perception of identity; therefore, they are crucial in explaining actors' behaviors.

The history of being a self-governing entity for more than 70 years, is the major factor that creates and consolidates Taiwanese identity. This historical period also changes the demography, which gives most of the residents on the island of Taiwan no memory related to China. Smith (1993, p. 16) points out that "the nation is called upon to provide a social bond between individuals and classes by providing repertoires of shared values, symbols and traditions." He explains that the use of symbols includes flags, coinage, anthems, uniforms, monuments, and ceremonies. Through those symbols, "members are reminded of their common heritage and cultural kinship and feel strengthened and exalted by their sense of common identity and belonging." Taiwan, or the Republic of China, has all the symbols mentioned above, which are different from those of Mainland China. Furthermore, Social Identity Theory (SIT) points out that individuals automatically sort themselves into categories in a social setting. After 70 years of separation, a social bond has formed in the Taiwanese society and reinforced the consolidation of Taiwanese identity. The category that the people in Taiwan would automatically sort themselves into is Taiwanese instead of Chinese.

However, except for the factor of time in separation, in the case of Cross-Strait Relations, other factors also have great influence in shaping Taiwanese identity. This time of the COVID-19 pandemic provides the best opportunity to observe the development of Taiwanese identity and allows people to understand the identity drivers that emerged in the past 70 years. In the year 2020, Taiwanese identity has risen 8.5 percent (Figure 1), which breaks yet another record high in the island's history. The following section initially demonstrates COVID-19 measures that allow Taiwan to achieve success in public health using social constructivism to analyze the ways in which the rise in Taiwanese identity as a driver was generated during the pandemic.

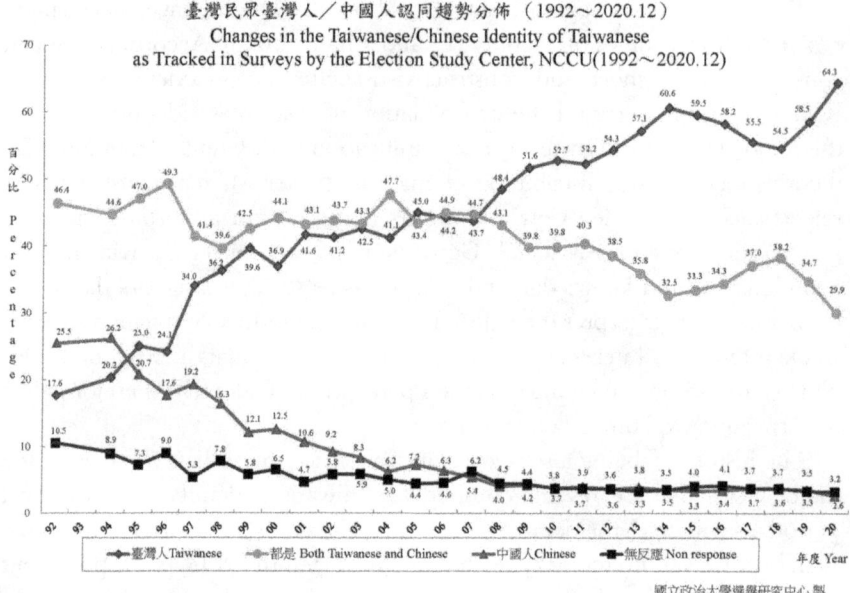

Figure 1 Chinese/Taiwan Identity Survey (1992–2020.06).
Source: Election Study Center, National Chengchi University (Taiwan).

The Taiwan Model

Taiwan, an island with 23.78 million population, is only 81 miles away from Mainland China, with a huge number of people traveling back and forth every day. Early in 2020, John Hopkins University modeled the spread of the virus and predicted that Taiwan would have the second most confirmed number of cases in the world (PBS, 2020). Yet, Taiwan flattened the curve before infection rates soared exponentially and the accumulated confirmed cases exceeded a thousand 15 months after the first case reports in Wuhan. Although an outbreak occurred in May 2021, the death toll remained as low as 12, as recorded on May 15.

Taiwan's success has rested on a fusion of technology, civic participation, and the vigilance of government and people due to the tragic experience during the outbreak of SARS in 2003. Back then, Taiwan was hit hard by SARS, a respiratory epidemic, as 11 health workers died during the crisis. Given this heartbreaking experience, when informed of a SARS-like pneumonia outbreak in Wuhan, China, Taiwanese officials quickly formed the Central Epidemic Command Center (CECC) to coordinate swift responses across government agencies and keep citizens well informed about the disease as well as any official measures. The CECC implemented border controls before a single case was confirmed and was the first in the region to ban exports of surgical masks to ensure mask supply. The government also created a "national face mask production team," producing ten million masks per day. Technology plays a central role in the government's responses. For example, at the beginning of the pandemic, masks were in short supply. The Taiwanese government developed a rationing system in which each adult resident was allowed to purchase three masks per week. Masks can be purchased at designated pharmacies, drugstores, and medical centers. These locations were equipped with the facilities digitally to scan National Health Insurance (NHI) cards, which allows the government to record the purchase history of each citizen. Along with the rationing system, the government also conducted trials for online mask ordering or a "name-based rationing system." Residents with NHI cards were able to preorder masks online and collect them at convenience stores. During the outbreak in May 2021, an app called "Taiwan Social Distancing app" was widely downloaded. With Bluetooth technology, the app delivers notifications to device holders if they are exposed to any confirmed cases less than two meters away for more than two minutes over the previous 14 days. Other measures that make use of technology include using phones to track arriving travelers during the 14-day quarantine as well as merging the national healthcare database with the immigration and customs database to keep track of people's health conditions while allowing doctors to see patients' travel history.

Besides government efforts, the value of Taiwan's tech-enabled civic culture became abundantly clear during the outbreak. Dozens of community-created apps helped complement and strengthen the government. Face Mask Map, a national real-time map for every Taiwanese citizen to track the stock of masks in every pharmacy, is one of the most celebrated examples. At the beginning, the app was developed by a Taiwanese programmer for his friends and close relatives. Soon after, Audrey Tang, Taiwan's digital minister, reached out to this programmer, thereby making this idea available for every Taiwanese citizen. Another platform, which allows individuals voluntarily to share reports about symptoms, was later created to help citizens reduce their exposure to the virus. Information on the platform was verified and collated. The result was then combined with more community-created apps that enable users to download their smartphone location history to determine if they may have been exposed. The government has assured that privacy was carefully protected in these apps and platforms; the movements of individuals were not visible to other users.

With (1) the fast and vigilant measures from the CECC, (2) the collaboration between the society and the government, and (3) the frequent communication to the public from a trusted official to reduce public panic, Taiwan successfully contained the spread of virus in the early stages and kept the economy operating. More importantly, this early success created multiple factors to reinforce the consolidation of Taiwanese identity and its differentiation from that of the Chinese identity.

Identity Formation in the Time of COVID-19

The following section points out major factors that reconsolidate Taiwanese identity during the pandemic and use Constructivism to explain the social context that allows these factors to be effective.

Success based on democracy

In this global crisis, Taiwan's counterpart, the People's Republic of China, also contained the outbreak. Given the massive population in the PRC and the fact that the pandemic broke out during the Chinese New Year, when millions of people travel back to their hometown, the time that the Beijing government took to flatten the infection curve was phenomenal. However, Beijing's success did not produce any incentive for people in Taiwan to adopt the Chinese identity. One major reason is that its success was perceived to be accomplished through inhuman and draconian control on citizens. This stands in contrast to the Taiwanese identity at present in which values of democracy and liberalization are integral.

The formation of Taiwanese identity has gone through three stages (Wakabayashi, 2005, p. 4). First, during Japanese colonization, Taiwanese was an identity that was limited to the Han ethnic group on the island of Taiwan. The second stage began after the Japanese handover to the KMT Party in 1945. In the early years of the KMT's rule, the Party imposed a segregation policy between the "*waishengren* (外省人, the newly arrived mainlanders from China after Japan's handover)" and "*benshengren* (本省人, people whose fathers had immigrated to Taiwan before the KMT retreated to Taiwan)." The KMT also ensured *benshengren's* inferiority within the domestic political structure. Therefore, during that time, Taiwanese was a term that was largely linked to the *benshengren*, whereas the *waishengren* held on to the Chinese identity, as their hope to retake Mainland China endured. As time passed, the division between *waishengren* and the *benshengren* had blurred through decades of social interaction and intermarriage. Meanwhile, *waishengren's* hope of reclaiming Mainland China had also faded as the PRC consolidated its sovereignty of Mainland China. A Taiwanese identity that includes all residents on the island gradually formed. However, the third stage, the current one, did start until the lifting of martial law in 1987 when Taiwan began a democracy transition process. Since democratization introduced the first presidential election in Taiwan, in which the election of a president promoted Taiwanese identity, a non-decremental Taiwanese identity grew rapidly during the third stage. What really differentiates the second and third stages of Taiwanese identity is the value of democracy and liberalization. Third-stage Taiwanese identity consolidates during a series of democratic movements; moreover, economic development also contributes to the pursuit of democratic values. Ronald Inglehart (2015, pp. 116–48), a political and social scientist, posited that a major trend of value change in developed societies is from "materialist" to "post-materialist" values. With economic affluence, the stress on economic and physical security and bread-and-butter (materialist) issues in the Industrial Age gradually gave way to self-expression values and quality of life (post-materialism) issues in postindustrial societies. During the latter half of the twentieth century, Taiwan went through a rapid industrialization and created an economic miracle. Therefore, people born after 1978 were also the generation that grew up in a relatively affluent environment. Accordingly, they give priority to non-materialistic values, such as democracy, freedom of expression, and participation in public affairs, over material needs.

In response to the COVID-19 pandemic, Taiwan successfully contained the spread of the virus through democratic measures and transparency. The political and public health system differentiates the value of Taiwan from China and consolidates Taiwanese identity, which is built on the value of democracy. As Burton's Basic Human Needs theory (1990, p. 38) points out, "while interest is tradable, needs and values are not." Beijing's attempt to win the Taiwanese people's hearts will not work if the CCP government does not recognize the identity needs and democratic value of Taiwan.

International perception

While the world is inundated with negative news stories of cities in lockdown and growing infection rates, most residents in Taiwan carry on their lives as normal. Taiwan also successfully maintained its GDP growth above 3 percent in 2020. Restaurants, gyms, and cafes were still bustling, although most premises take temperatures and spray hands with sanitizer before allowing customers inside their locales. With the outstanding performance and the striking contrast, as compared to many countries, news media around the globe began to recognize and reference the Taiwan Model. Posts and videos expressing gratitude for being Taiwanese or being able to live in Taiwan appeared everywhere on social media. A graph, showing names of the foreign major news media that reported Taiwan's success, spread widely as well (Figure 2).

Figure 2 The graph that lists the foreign media that praise Taiwan's response to the pandemic.
Source: Ministry of Foreign Affairs Republic of China (Taiwan).

Moreover, Taiwan earned recognition and support within a system fully independent from China, which boosted the sense of Taiwanese pride.

In fact, before the pandemic, the difference in international perception toward China and Taiwan was a major factor shaping the Taiwanese identity. According to Pew Research (Silver et al., 2019), the opinion of China is, on balance, negative in Western Europe. The share of people who view China positively has dropped since 2018 by double digits in nearly half of the Western European countries surveyed, including Sweden (down 17 percentage points), the Netherlands (−11 points) and the United Kingdom (−11). In Greece and Italy, opinions of China have improved. Central and Eastern Europeans show more divisions in their assessments. More Bulgarians, Poles, and Lithuanians have favorable than unfavorable views of China, whereas Hungarians are nearly evenly divided. Conversely, a plurality of Slovaks and the majority in Czech society have unfavorable views of China.

In North America, negative views of China dominate in both the United States and Canada (Figures 3 and 4). In the respective populations, 73 and 67 percent view the country unfavorably. The decline in perception may be caused by those countries' domestic issues or bilateral relationship with China. In Canada, unfavorable opinions increased 22 points in the wake of the trade

Figure 3 Negative views of China in Canada and the United States.
Source: Spring 2019 Global Attitudes Survey. Q8b, Pew Research Center.

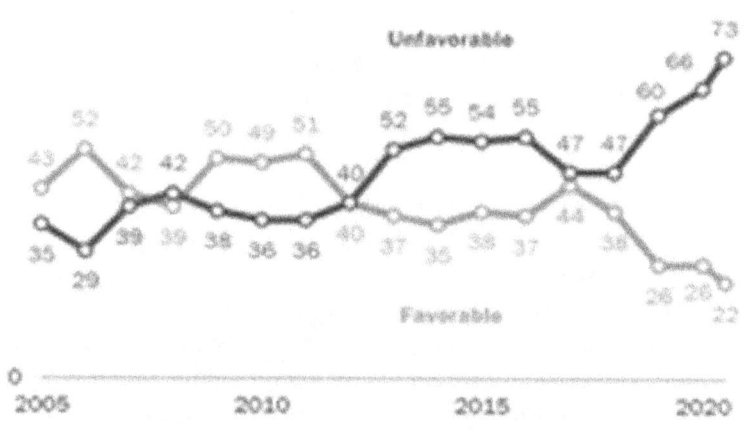

Figure 4 Negative views of China in United States.
Source: June 16–July 14, 2020 Global Attitudes Survey. Q8b, Pew Research Center.

conflict with China. As for the United States, the pandemic is one of the major causes for the rise in an unfavorable view of China. Yet, recent inhumane measures taken by the CCP government, including imposing a national security law in Hong Kong, mass detention of ethnic Muslim Uighurs, drastic responses to the novel coronavirus, and the mistreatment of Africans in the country also contributed to this rise. In the research cited by Figure 4, Pew Research asked the interviewees "whether the U.S. should prioritize economic relations with China or promote human rights in China"; nearly three-quarters of Americans chose human rights even if this choice harms economic relations with China.

The poll shows Western thinking countries hold a relatively negative view of China. Taiwan has developed into a democracy; people, especially in the younger generation, pursue liberalism, which is more aligned with the Western idea. Thus, the decline of favorable views regarding China in Western Europe coincides with the rise of Taiwanese identity poll in Taiwan. In an interview, a 23-year-old man said,

> I will tell people that I'm Taiwanese without a doubt. From my personal life experience, it is hard for me to recognize that I'm Chinese. Even though many people think they are ethnically or culturally Chinese, when you go abroad and tell people that you are Chinese, they will think that you come from Mainland China which is under the rule of the PRC. But the fact that we have our own president, we are not under the communist system and we do not do anything that abuses human rights. Thus, if you still tell people that you're a Chinese, it would cause huge confusion.

The negative view toward Chinese among Western countries serves as a huge barrier for Taiwanese people to adopt the Chinese identity.

In some countries, the visa application administration also differentiates Taiwanese and Chinese people. For example, the Australian government gives each country an assessment level when granting students visas and citizenship. Level one represents the lowest immigration risk and level five is the highest. In the assessment, Taiwan is rated as level one, whereas China is at level three. In this case, it is hardly possible for Taiwanese people to adopt the identity of the Chinese. This choice would degrade Taiwanese identity and bring immediate and real-life inconveniences to the applicants (Déloye, 2013). When Taiwan and China are taken as different entities by foreign governments, the differentiation in fact diluted the formation of "Chinese" identity in Taiwan and reinforced in-group favoritism of the Taiwanese identity.

The foreign policy strategy of Taiwan and the political support from foreign countries have also helped strengthen the Taiwanese identity. To showcase its readiness and ability to contribute to multilateral initiatives, Taiwan launched a UN Sustainable Development Goals (SDG) campaign, known as Taiwan Can Help, which highlighted Taiwan's efforts to help other nations accomplish these goals. During the May World Health Assembly (WHA) seasons in 2020 and 2021, Western countries echoed this initiative. In 2020, the US Department of State mobilized a social media campaign, using the #TaiwanCanHelp hashtag to support Taiwan's participation in the WHA. In 2021, the State Department also called for Taiwan's inclusion in the WHA with the slogan "Let Taiwan Help." Across the Atlantic, the French Senate adopted a resolution, with a 304–0 vote and 19 abstentions, to support Taiwan's participation in activities of international organizations, including the World Health Organization (WHO). Meanwhile, a resolution to back Taiwan's participation in the WHA was passed by the Foreign Affairs Committee of Slovakia's National Council. In contrast, during the time of the COVID-19 pandemic, China's role as a responsible stakeholder in the international system has once again been questioned. The CCP government received numerous critiques of its inhumane measures against Hong Kong and the Uyghurs. Its vaccine diplomacy is also controversial due to the quality of the vaccines and the purpose of the policy. As Taiwan's success has been referenced and praised globally, this success creates opportunities to differentiate the Taiwanese from the Chinese identity, which leads to a rise in the superiority of the Taiwanese identity.

Superiority

Social Identity Theory predicts that the categorization process leads to prejudicial and discriminatory attitudes toward the out group. Superiority in Taiwanese identity has existed since the second stage of its development, due to the Japanese colonial legacy and the difference in value. In recent years, media propaganda has greatly reinforced the superiority, which is entrenched in Taiwanese society. During the COVID-19 pandemic, a number of YouTubers also joined the media effort to harden the superiority. For example, the Nas Daily, a Facebook video channel with 17M followers run by an Israeli-Arab blogger, published two videos titled "Asia's Secret Countries" and "Why this Country is a Coronavirus Hero" during August 2019 and May 2020. The two videos received 2.7M and 16M views, respectively. Thousands of comments appeared from Taiwanese people expressing their pride in being Taiwanese and from foreigners to praise Taiwan. In addition to the recognition from YouTubers, global politicians and journalists published articles and journals urging Taiwan's participation in the WHO given its public health success and for the sake of global health. All these reports and video reinforced the superiority within Taiwanese society (Figure 5).

Figure 5 Comments under the Nas Daily videos.
Source: Screenshot by the author.

IV. Unification approaches from China—carrot-and-stick tactics

In the past year, China has been using "carrot-and-stick tactics" as a unification approach. For example, while providing a series of incentive measures to lure Taiwanese professionals and investments across the Strait, there are thousands of missiles on the East Coast of China aimed at Taiwan. However, both carrot-and-stick measures have little effect, especially the stick. In the time of the COVID-19 pandemic, Chinese pressure kept Taiwan from attending the WHA. China stands firm that Taiwan can participate only under the "one China" principle, which involves the acceptance that Taiwan is a part of China. Beijing's insistence caused outrage in Taiwan. Taiwan has demonstrated its strength in containing the COVID-19 outbreak and showed the island's excellent medical capacity. This capacity includes synthesized Remdesivir, which is an effective treatment for COVID-19 suggested by the WHO, and Taiwan's development of antibodies for the COVID-19 virus test in 19 days.

Burton suggests that deprivation of individual and group needs can lead to intractable conflict. These needs include physiological ones as well as "self-esteem and self-actualization." And if these needs are deprived, they lead "naturally to setting goals with the aim to satisfy them." Beijing's objections to Taiwan's global participation deprives the Taiwanese of self-esteem. On April 9, Dr. Tedros, the head of the WHO elected with the support of China, accused Taiwan of a racist and personal attack campaign against him lasting several months. Soon after the accusation, several Taiwanese YouTubers and graphic designers began a crowdfunding campaign to buy a full-page advertisement on the *New York Times*. The ad aimed to raise global awareness of Taiwan's willingness and ability to provide medical expertise to the world. In the 15 hours since the crowdfunding campaign started, nearly US$1,000,000 from 26,980 sponsors was generated.

The campaign and the strong support from the Taiwanese public are actions that satisfy the self-esteem needs the Taiwanese people have been deprived of for so long. Beijing's effort to block Taiwan from joining international organizations does not intimidate or scare the Taiwanese people. Instead, as the CCP government deprived the Taiwanese of their basic human needs, this deprivation created grievances toward the CCP government and generated momentum for the Taiwanese people to strive for international recognition.

Outcomes

In the previous analysis, this chapter underlined the factors that reinforced the consolidation of Taiwanese identity during the pandemic using constructivism to understand the underlying social context that produced these factors.

With the difference in value, the pressures from China, and the growing sense of pride in Taiwan, the consolidation of Taiwanese identity is an unstoppable trend. The placement of the "self" in one category, in turn, immediately creates an "other" (Rousseau and Garcia-Retamero, 2007, p. 747). In the Cross-Strait scenario, the majority in Taiwan have put themselves into the self-category of Taiwanese as the Chinese have gradually become the category of "other." According to the identity survey done by the Election Study Center at NCCU, the percentage of people recognizing themselves as Taiwanese has risen from 17.6 percent in 1992 to 67 percent in 2020. In this year of COVID-19, the rise is 8.5 percent. In contrast, the Chinese identity has fallen from 25.5 to 2.4 percent (Figure 1), reaching a record low.

The factor of identity plays a huge role in shaping Cross-Strait Relations in the future. How Taiwanese identity evolves in the post-pandemic era is worthy of researchers' and observers' attention in the analysis of its development through the lens of social constructivism. The following section continues to use the social constructivist lens to dive into Taiwan's COVID-19 responses and to understand the cornerstone of its success.

Information Technology and Personal Data Protection: The Paradox in Taiwan

During this global pandemic, the spread of the novel coronavirus has proven Slaughter's argument (2018, p. 9) that humankind is at the dawn of a "Networked Age" when "all humanity is connected beneath the surface like the giant colonies of aspen trees in Colorado that are actually all one organism." The grand strategy for the Age, Slaughter proposes, is an international order based on three pillars: open society, open government, and an open international system. Openness means participation, transparency, autonomy, and resistance to controls or limits on information. Taiwan's successful model is the best testimony for the power of openness. This model also offers a template of "government *with* the people rather than government *for* the people" (Slaughter, 2018, p. 215). The successful response has drawn countries to come and learn. However, the Taiwan Model may not be duplicated easily, especially for the Western world. This is not because of its openness; its culture leads to a different view on "democracy" and attitude toward "data/personal information security." This cultural difference also creates a paradox of democracy in Taiwan.

Democracy and Liberalism: Drivers to Protect Data Security in the West

To prevent the abuse of power by government as well as fear of the misuse of personal data drives the public to protect data privacy in Western countries

(Menand, 2018). These two drivers also show the people's strong will to protect democracy and the idea of liberalism. In their volume *The Making of Global International Relations*, Acharya and Buzan (2019, p. 9) point out that "Liberalism was associated with the leading-edge society of the revolution of modernity, Britain. It evolved into a complicated package of concepts that had its roots in two central ideas: that the rights of the individual should be foundational to society and politics." At present, individualism is considered as associated with democracy.

Acemoglu, an economist and institute professor at MIT, also argues that democracy and liberty require a strong civil power. "True democracy and liberty don't originate from checks and balances or from clever institutional design [...] They originate [and are sustained] in the much more messy process of society mobilizing, people defending their own liberties, and actively setting constraints on how rules and behaviors are imposed on them" (Dizikes, 2020). In Acemoglu and Robinson's book, *The Narrow Corridor to Liberty*, they use ancient Mesopotamian mythology to explain the importance of citizens and society itself to control the despot. In the story of Gilgamesh, king of Uruk, he created a rich, secure, and powerful city on the banks of the Euphrates. However,

> The city in his possession, he struts through it, arrogant, his head raised high, trampling its citizens like a wild bull. He is king, he does whatever he wants, takes the son from his father and crushes him, takes the girl from her mothers and uses her [...] no one dares to oppose him.

So, the people cried out to heaven to Anu, the god of the sky, to stop this despotism. Anu came up with a great idea of "checks and balances" to contain Gilgamesh.

> [He] creates a double for Gilgamesh, his second self, a man who equals his strength and courage, a man who equals his stormy heart. Create a new hero, let them balance each other perfectly, so that Uruk has peace.

In the story, Enkidu, Gilgamesh's double, indeed beats him and contains him. Yet Anu's solution is impractical. In the end, Enkidu together with Gilgamesh oppress the citizens of Uruk. Therefore, Acemoglu and Robinson (2019) suggest, the power of citizens is a much better way to contain despotism. It also paves the way to the Shackled Leviathan, which is liberty—meaning freedom from violence, the threat of violence, and dominance.

The graph in Figure 6 shows that the United States and the UK are both in *The Narrow Corridor to Liberty*, where the civic power is strong enough to

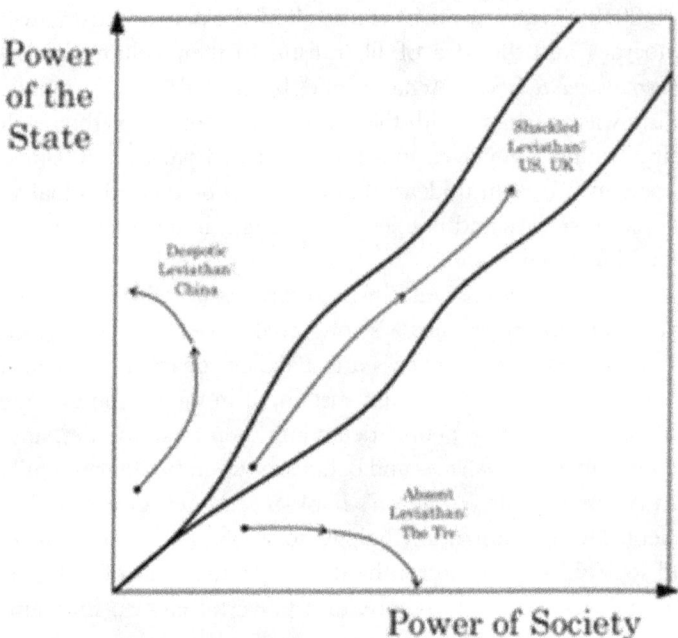

Figure 6 The Evolution of Despotic, Shackled, and Absent Leviathans.
Source: The Narrow Corridor State, Society, and the Fate of Liberty.

secure their liberty. On the issue of data privacy and information collection, people in the UK, United States, and other Western countries have also held their governments responsible. Proliferating breaches from global high-tech companies including Uber, Google, and Facebook have led to the demand of consumers for data privacy and control of their own data. Governments have later adopted new regulations, with General Data Protection Regulation (GDPR) in Europe and the California Consumer Privacy Act (CCPA) in each US state. The GDPR has been considered a bellwether for data privacy regulation and was implemented in Europe in May 2018. This legislation gives consumers easier access to data that companies hold and makes it easier for consumers to ask companies to delete their data. Shortly after GDPR's institution, a similar law emerged in California—the CCPA. Based largely on the GDPR, the CCPA brought Europe's push for better transparency, user control, and accountability into US borders. However, the California law is notably less extensive and less stringent than its EU predecessor, earning the nickname "GDPR Lite."

GDPR set an unprecedented standard for transparency, user control, and accountability. Its "lite" version also demonstrates a huge improvement in personal data protection. However, even with these regulations implemented, concerns over data privacy remain high. Research from SurveyMonkey (Gebhardt, 2019) shows that one year after GDPR was implemented, 45 percent of EU citizens still do not feel confident in their internet privacy and doubt the effectiveness of this new legislation. As for the United States, according to Pew Research (Auxier et al., 2019), a majority in society feel that they have little control over data collected about them by companies and the government. The research also indicates that in the United States, there is a collective sentiment that data security is more elusive today than in the past. Currently, the United States does not (yet) have a federal-level general consumer data privacy law, let alone a data security law. California, Nevada, and Maine are the only three states that have privacy laws in effect. While states are taking it upon themselves to innovate in this area, more human rights organizations, investigative reporters, and movies have increased attention on the matter, raising peoples' awareness to protect their data privacy. During the pandemic, human rights organizations have also raised concerns about the use of data to contain the spread of the virus. However, similar attention to data security issues does not exist in Taiwan where data technology plays an essential role in the government's responses.

The Paradox of Taiwan

Taiwan is considered as "the beacon of democracy in Asia" and is known for its vigorous public participation. Many scholars argue that Taiwan is among the members in the "Narrow Corridor." On the issue of data security, society is lacking civic power to balance the government. During the pandemic, privacy concerns emerged among the government's measures to contain the COVID-19 pandemic. The initial 14 days during which anyone arrived in Taiwan from overseas, perhaps, can best demonstrate these concerns.

Once arriving at the airport, the person must hand over his/her mobile phones to allow health authorities to record the details and use the GPS signals provided by telecom operators to track the phone's owners. To make sure the person stays isolated during 14 days of mandatory quarantine, a county worker calls the person around 10 am every morning. If he or she does not answer the phone or text messages, or the reception is poor, or the phone runs out of battery power, police show up within minutes. Violations of home quarantine regulations result in fines and mandatory placement. After the 14-day quarantine, the person is free to go anywhere. Yet, from post offices and banks to office towers and sports centers, there are people checking temperatures. Anyone with a fever is reported to the government. With these strict measures, there has been no lockdown in Taiwan. Yet, the shadow of the government is literally everywhere.

Other measures also have considerable privacy concerns. For example, Taiwan's CDC discloses the travel history data of almost each confirmed case; the relationships between cases and their affiliations are revealed as well. Furthermore, the integration of health and immigration databases, the use of GPS tracking systems, and the data of people's purchase history all indicate that the central government is being granted higher control over citizen's data. However, little debate has been raised against the potential abuse of the power of government and little attention has been given to the privacy concerns of disclosing confirmed cases' travel history and the data of their identity.

A social constructivist lens is required to find the explanation of such a paradox, as the development of data security is often related to the region's historical context. Ching-Kuen Ueng (2010, 2018, and 2020), a professor at FuJen School of Law, pointed out that the Europeans' leading approach to privacy can be traced back, in large part, to German history. During the Second World War, the Nazis systematically exploited private data to identify Jews and other minority groups. In the 1930s, German census workers went door to door filling out punch cards that indicated residents' information, which included nationality, native language, religion, and profession. When the war ended, the surveillance system remained intact and was carried out by the East German secret police force—the *Stasi*. *Stasi* officials screened mail, searched people's apartments, and tortured those they suspected. In response, in 1970, the West German government approved the first modern data privacy legal protections in the country (Palmer, 2012). Numerous laws and acts serving to protect residents' data were later carried out, including the Federal Data Protection Act in 1977. The Federal Constitutional Court declared the right of "self-determination over personal data" as a fundamental right in 1983.

During the Second World War, Taiwan was also under state surveillance when Japanese colonization occurred. The Japanese government gave each person a serial number and an ID card. The serial number was linked to the civil registry system called *HuKou*, which included information such as address, fingerprint, blood type, family members, gender, family ranking, health condition, as well as whether the person practices foot binding or smokes opium. The system was organized by the police department. Residents were required to bring their ID card when traveling outside the city. After the KMT-ruled ROC took over Taiwan, the government continued to use the system when ruling the Taiwanese people. The system of *HuKou* still exists today; each person also has a serial number (ID number) linking to all kinds of data. The *HuKou* system is a legacy of authoritarianism. Since inhumane events and governmental control that happened under the totalitarian rule of Japanese and KMT governments were not directly linked to the *HuKou* system, little voice was raised against the system. Surprisingly, even after a data breach from the government was reported, discussion to contain or to question the government's control on personal data remains limited. In 2018, the servers of Taipei Department of Health were hacked. The personal information of more than 2.98 million people was hacked. This information included the name, date of birth, ID number, and address. The bureau later traced the source of the attack to IP addresses in Shanghai. On June 22, 2019, the Ministry of Civil Service reported that 243,376 civil servants' information was compromised and made available on foreign websites. The compromised information included ID numbers, names, agency information, job designations, and the agencies that employed the civil servants. The government received criticism due to the incidents, while civic forces to hold the government responsible did not last long. No victim claimed compensation. Ueng (2020) points out that the compensation was too low to provide incentives to make claims for damages. The deep-rooted Chinese culture is the fundamental reason that explains why citizens of such highly rated democratic countries do not show the same degree of concern for data privacy and the potential abuse of power by the government.

Chinese Collectivism Culture

Democracy and liberalism spread to China in the late nineteenth century. Meanwhile, more and more revolutionists, mostly of Han ethnic origins, in Taiwan had demanded higher political participation under Japanese rule. The concept of democracy was written in the Constitution of the Republic of China. Only 47 years after the KMT party withdrew to Taiwan, the ROC had its first presidential election. Democracy in Taiwan is relatively young; together with the idea of liberalism, democracy is deeply affected by the Chinese culture. Therefore, while Acharya and Buzan consider that individualism is associated with democracy, the linkage between individualism and democracy does not have the same significance in countries influence by Chinese culture. The notions of liberty or bottom-up politics are not significant in the context of Chinese history. Acharya and Buzan suggest that "Whereas Western thinking and practice have been drawn more toward sovereignty, territoriality, international anarchy, war and international society, Chinese theory and practice have been drawn more towards unity, hierarchy, *Tianxia* (all under heaven) and tribute system relations." Under the concept of *Tianxia*, Chinese-majority societies are "collectivism" or "low individualism" (Hofstede, 1984). Group orientation is considered a key feature of Chinese culture and is common to the PRC, Hong Kong, Taiwan, and overseas Chinese (Lockett, 1988, pp. 475–96).

For individualism, having control over private life and independence from the collective can be considered a key element (Hofstede, 1991). Individuals are eager to have control over their lives and personal data and are more likely to avoid privacy risks. In contrast, the collectivist is motivated by group goals. People tend to sacrifice individual benefit or praise to recognize and honor the team's success. In fact, being singled out as an individual from the rest of the team may be embarrassing. During the pandemic, videos, capturing those who violate the government's order to wear a mask on public transportation, went viral on social media platforms. These posts received overwhelming criticisms from the public; many of these posts and comments blame the people for "ruining the success of Taiwan" or calling them the "bad apple."

The ideas of democracy and liberty, which are linked to individualism, are relatively young in Taiwan; hence, the public's awareness of personal data protection remains low. And with the underlying collectivist orientation, the goal successfully to contain the virus has a higher priority than protecting personal rights. Consequently, this context creates a paradox as with other members in the Narrow Corridor. However, with the absence of a public role in demanding data protection, the Taiwanese government's efforts to improve data protection have been nonstop.

Taiwan's Unique International Status, Not Democracy, Helps Propel Its Data Protection Development

Instead of the value of democracy, the unique international status of Taiwan became the force to push the development of data protection laws forward. Due to pressure from China, Taiwan's requests to join international and regional economic partnerships, including RCEP and CPTPP, were often rejected. Yet, Taiwan relies hugely on international commerce. In recent years, Taiwan's foreign trade dependency ratio has been over 100 percent, except for 2009, 2015, and 2016. To ensure its economic growth under the challenges from China, making the market more friendly and safer for data transmission became the way to secure and attract foreign investment. In 2018, Taiwan was admitted into the Cross-Border Privacy Rules (CBPR) system under the Asia-Pacific Economic Cooperation (APEC) forum. CBPR is a data privacy certification that APEC members can join to demonstrate compliance with internationally recognized data privacy protections. Currently, the GDPR is considered as the world's strongest set of data protection rules. The "reciprocal adequacy" decisions are required to allow personal data to flow between companies in the EU and non-GDPR member countries. Otherwise, the data is subjected to additional safety checks. In January 2019, Japan became the first country to earn an adequacy decision from the European Commission

(EC). The decision indicates that Japan's existing information protection legislation, Act on the Protection of Personal Information (APPI), is recognized as having "adequate safeguards" in place for data protection.

Taiwan has considerable business with the EU. In 2018, Taiwan became the EU's 15th trading partner around the globe, larger than Australia (19th) and Hong Kong (20th). The EU also is the largest investor in Taiwan. By the end of 2018, Foreign Direct Investment (FDI) stock from the EU (US$51.4 bn) accounted for 30.4 percent of total FDI stock (US$169.1 bn) in Taiwan. In response to the EU's enforcement of the GDPR, Taiwan's National Development Council (NDC), a policy-advising agency affiliated with the Executive Yuan (the highest agency of the executive branch), established the Personal Data Protection Office in July 2018. The office has been working to amend Taiwan's current data protection regulations—the Personal Information Protection Act (PIPA)—to comply with the EU's standard. Taiwan has sent the request to the EC to obtain the reciprocal adequacy decision. The adequacy talks with the EC are ongoing.

Once Taiwan earns the adequacy decision from the EC, this development will facilitate Taiwan's exploration of more business opportunities overseas and enhance the country's image in personal data protection. This decision will also be another symbol of Taiwan's recognition by other countries. The judiciary autonomy of Taiwan will be more evident. In addition, as most of the counties (or economies) that were admitted by the CBPR and GDPR were considered "like-minded" democracies by the Western world, the decision will, once again, differentiate Taiwan from Mainland China and consolidate Taiwanese identity.

Conclusion

This chapter demonstrated the strengths of Social Constructivism to analyze the identity-based conflict and data protection development in Taiwan. The research points out the principal variables forming and consolidating Taiwanese identity. The variables can be divided into internal and external ones. Internal factors include institutional and educational change, which was introduced after the political democratization began in 1978, demographic change, and the shared memories of people in Taiwan. External factors include the negative international perception of China among Western countries and military pressures from China against Taiwan. All these variables, developed during the last 70 years, led to the consolidation of Taiwanese identity, which in turn prevents the adoption of Chinese identity by the Taiwanese people. Therefore, the current nationalistic narratives of President Xi to pursue unification only create grievances experienced by the Taiwanese people and increase tensions between the Taiwan Strait. In the time of the COVID-19 pandemic, this evolution provides the best opportunity to verify the utility of this study. As Slaughter argues, open versus closed is the fault line of the digital age, the way capitalism versus Communism was in the last century. In the past year, we can easily see that the open system allowing Taiwan to establish the Taiwan Model has, again strengthened the Taiwanese identity and creates the sentiment to prevent reunification.

However, although Taiwan has differentiated itself from Mainland China, the deep-rooted Chinese culture still influences its development. The last section placed the focus on Taiwan's data protection development where public awareness of the issue remains low due to its Chinese legacy. Interestingly and ironically, this study underlines that pressure from China to prevent Taiwan from joining international partnerships has propelled Taiwan's political and economic system to be more aligned with the Western world.

Taiwan's crucial strategic position has put the island at the center of regional geopolitical competition for centuries. To conclude, the author urges further research on Taiwanese identity, especially on Taiwan's data protection development. In the era of big data and information technology, the importance of data protection in international and Cross-Strait Relations can only increase. These efforts are critical, continuously over time, for global stability and the full exercise of human rights.

References

Acemoglu, D., and Robinson, J. A. (2019). *The Narrow Corridor States, Societies, and the Fate of Liberty*. New York: Penguin Press.

Acharya, A., and Buzan, B. (2019). *The Making of Global International Relations: Origins and Evolution of IR at Its Centenary*. Cambridge: Cambridge University Press.

Auxier, B., Lee, R., Anderson, M., Perrin, A., Kumar, M., and Turner, E. (2019). *Americans and Privacy: Concerned, Confused and Feeling Lack of Control over Their Personal Information*. New York: Pew Research Center. https://www.pewresearch.org/internet/2019/11/15/americans-and-privacy-concerned-confused-and-feeling-lack-of-control-over-their-personal-information/ (accessed March 25, 2020).

Burton, J. W. (1990). *Conflict: Resolution and Prevention*. Hampshire: Macmillan.

Déloye, Y. (2013). "National Identity and Everyday Life," in J. Breuilly (ed.), *The Oxford Handbook of the History of Nationalism*. Oxford: Oxford University Press, pp. 615–31.

Dizikes, P. (2020). "The Fragility of Freedom," *MIT Technology Review*, Cambridge, MA: Elizabeth Bramson-Boudreau. https://www.technologyreview.com/2019/12/27/238226/the-fragility-of-freedom/ (accessed March 25, 2020).

Gebhardt, J. (2019). *GDPR, One Year Out*, SurveyMonkey, https://www.surveymonkey.com/curiosity/gdpr-one-year-out/ (accessed March 23, 2020).

Glaser, B. S., Funaiole M. P., and Hart, B. (2020). *Breaking Down China's 2020 Defense Budget*. Washington, DC: Center for Strategic and International Studies. https://www.csis.org/analysis/breaking-down-chinas-2020-defense-budget.

Hofstede, G. (1984). *Culture's Consequences: International Differences in Work-related Values.* Beverly Hills, CA: Sage.

———— (1991). *Cultures and Organizations: Software of the Mind.* London: McGraw Hill.

Inglehart, R. (2015). S*ilent Revolution: Changing Values and Political Styles among Western Publics.* Princeton, NJ: Princeton University Press.

Li, Y., and Zhang, E. (2016). "Changing Taiwanese Identity and Cross-Strait Relations: a Post 2016 Taiwan Presidential Election Analysis," *Journal of Chinese Political Science,* 22(1), pp. 17–35. https://doi.org/10.1007/s11366-016-9452-9.

Lockett, M. (1988). "Culture and the Problem of Chinese Management," *Organization Studies,* 9(3), pp. 475–96.

Menand, L. (2018). "Why Do We Care So Much about Privacy?" *New Yorker,* New York: New Yorker.

Palmer, E. (2012). *Online Privacy Law: Germany.* Germany: Law Library of Congress. https://www.loc.gov/law/help/online-privacy-law/2012/germany.php.

PBS NewsHour (2020). How Taiwan Has Become a COVID-19 Success Story. *PBS.* Available at https://www.pbs.org/video/a-different-approach-1585775995/ (accessed March 25, 2020).

Rousseau, D. L., and Garcia-Retamero, R. (2007). "Identity, Power, and Threat Perception: A Cross-National Experimental Study," *Journal of Conflict Resolution,* 51(5), pp. 744–71. doi: 10.1177/0022002707304813.

Silver, L., Devlin, K., and Huang, C. (2019). People around the Globe Are Divided in Their Opinions of China. *Pew Research Center.* Available at https://www.pewresearch.org/fact-tank/2019/12/05/people-around-the-globe-are-divided-in-their-opinions-of-china/a.

Slaughter, A. M. (2018). *The Chessboard and the Web: Strategies of Connection in a Networked World.* New Haven, CT: Yale University Press.

Smith, A. D. (1993). *National Identity.* Reno: University of Nevada Press.

Ueng, C. K. (2010). "Globalization of Data Protection Standard," *SooChow University,* 22(1), pp. 1–60.

———— (2018). "The Strengths and Weaknesses for Granting Property Rights in Personal Information to Data Subject: Focusing on the U.S. Laws," *National Taiwan University Law Journal,* 47(3), pp. 941–1051.

———— (2020). "The Challenge of Big Data to Personal Information Protection," *SooChow University,* 31(3), pp. 79–159.

Wakabayashi, M. (2005). "Taiwanese nationalism and the 'Unforgettable Others,'" inE. Friedman (ed.), *China's Rise, Taiwan's Dilemma's and International Peace.* London: Routledge, p. 4.

Chapter 5

REEDUCATION CAMPS IN XINJIANG, CHINA: AN INTERSECTIONAL CONSTRUCTIVIST APPROACH

Mary Davis

Introduction

How to prevent genocide is a question we have yet to answer, but it is a gray rhino nonetheless—predictable in its coming and impactful worldwide (Wucker, 2016). The mere existence of genocide in our world presents a threat to the fundamental concept of human security, something that strongly clashes with liberalism-informed states and actors whose primary concerns are centric to the ideals of personal freedoms. It goes without saying that sans basic human security, the protection of personal freedom is a pipe dream. In the case of Xinjiang's "reeducation" camps, which have gained substantial international attention in recent years, the gray rhino of genocide is particularly complex due to the meta-rhino of Chinese–American relations, China's unique position in the GIS as an "enigmatic outsider" (Acharya and Buzan, 2019), the constraints of the UN's conflicting principles of non-interventionism and the "responsibility to protect" (R2P), and the gray area within the Chinese Communist Party to regard ethnic conflicts in autonomous regions as domestic or foreign affairs. These are the four main challenges that the present policy analysis aims to address while expressing the intense intersectionality of these challenges and acknowledging that it is by no means an exhaustive list of issues to address but rather a starting point for considering overarching themes that feed into China's treatment of the Uyghur people in Xinjiang, which are for the purposes of this analysis qualified as genocide.

Literature Review

Genocide and mass atrocities are a kind of human phenomena that we can almost universally agree are evil and something to at the very least be avoided at all costs, but the solution to preventing genocide and an agreement of how to address it seem to elude us to date. The theoretical underpinnings of addressing genocide in this analysis are not new: they rest with Judith Shklar and Hannah Arendt in the beginning. While Arendt and Shklar did not often agree in their political and theoretical logic, both bring poignant and unique approaches to the discussion from within their respective paradigms. Arendt embodies a more realist approach—what scholars have coined as "agonistic realism" and largely keeps conflict in the center of her theory (Royer, 2020). Shklar, on the other hand, operates within the liberalist paradigm while simultaneously rejecting it. Her definition of the "liberalism of fear" or the "liberalism of permanent minorities" places the human and civilian experience in the center of her theory, rather than states (Benhabib, 1994). In my opinion, despite Arendt and Shklar in some ironic way embodying the age-old realist–liberalist oppositional debate, they both show an important preoccupation with the concept of evil—what makes evil, how we process and experience it, and what we as global citizens or states are morally and legally obligated to do about it. Both acknowledge the great capacity for evil on the part of humanity and governments as well as the search for a possible response to this dilemma. For Arendt, this evil is inextricable from international relations and politics, and may even be akin to the thread that ties us all together. For Shklar, this *summum malum* should be our primary concern to avoid rather that the *summum bonum* being the object of our pursuit (Hess, 2020). Regardless of whose theoretical foundation speaks to us most on a personal level, keeping the propensity of evil—the ability to perpetrate mass atrocity—at the forefront of our concern in analyzing Uyghurs' abuse in Xinjiang is essential.

Moving forward, having identified some Western philosophy and theory surrounding cruelty and genocide, we must then establish the necessary link of humanitarianism to mass atrocities. In the twentieth century, the impetus to intervene in mass human rights violations—beginning with the Armenian genocide—was one of the footholds of humanitarian intervention on a global scale (Tusan, 2014). This coincides, causally or not, with a perceived increased demand for citizens' justice from individuals throughout the 1900s, noticeably coming to a peak in the 1990s (Baylis et al., 2020) when significantly the Bosnian and Rwandan genocides were at the forefront of humanitarian concern. This pressure from the public can be interpreted as a kind of global foreign policy paradigm shift toward one of stronger interventionist policy rooted in liberal ideals that a state or nonstate actor must be motivated to act to preserve nascent human rights rather than advance its own agenda. We see the spirit of this shift in the 1948 Genocide Convention of the UN (United Nations High Commissioner for Refugees, 2019), which charges states to intervene and stop genocide when it occurs domestically while simultaneously putting a certain onus on other international members to suppress genocide if the domestic state cannot or does not (or is the entity perpetrating the atrocity). The universality of the Genocide Convention's charge unfortunately is directly in conflict with the United Nations charter, which lays out a clear noninterventionist policy for the organization (United Nations, 2019). Five decades later, the same contradictory paradox presents itself to the UN in the form of the R2P commitment, with which China has a complicated relationship.

China did not officially support the R2P commitment until four years after its inception in 2001—no insignificant delay as a member of the Power Five (P5). Most of China's resistance to adopt or invoke R2P is centric to two main concerns: (1) agreeing that in general states have a right to protect and agreeing that certain states should be able to nonconsensually intervene in another state's domestic affairs are not mutually inclusive and (2) each R2P question is essentially case by case and so there is a general unwillingness to establish a blanket procedure of evoking R2P (Teitt, 2011). Not even a decade later, China was scrutinized in the global eye for its abstinence from voting to enact R2P in Libya and for vetoing intervention in Syria (United Nations Meetings Coverage and Press Releases, 2011). This ties into Acharya and Buzan's description of China as an "enigmatic outsider"—having the qualities of both a core and peripheral state but undeniably a Great Power. In the matter of their position in the UN, China is the only truly non-Western state with veto power in the Security Council (barring Russia, which is somewhat ambiguously aligned being politically tied to the West but partially culturally and geographically rooted in the East). Therefore, enacting R2P can, in the instances that China opposes or abstains, be perceived as Western intervention, echoing imperialist legacies left behind by the United States, France, the UK, and Russia. China's identity in such a case may more closely align with the "third world," bearing resentment toward the colonizing states but having the power of the first world to obstruct foreign intervention. Its unique position allows China and the rest of the P5 a kind of safety net, which ensures that R2P will never be enacted against them or, if entertained, could be blocked by way of a veto. We can assume that no such motion would be brought to the P5 to address Xinjiang's current situation, operating under the knowledge that any kind of intervention would surely be rejected, but to date, the motion hasn't even been symbolically brought to the table.

The ability of all P5 nations to completely shut the UN SC down with a single veto is problematic for many reasons. In considering human rights abuses in Xinjiang, it can be viewed as a kind of mechanic that has potential to increase tensions between nations of the P5. Given the global economic influence of both the United States and China, the escalation of tensions between the two nations is a kind of meta-rhino: a problem on a large enough scale that, while it is its own issue to address, it also intersects with other gray rhinos and has the propensity to make those concerns more impactful—often worse. Wucker herself projected United States–China tensions to be one of the top five most threatening gray rhinos of the year 2019 (Wucker, 2019). The Security Council P5's veto power isn't probably one of the most tense dynamics between the nations but embodies the oppositional stalemate that United States–China relations have the capacity to achieve ideologically (Kroenig, 2020)—the sense that a liberal democracy and authoritarian autocracy which have the world's first and second largest economies can "cancel" each other out, or clash and create the scale of total war that was so narrowly avoided with the USSR and the United States less than a century ago. In a capitalist global economy, the two would naturally be economic competitors, but this competition can carry over into their foreign policies toward each other, particularly from a realist approach wherein each seeks absolute gains over the other to preserve its own interests. It's this trajectory of reason that leads us to the Thucydides Trap—the idea that the United States as existing economic superpower would be threatened by China as an "up-and-coming" economic superpower and seek to act to preserve the existing hierarchy that favors its own state (Persaud and Sajed, 2018). While many would argue that the Thucydides Trap is an overly simplistic analogy of power transition theory, it brings its own merits in showcasing the emotional stakes between the ruling and rising states in question (Zhang, 2019). Within this analogy, the suspicion of each other drives increased hostility, which would at some point permeate all of foreign affairs since there are essentially no states that do not maintain economic ties to each or both nations. Particularly in Central and South Asia, the ties to China are intricately woven and China is continuing to gain political influence in regional conflict as well as economic influence through its vast lending to infrastructure projects (Staats et al., 2020). Considering how China practices economic diplomacy with its geographical neighbors is paramount when trying to identify the driving factors of human rights abuses in Xinjiang.

The approach that the Chinese Communist Party takes in handling conflict between itself and the autonomous regions of China is a blended balance of foreign and domestic affairs. In some respects, China must acknowledge that any such friction between itself and Tibet or Xinjiang is a domestic issue—the premise upon which it refrains from evoking R2P in the Security Council for other nations is the unwillingness to interfere without invitation per the Charter rather than the R2P commitment (Perisic, 2019), which ought to be upheld internally as well. The "One China" dream relies on the enforcement of a single Chinese identity (which includes absolute loyalty to The Party), by which autonomous regions must abide or face consequences of being perceived as separatist terrorists and enemies of the state. Crossing this line triggers an almost foreign-affairs-driven response on behalf of the CCP, including increased military intervention within its own borders. There is historical precedent in modern history for China to use military force to bend autonomous regions to the will of The Party (Griffiths, 2018), and the "bad blood" between the two can act as a kind of accelerant when conflict erupts. The precarious nature of interrelations between Xinjiang and Beijing specifically goes far back—Eastern Turkestan was not considered part of "China" as it was geopolitically drawn until it was annexed in the last decades of the Qing Dynasty, then dubbed "Xinjiang." In the midst of the civil war before the establishment of the PRC, Eastern Turkestan had a brief period of declared independence in the twentieth century. Uyghurs who maintain this identity for themselves are often labeled as separatists and designated as enemies of the state. Since 2016, China's "War on Terror" has been the flagstaff of its zero-tolerance approach to quashing separatism in the northwest once and for all. Necessarily, depending on each side's perspective, this is both a domestic and foreign dispute, making the policy applied something of a mix between the two. Conflicts between Tibet and Beijing offer some kind of context for what this blended policy looks like—seizure of control at the state and federal level, essentially, but one could argue that the stakes are even higher currently in Xinjiang. Some elements remain the same: ostracization of ethnic minorities, The Party's wariness of religious influence in the region that could divide the region from Beijing, and a growing tension in the West whose liberal ideals demand a type of humanitarian intervention yet never quite follows through with actionable measure (Charbonneau, 2008). However, Xinjiang has an economic multiplier: it is the geopolitical key to unlocking the Belt Road Initiative (Ma, 2019). For China and the surrounding Central and South Asian states, this is a huge economic undertaking to accessing regional markets, thereby giving smaller, less stable countries the opportunity for growth and giving China the opportunity to solidify its control over the markets by tying most regional trade back to and routed through itself. For the West, however, economic rhetoric is centric to concerns of "debt traps" and questioning whether the balance of debt to the PRC and the countries' infrastructure development is sustainable for the region long term (Staats et al., 2020). If we look back to the analogy of the Thucydides Trap, this project would be a significant threat to the United States, who has no competitive heartland-based alternative to the BRI and can anticipate a certain amount of being "boxed out" of the region.

With these four intersecting challenges, we have laid out a general (although not nearly comprehensive) picture of "the problem in Xinjiang" and, like Arendt and Shklar, position this conflict at the heart of our analysis, particularly acknowledging both the state and civilian experiences. With these underpinnings in mind, our following data should and could be interpreted for pluralistic perspectives.

Data and Methodology

One of the key challenges of gathering data (or establishing a best method by which to gather data) from Xinjiang's reeducation camps is the CCP's relative control over what information comes out of China. This is arguably one of the great sources of strength for the Party—unification of the Chinese people and construction of the Chinese-with-a-capital-C identity hinges on the Party's diligent control over the political rhetoric of the country. Like with Tibet, this control eventually turns into a manipulation of the country's history (Macmillan, 2010), which will then cycle into a stronger rhetoric by which to unify (or manipulate) citizens of China. As such, a large amount of our data presently comes from non-Chinese, Western sources.

Journalistic reports and leaked documents

Adrian Zenz, a German theologian and philosopher, is a key actor in many of the reports coming from the Xinjiang-Uyghur Autonomous Region (XUAR). His data has been cited by major news outlets like CNN (Griffiths, 2019) (Watson et al., 2020) and *The New York Times* (Buckley, 2019; Buckley and Mozur, 2019) and is hosted by The Jamestown Foundation (Jamestown, n.d.) in Washington, DC. One of Zenz's most cited reports from 2017 show dramatic increases in domestic security spending per capita in Xinjiang in the year 2017—more than three times greater than the rest of the country (Zenz, 2018), despite Xinjiang being a relatively rural/unpopulated region. In another report, Zenz analyzes open job positions for law enforcement in XUAR, where a distinct and alarming spike shows that in the year 2016, there were more than 30,000 law enforcement positions for hire—more than three previous years combined (Zenz and Leibold, 2017b). Both these timelines overlap with the anticipated start of the Uyghur "reeducation" camps en masse in 2016. At the time, the official rhetoric of the CCP was denying the existence of the camps—they are still largely referred to as vocational training centers—but the report clearly showed that the rhetoric did not match the numbers. Zenz and other Western critics of the CCP's actions in Xinjiang draw a connection between this increased militarization with the promotion of Chen Quanguo from party secretary of Tibet to the party chief of Xinjiang (Zenz and Leibold, 2017a) (International Campaign for Tibet, 2018)—similar military surveillance grids were first implemented in Tibet c. 2008 before Chen moved to his position overseeing XUAR in 2016. Another significant contribution of data from Adrian Zenz is the report regarding intentional declining birth rates and forced sterilization among Uyghur women in Xinjiang (Zenz, 2020b) and disproportionate incarceration rates among Uyghurs in Xinjiang at large (Zenz, 2020c). Despite making up less than 2 percent of the national population, Uyghurs account for roughly 20 percent of the incarcerated population in China and an estimated 1–2 million currently reside in detention centers (Buckley, 2019). There are continuing emerging reports of forced labor being facilitated through these reeducation camps (Zenz, 2020a) and suspicions of organ harvesting that resulted in a UN Human Rights Tribunal in 2019, ultimately not imposing any action upon Beijing (Martin, 2019).

By the 1948 Genocide Convention (United Nations, 2018), these reports are significant in their applicability to the definitions of genocide in article II, namely the points which concern *"deliberately inflicting on the group conditions of life calculated to bring about its physical destruction in whole or in part [and] imposing measures intended to prevent births within the group."* Zenz and others have also sought to investigate what happens to the children whose parents are detained by authorities in reeducation centers and have followed trails of increased elementary enrollment at state-run boarding schools in Xinjiang and western Chinese provinces, finding other locations as far west as Turkey (Griffiths, 2019) (Zenz, 2019). This concerns the fifth of the acts constituting genocide, defined by the UN Convention: *"forcibly transferring children of the group to another group"*—disrupting the family dynamic, culture, and Uyghur identity is the necessary outcome of separating children from their roots. There are further elaborations in these same reports that speak of cultural and linguistic imperialism—forbiddance of speaking non-Mandarin languages or participating in any overtly religious activity.

Other journalistic contributions to uncovering the ongoings of the internment camps include the *China Cables*: documents leaked from the International Consortium of Investigative Journalists (ICIJ), which detailed disturbing military strategy for detaining suspicious Uyghur individuals—this may include knowing someone who had studied abroad, exceeding the birth limit per family, owning a passport, using a VPN, or having certain communications apps on a person's cellular device. Many of these investigative reports that attempt to gather generalizable or wide-scale data align with individual accounts that are more typically championed for justice by NGOs and IOs, detailed as our second main source of data.

Firsthand accounts and advocacy from humanitarian organizations

Organizations like Amnesty International champion for a more grassroots approach to Xinjiang's crisis. Using individual experiences to pursue routes to justice and garner attention from the international community is a strategic attempt to address and stop the human rights violations ongoing in northwest China. For instance, Amnesty International began a letter writing campaign to PRC's President Xi Jinping to seek the release of Uyghur activist Rebiya Kadeer's family (Amnesty International USA, 2019)—some 30 relatives who were imprisoned for their relation to Kadeer. She herself escaped detention by fleeing the country but has had no contact with her family ever since.

Human Rights Watch employs a similar strategy—they publish reunification stories and interviews with separated families (Human Rights Watch, 2019), presumably to advance a more empathetic understanding of the threat to human security for Uyghurs in Xinjiang today. There are plenty of smaller NGOs and nonstate actors who pursue advocacy using such methods of highlighting the civilian experience in Xinjiang (Justice for All, 2020); however, these NGOs are also in a unique position to apply unopposed pressure to the UN General Assembly as well as their state and national governments to take formal action to investigate or condemn Chinese actions in Xinjiang.

Researchers and *outsiders* are less welcome in XUAR since 2017; one PhD candidate recalls leaving her research site in the capital of Urumqi ahead of schedule, due to the discomfort of being frequently stopped, questioned, and investigated by the state police (Tynen, 2020). As these reports from survivors and firsthand accounts of researchers, journalists, or travelers become more difficult to obtain, our data set wants for a category of data to illuminate the situation in Xinjiang that is less susceptible to the CCP's clampdown.

Satellite imagery analysis

Thanks to modern technology, satellite imagery analysis is likely the closest thing existing to nonbiased evidence of the abuses in Xinjiang. Time lapses of detention centers observed from orbit obviously lack the qualitative part of data analysis—it can seem almost removed from the human experience entirely. However, it's still an incredibly worthy pursuit. In line with the pressure that humanitarian NGOs are able to apply to the UN and other nations to promote just intervention, modern methods like information and communications technologies (ICTs) offer the kind of indisputable evidence the ICC may be looking for. Amnesty International has successfully used satellite imagery analysis to capture human rights abuses in North Korea and Nigeria, the latter leading to a case brought to the ICC (Koettl, 2017). Similarly, the Australian Strategic Policy Institute (ASPI) has captured and analyzed satellite data of Xinjiang camps to document their growth (Australian Strategic Policy Institute, 2020), contrary to the CCP's rhetoric that the centers are being closed down. These ICT data don't capture the firsthand experience of those detained like the humanitarian groups do and they don't have (much) circumstantial data to tie to current events like the investigative journalists provide, but they even out the data set we have available with hard numbers—images of centers, evidence of activity, and calculable growth in square meters over time. The state media in China denounced the legitimacy of the ASPI images, asserting that the West was attempting to demonize China for its own gain (Global Times, 2020).

Analysis and Conclusion

Despite the relative difficulty of obtaining unbiased, quality data to illustrate the breadth of the human rights abuses in Xinjiang, since 2016 the major data sets and methods of collection outlined here have gathered significant international attention. Frustratingly, there seems to be no actionable solution when considering China's unique position in the GIS, the ideologic and economic factors at stake that drive further tension between the United States and China, and an understanding of the complex relationship between The Party and ethnic minorities in the mainland. This analysis recommends employing a constructivist approach to accommodate the interdimensional nature of the present gray rhino while keeping the conceptual underpinnings that place the conflict of the people and the propensity for cruelty by the government at the center of our analysis. Constructivism will allow us the fluidity needed to accommodate the bipolar nature of even identifying the problem. This is to say that the severity of human rights' abuses and even the definition of genocide is somewhat determined by the social construction of the relationship between the PRC and another entity (namely the West, specifically, the United States and the Uyghur peoples of XUAR). Constructivism allows us to account for the power dynamics at play—the potential Thucydides Trap in regard to the United States but also the few options available to Uyghurs in northwestern China. Because this approach accounts for that entity's ability or agency to incite change in the present situation, it can provide a kind of weighted formula to project outcomes of this conflict, depending on the actors in question.

Undeniably one key actor will be the CCP, but others would potentially be the UN, the United States or other Western states, as well as the Uyghur and other ethnic minority groups like the Tibetans who have lived, and still live, in similar conditions. These are who I believe would be the most significant actors in a constructivist analysis of a solution to the reeducation camps in Xinjiang. Each stakeholder bears some kind of weight or role in addressing the widespread cruelty imposed upon Uyghurs now. The UN and the West are similarly constrained—one by a Schrodinger's intervention-type paradox and the other by neoliberal–democratic ideology. While searching for a solution, the role that makes the most probabilistic sense to me for the United States and UN to play is that of an external pressure. It seems like a scant chance that the UN or United States would be willing or able to intervene in Xinjiang; even if so, the question remains whether it would be beneficial to the conflict or the Uyghur people. The Trump Administration passed the Hong Kong Autonomy Act and the Uyghur Human Rights Act (UHRA) in 2020—both attention-grabbing news pieces that keep the international spotlight on Xinjiang. Although the UHRA lacked a lot of follow-up—for instance sanctions and consequences for US-based companies whose supply chains ran through the forced labor markets in Xinjiang—it was a source of pressure nonetheless. Using still a constructivist approach, such pressure from the West borders on postcolonial/imperialist interpretation. The rhetoric from the state-approved media outlets has been explicitly offended by the West's criticism of the CCP reeducation centers in Xinjiang. *The Global Times* regularly and consistently refutes claims from the UN and the United States: first denying that the camps existed at all, then attributing them to antiterrorist campaigns in the region, and finally criticizing the United States for its hypocrisy to condemn China for taking a firm stance against "religious extremism" in an attempt to stigmatize China and its growing power.

Echoing MacMillian's book referenced before, constructivism would have us pay special attention to the skew of how the information that informs our analysis is filtered to us and who, ultimately, is writing the "history" to be repeated—is it the history of ethnic minorities in Tibet, the history of the Cultural Revolution's "reeducation" campaign, the history of any other genocide that preceded Xinjiang, or all of the above? Regardless, constructivism allows us a healthy margin of skepticism that is inherently needed in such a circumstance where data is sparse and tensions are high. In essence, *The Global Times* accounts of the "reality" of the detention centers in XUAR are as biased and ulterior as some of the information coming from the US White House.

Ultimately, some kind of peace would need to be brokered between Uyghurs and the CCP for a positive solution to cease the abuses perpetuated by the reeducation centers in XUAR. The objective, according to our conceptual underpinnings, could be satisfied if the solution subverts a continuation of the cruelty of the PRC government in favor of restoring human rights to the Uyghurs whose rights have been violated. The authoritarian structure of the government makes this conflict especially one-sided and challenging, not just by its convoluted domestic/foreign policy in handling autonomous regions but in its potentiality to pursue traditional peacebuilding strategies. Where IOs and NGOs are already involved in spreading survivors' stories and advocating for their rights, there is an unexplored opportunity for the NGOs to open space for the CCP to connect with the Uyghur people. Contrary to what intervention from the UN or United States would be—inherently political and shifting our approach to a more traditional liberal or realist view—NGOs, particularly those that are based in China and Central Asia, are well-positioned to maintain our constructivist approach, keeping the conflict and human experience at the center, to build narratives from the perpetrator and victims' sides.

Conclusion

There are glaring gaps in the literature and in the data surrounding the modern internment camps in Xinjiang today. For many of the reasons highlighted above, access is an unavoidable issue. However, it is important to note that using Western-centric theories and paradigms as the conceptual underpinnings of our policy analysis is not ideal and biases our observations to be less encompassing of IR theory, which emerges from the periphery and from China itself. While it is exceptionally difficult to find robust political analysis from Chinese scholars, especially in the case of ethnic minority relations with the Chinese Communist Party, it is not as much of an accessibility issue as procurement of the data itself could be. The CCP is a relatively small, close-knit group, but it isn't impossible to gain firsthand insight to the inner workings of the CCP. Notably, the few scholars who have achieved and published interviews from within the high ranks of the CCP in recent decades have also been Western scholars (Feng and He, 2020). Feng and He propose a meta-analysis of the topics, findings, and research of Chinese scholars of foreign affairs as a new way to gain a clearer understanding of the state of IR and the current dialogue within the discipline to understand Chinese IR methodology today, but such an undertaking has not yet been completed. Meanwhile, China's ancient history provides a wealth of philosophical underpinnings that we can look to in search of applicability to modern IR. For instance, one such piece that is rooted in Confucianism applies well to our present analysis: from the *Three Character Classic*—a staple of all young Chinese learners—we find commentary that runs completely contrary to Arendt and Shklar's relative realisms and liberalisms. One lesson begins: "人之初，性本善"—roughly translating to "humanity is inherently good." We would not assume that this single example alone has significant influence in China's policymaking, but if we were able to carry out Huiyun and Kai's proposal, we could almost certainly find remnants of centuries of rich philosophy at the roots of Chinese IR theory, the same way we can with Western writers. There is a desperate need for more robust, accessible literature on the topic of domestic and foreign affairs that is sourced from Chinese scholars using IR theory that represents the structures and paradigms within which Chinese politics operates.

References

Acharya, A., and Buzan, B. (2019). *The Making of Global International Relations: Origins and Evolution of IR at Its Centenary*. Cambridge: Cambridge University Press.

Aleci, S. (2019). *China Cables | China's Operating Manuals for Mass Internment*. (online) ICIJ. Available at https://www.icij.org/investigations/china-cables/.

Amnesty International USA (2019). *Urgent Action Update: Uyghur Activist's 30 Relatives Still Detained (China: UA 251.17)*. (online). Available at https://www.amnestyusa.org/urgent-actions/urgent-action-update-uyghur-activists-30-relatives-still-detained-china-ua-251-17/.

Australian Strategic Policy Institute. Cave, D., Ruser, N., and Ryan, F. (2020). "*Mapping Xinjiang's 'Re-Education' Camps*," Australian Department of Defense, Canberra, Aus.

Baylis, J., Smith, S., and Owens, P. (2020). *The Globalization of World Politics*, 8th ed. Oxford: Oxford University Press.

Benhabib, S. (1994). Judith Shklar's Dystopic Liberalism. *Social Research*, 61(2), pp. 477–88.

Buckley, C. (2019). China's Prisons Swell after Deluge of Arrests Engulfs Muslims. *New York Times*. (online). August 31. Available at https://www.nytimes.com/2019/08/31/world/asia/xinjiang-china-uighurs-prisons.html.

Buckley, C., and Mozur, P. (2019). How China Uses High-Tech Surveillance to Subdue Minorities. *New York Times*. (online). May 22. Available at https://www.nytimes.com/2019/05/22/world/asia/china-surveillance-xinjiang.html.

Charbonneau, L. (2008). *U.N. Council Keeps Silent on Tibet Protests*. (online). Available at https://www.reuters.com/article/us-china-tibet-un/u-n-council-keeps-silent-on-tibet-protests-idUSN1758766020080317.

Feng, H., and He, K. (2020). The Study of Chinese Scholars in Foreign Policy Analysis: An Emerging Research Program. *Pacific Review*, 33(3–4), pp. 362–85.

Global Times (2020). *Anti-China Australian Think Tank's Malicious Lies Cannot Escape Justice: Chinese FM*. (online). Global Times. Available at https://www.globaltimes.cn/content/1203607.shtml.

Griffiths, J. (2018). *China's Paranoia and Oppression in Xinjiang Has a Long History*. (online). CNN. Available at https://www.cnn.com/2018/10/11/asia/xinjiang-reeducation-muslim-china-intl/index.html.

——— (2019). *Children of Detained Uyghurs Held in Mass Boarding Schools in Xinjiang, Research Claims*. (online). CNN Digital. Available at https://www.cnn.com/2019/07/05/asia/xinjiang-muslims-china-intl-hnk/index.html.

Hess, S. (2020). *Discovering Judith Shklar's Skeptical Liberalism of Fear—Samantha Ashenden & Andreas Hess | Aeon Essays*. (online). Aeon. Available at https://aeon.co/essays/discovering-judith-shklars-skeptical-liberalism-of-fear.

Human Rights Watch (2019). *UN: Unprecedented Joint Call for China to End Xinjiang Abuses*. (online). Available at https://www.hrw.org/news/2019/07/10/un-unprecedented-joint-call-china-end-xinjiang-abuses.

International Campaign for Tibet (2018). *The Origin of the "Xinjiang Model" in Tibet under Chen Quanguo: Securitizing Ethnicity and Accelerating Assimilation*. (online). International Campaign for Tibet. Available at https://savetibet.org/the-origin-of-the-xinjiang-model-in-tibet-under-chen-quanguo-securitizing-ethnicity-and-accelerating-assimilation/.

Jamestown (n.d.). *Adrian Zenz*. (online). Available at https://jamestown.org/analyst/adrian-zenz/ (accessed 2021).

Justice For All (2020). *Islamophobia in Three Asian Contexts: India, Myanmar (Burma) and China*. (online). Available at https://www.justiceforall.org/human-rights/islamophobia-in-three-asian-contexts-india-myanmar-burma-and-china/.

Koettl, C. (2017). Sensors Everywhere: Using Satellites and Mobile Phones to Reduce Information Uncertainty in Human Rights Crisis Research. *Genocide Studies and Prevention*, 11(1), pp. 36–54.

Kroenig, M. (2020). *The Power Delusion*. (online). Foreign Policy. Available at https://foreignpolicy.com/2020/11/11/china-united-states-democracy-ideology-competition-rivalry-great-powers-power-delusion/.

Ma, A. (2019). *This Map Shows a Trillion-Dollar Reason Why China Is Oppressing More Than a Million Muslims*. (online). Business Insider. Available at https://www.businessinsider.com/mapt-explains-china-crackdown-on-uighur-muslms-in-xinjiang-2019-2.

Macmillan, M. (2010). *Dangerous Games: The Uses and Abuses of History*. New York: Modern Library.

Martin, W. (2019). *China Harvesting Organs of Uighur Muslims, China Tribunal Tells UN*. (online). Business Insider. Available at https://www.businessinsider.com/china-harvesting-organs-of-uighur-muslims-china-tribunal-tells-un-2019-9.

McNeill, S. (2020). *Uyghur Family Kept Apart by China's Xinjiang Policies Reunites*. (online). Human Rights Watch. Available at https://www.hrw.org/news/2020/12/10/uyghur-family-kept-apart-chinas-xinjiang-policies-reunites.

Perisic, P. (2019). Intervention by Invitation—When Can Consent from a Host State Justify Foreign Military Intervention. *Russian Law Journal*, 7(4), pp. 4–29. Available at http://search.ebscohost.com.proxy.library.nyu.edu/login.aspx?direct=true&db=edshol&AN=edshol.hein.journals.russlj7.32&site=eds-live.

Persaud, R. B., and Sajed, A. (2018). *Race, Gender, and Culture in International Relations Postcolonial Perspectives*. London Routledge.

Royer, C. (2020). Evil as an Expression of and a Threat to Human Plurality: Hannah Arendt's Agonistic Realism. *Distinktion: Journal of Social Theory*, 21(3), pp. 257–75.

Staats, J., Olson, R. G., Schriver, R. G., Ayres, A., Cronin, P., Lalwani, S., . . . Stokes, J. (2020, December 15). *China's Influence on Conflict Dynamics in South Asia*. Lecture presented at USIP Senior Study Group on China and South Asia Launches Final Report in Online.

Teitt, S. (2011). The Responsibility to Protect and China's Peacekeeping Policy. *International Peacekeeping*, 18(3), pp. 298–312.

Tusan, M. (2014). Humanitarianism, Genocide and Liberalism. *Journal of Genocide Research*, 17(1), pp. 83–105.

Tynen, S. (2020). Dispossession and Displacement of Migrant Workers: The Impact of State Terror and Economic Development on Uyghurs in Urban Xinjiang. *Central Asian Survey*, 39(3), pp. 1–21.

United Nations (2018). *United Nations Office on Genocide Prevention and the Responsibility to Protect*. (online). Un.org. Available at https://www.un.org/en/genocideprevention/genocide.shtml.

——— (2019). *Charter of the United Nations*. (online). Refworld. Available at https://www.refworld.org/docid/3ae6b3930.html.

United Nations High Commissioner for Refugees (2019). *Convention on the Prevention and Punishment of the Crime of Genocide*. (online). Refworld. Available at https://www.refworld.org/docid/3ae6b3ac0.html.

United Nations Meetings Coverage and Press Releases (2011). *Security Council Fails to Adopt Draft Resolution Condemning Syria's Crackdown on Anti-Government Protestors, Owing to Veto by Russian Federation, China | Meetings Coverage and Press Releases.* (online). Un.org. Available at https://www.un.org/press/en/2011/sc10403.doc.htm.

Watson, I., Wescott, B., Lee, L., and Xiong, Y. (2020). *China's Xinjiang Records Revealed: Uyghurs Thrown into Detention for Growing Beards or Bearing too Many Children, Leaked Chinese Document Shows.* (online). www.cnn.com. Available at: https://www.cnn.com/interactive/2020/02/asia/xinjiang-china-karakax-document-intl-hnk/.

Wucker, M. (2016). *The Gray Rhino: How to Recognize and Act on the Obvious Dangers We Ignore.* New York: St. Martin's Press.

——— (2019). *The Top Gray Rhino Risks of 2019 | The Gray Rhino.* (online). Gray Rhino & Company. Available at https://thegrayrhino.com/the-top-gray-rhino-risks-of-2019/ (accessed January 27, 2021).

Zenz, A. (2018). Xinjiang's Re-Education and Securitization Campaign: Evidence from Domestic Security Budgets. *China Brief.* (online), 18(17), pp. 4–9. Available at https://jamestown.org/wp-content/uploads/2018/11/Read-the-11-19-2018-CB-Issue-in-PDF.pdf?x44883.

——— (2019). Break Their Roots: Evidence for China's Parent-Child Separation Campaign in Xinjiang. *Journal of Political Risk*, 7(7), pp. 1–36.

——— (2020a). *Coercive Labor in Xinjiang: Labor Transfer and the Mobilization of Ethnic Minorities to Pick Cotton.* (online). Center for Global Policy. Available at https://cgpolicy.org/briefs/coercive-labor-in-xinjiang-labor-transfer-and-the-mobilization-of-ethnic-minorities-to-pick-cotton/.

——— (2020b). *Sterilizations, IUDs, and Mandatory Birth Control: The CCP's Campaign to Suppress Uyghur Birthrates in Xinjiang.* (online). Available at https://jamestown.org/wp-content/uploads/2020/06/Zenz-Internment-Sterilizations-and-IUDs-UPDATED-July-21-Rev2.pdf?x60903.

——— (2020c). China Suppression of Uighur Minorities Meets U.N. Definition of Genocide, Report Says [Interview by 1135457596 855630749 S. Simon]. Retrieved from https://www.npr.org/2020/07/04/887239225/china-suppression-of-uighur-minorities-meets-u-n-definition-of-genocide-report-s.

Zenz, A., and Leibold, J. (2017a). *Chen Quanguo: The Strongman Behind Beijing's Securitization Strategy in Tibet and Xinjiang—Jamestown.* (online). Jamestown. Available at https://jamestown.org/program/chen-quanguo-the-strongman-behind-beijings-securitization-strategy-in-tibet-and-xinjiang/.

——— (2017b). *Xinjiang's Rapidly Evolving Security State.* (online). Jamestown. Available at https://jamestown.org/program/xinjiangs-rapidly-evolving-security-state/.

Zhang, B. (2019). The Perils of Hubris? A Tragic Reading of "Thucydides' Trap" and China-US Relations. *Journal of Chinese Political Science*, 24(1), pp. 129–44.

Part III

Chapter 6

SMARTPHONES AND DATA PRIVACY ETHICS: INTERNATIONAL REGULATIONS IN A "CHESSBOARD-WEB" ENVIRONMENT

Andrea Adams

Introduction

As early as 1969, legal scholars were concerned about the emerging information age and its effect on privacy. Miller's (1969) review of computer privacy is surprisingly accurate in projecting the effect of the then-coming computer and information age on traditional privacy promises. Initially, nonpersonal data did not require protection primarily because it lacked the personal data attributes that would allow easy identification. Moreover, data ownership distinctions are increasingly blurred (Hummel et al., 2020) and are now attributed to confusing data ownership linked to process centricity definitions (Fadler and Legner 2020, p. 673). Fifty-one years later, many of those same privacy concerns discussed in Miller's review are present. However, the volume and complexity of data and information are well beyond Miller's vision, especially since the advent of the "smartphone."

Though data privacy regulation is widely acknowledged as critical (Jensen, 2013), party-based gridlock and presidential policies in the United States seem to prevent implementing a clear global regulatory privacy framework to address the emerging concerns of data from smartphone and smart device technology (Fefer, 2019). However, the European Union's Global Data Privacy Regulation (GDPR) covers its member states and citizens and covers multinational corporate businesses and cross-border data flows between countries. In addition, other nation-states are building privacy frameworks to address similar global concerns (Hunton Privacy Blog, 2020). The lack of international leadership regarding global concerns by the United States supports Acharya and Buzan's description of the shift from international to domestic-focused priorities (Acharya and Buzan, 2019).

Under President Donald Trump, the US regulatory parameters sought to limit privacy regulation to promote business innovation. However, the limited regulatory guidance includes a legacy of data classifications that seem irrelevant compared to how data is currently used. Piecemeal enforcement has not kept up with innovative ways data is created and utilized. Moreover, increased cross-border flows of data have led to greater privacy risks, but these risks may be considered "trade" and not "conflict" based (Yakovleva and Irion, 2020).

Moreover, single nation-states are not the only actors and stakeholders in the data privacy arena. The new landscape of actors can be represented by what Anne Marie Slaughter (2017) calls a "chessboard and web" structure of vertical and horizontal influences on shared-fate issues. The chessboard represents the conflict-based posture of nation-states, where the web represents groups of individuals, businesses, and organizations whose actions impact the regulatory environment. Slaughter's perspective provides a method to dissect how these influences and perspectives impact the new regulatory landscape in and between nation-states. It uses network theory to explain web-based influence, identifying technology as both a means of influence and the specific networks that own technology as a topic of inquiry. To that end, owners of technology can influence how privacy is understood as well as how it is operationalized.

Notwithstanding privacy risks, the web networks have produced positive developments. Smartphones have created new connection pathways for like-minded individuals and groups, rewarding users that grow and manage them. Apps connections facilitate many social and business services. Social connections enable social discourse and exchange ideas between individuals and groups living in vastly different countries and environments. As the technology standardizes these exchanges, agency-based influences are created for users. Acharya (2018) argues that agency "involves conceptualizing and implementing new approaches to development, security, and ecological justice" and fosters local ideas and norms that form societies developed out of a particular context (p. 14).

Therefore, both "chessboard" and "web" influences provide a better way to understand how data privacy is being addressed in domestic and international environments. Uncovering the distribution of influence of chessboard regulations, technology-based networks in increased group agency might provide insight into how future regulation needs to be structured to achieve data privacy protection. First, the chapter reviews data privacy in the United States, including a limited review of agreements between the United States and the European Union and the future of current data classification schemes. Next, the chapter looks at the actions of data platforms as unique networks and influencers in the data privacy space. As an example, the chapter uses Slaughter's network centrality evaluation to understand data platforms' role during the COVID-19 tracing app development. In another example, network centrality is also used to understand a smartphone app's (Safecity.in) ecosystem to understand how their increased agency using the smartphone technology enabled the network to influence local government systems. The chapter comments on how future regulation should support integrating chessboard and network strategies to preserve privacy and concludes by briefly reviewing blockchain technology as a new way to give data ownership back to individuals.

Literature Review: The Chessboard Regulatory Scheme

"Chessboard" privacy regulations, data classifications, and tools for smartphones

Review of privacy regulations

The volume of data generated across digital devices continues to explode. The Cisco Visual Networking Index of 2012–23 (White Paper, 2020) indicates, among other statistics, that smartphones will surpass 90 percent of mobile traffic by 2022, and nearly 79 percent of the world's mobile data traffic will be in video format by the same year. They also project that global mobile data traffic will increase sevenfold between 2017 and 2022, with an annual growth rate of 46 percent from 2017 to 2022, reaching 77.5 exabytes per month by 2022. Similarly, the Middle East and Africa are expected to have the most substantial mobile traffic growth rate, 56 percent, of any region, followed by the Asia Pacific at 49 percent and Latin America at 43 percent. In addition, China's mobile traffic surpassed that of the United States at the end of 2017. Lastly, both mobile and wi-fi traffic will surpass fixed traffic devices (p. 4). The most recent report covering 2018 to 2023 also projected a faster-growing mobile traffic segment called MTM (machine-to-machine), accounting for transferring data between smart devices in homes and cars (Cisco Annual Report, 2018–23). These statistics suggest that device-generated data is primarily responsible for increased data traffic volume, spurred by device connections through apps.

The Cisco report confirms that future data types of video, alternative reality, and MTM applications will increase smartphone apps' demand. Though regulatory bodies have long acknowledged that app-mediated research using personal data is private (Health Information Accountability Act, 1996), they have declined to regulate nonpersonal, nonidentified data. Countries have addressed this issue in different ways. In the United States, privacy regulation for mobile app data is promulgated through different federal and state laws and enforced by various federal and state agencies. The Federal Trade Commission (FTC), the primary enforcement arm for data privacy in the federal government, issues guidance to protect consumer privacy, brings enforcement actions against companies that violate the law, and requires companies to take steps to remediate unlawful behavior. In 2016, the FTC released a tool to help app designers creating health-related mobile app to protect identified personal data (Mobile Health Act Interactive Tool). However, the tool was limited to helping app developers design health-related apps. As noted by Fefer (2019) in the Congressional Research Services' (2019) report, there is no globally accepted standard for the definition of privacy, and there are no multilateral rules about cross-border data flows.

The proposed agreement between the United States, Mexico, and Canada (USMCA), ratified on July 2020, requires adherence by businesses that voluntarily adopt the standard to privacy provisions based on the Asia Pacific Economic Cooperative's (APEC) Cross Border Privacy Rules (Gilbert, 2020). Though this agreement commits the United States to cooperate in enforcement across participating jurisdictions, the agreement is not connected to any overall privacy standard. Internally, as many as 16 federal agencies adhere to the restrictions on research under "Common Rule," Section 46.101 (b). Individual states specifically address some level of adherence to the federal scheme. Other states have created their parameters that exceed federal requirements (Kessler, 2019; Tovino, 2020) but remain silent about app-mediated research. On June 11, 2020, the California Legislature amended its law (CCPA), imposing new restrictions on the sale of deidentified information and expanding the exemption used for research purposes.

In 2018, the Trump Administration shifted away from protection-based guidelines, preferring outcome-based approaches designed to balance privacy protection and strengthen protections for private sector prosperity and innovation (Mulligan et al., 2019). However, there was no indication that this approach was related to the increased volume or the influence of smartphones or other technological impacts. Thus, this proposal sent to Congress includes similar prescriptive previsions but has yet to propose a way to accomplish them (p. 53).

The European Union passed the General Data Protection Regulation (GDPR, 2016). The GDPR defines sweeping and comprehensive changes to definitions of personal data and the corresponding protections afforded them while regulating data transferred between the member states, including mobile app data (Fefer, 2019). In 2019, the EU modified its regulatory privacy scheme by implementing the Digital Single Market Commission and published "Regulation on the free flow of non-personal data." With this regulation, the EU now permits the free flow of nonpersonal, nonidentified data throughout its member states to provide a stable legal and business environment for data exchange. In addition, the new regulation prevents EU member countries from passing laws that unjustifiably force data to be held solely inside the national territory. Consistent with providing regulatory guidance, courts in the EU sought to clarify these provisions for their member states. For example, Mourby et al. (2018) reported on Breyer versus Germany that for data covered by the GDPR, pseudonymized data (personal data with a pseudonym to mask identity) was personal, protected data. However, the GDPR courts held that anonymous information, "namely information which does not relate to an identified or identifiable natural person, or to personal data rendered anonymous in such a manner that the data subject is not or no longer identifiable," is not protected (p. 225).

Differences in privacy regulations between the United States and the EU are mediated by the Privacy Shield (2016), established in 2016. This agreement provides transparency and enforcement of privacy regulations between nations. The Privacy Shield established a voluntary program for businesses that included commitments, obligations, limitations, and transparency guidelines to help corporations address privacy disputes and ensure compliance with the Department of Commerce and the FTC's enforcement of standards. The FTC describes its international role as "protect[ing] consumers from harm while maximizing economic benefit and consumer choice." However, the Trump Administration has taken steps to weaken the Privacy Shield agreement by issuing Executive Order # 13768, limiting enforcement protections of individual or organizational complainants to US citizens, excluding EU companies (Butler, 2017).

Additionally, Mr. Trump failed to appoint members to the US Privacy and Civil Liberties Oversight Board (PCLOB). Without the full complement of membership, the board cannot review decisions regarding privacy-related disputes or violations (p. 2). These circumstances exist under the backdrop of interdependent companies and organizations with global footprints that need to sort out regulatory and ethical data exchange requirements. With the EU setting more precise guidelines for its member states regarding data flows, US businesses and organizations must manage the unknown impacts of a weakened Privacy Shield agreement. Now, because of *Scherns II* (Tracol, 2020), there is genuine uncertainty about companies achieving compliant international data exchange. Moreover, the Trump Administration's inaction regarding the Privacy Shield is also hard to reconcile, with the United States subsequently joining the USMCA agreement, which requires some enforcement promises between the United States, Canada, and Mexico since the administration refuses to support enforcement overseas.

According to Rustad and Koenig (2019), recent EU regulations' updates may drive a "disruptive wedge" between the EU and US privacy regimes. The authors explain that multinational entities may find it easier to adopt the most stringent data standard than satisfy divergent data privacy rules (p. 2). Moreover, the EU has also adopted many US innovations, such as Privacy by Design, suggesting that the EU's privacy directives could become the basis for a global privacy standard.

According to the Privacy Trust writers, the EU's ePrivacy regulation is currently being reviewed for adoption by member states. The ePrivacy regulation broadens the scope of the GDPR and aligns various online privacy rules across EU member states. The regulation encompasses all definitions of privacy and data within the GDPR and clarifies and enhances it. The regulation aims to align the online standard of privacy with the level covered under the GDPR. The same authority is responsible for the GDPR as is responsible for the ePrivacy regulations. The ePrivacy regulations are on track to replace the GDPR as the GDPR is redundant because of the all-encompassing coverage that the ePrivacy regulations establish. The current iteration of ePrivacy provisions suggests that location data generated in the context of electronic communication services (including smartphones) should not be considered metadata, owing to the sensitivity of that data. Further, the ePrivacy provisions propose that electronic communication mechanisms collect and process information that is a part of the end user's "private sphere" and so more protection is required. These new and potential clarifications about the unrestricted use of unidentified data indicate a change in the international privacy perspective.

Some wonder whether the change in leadership in the United States in 2021 will signal an immediate change in privacy regulation. Ropek (2020) conducted an interview with Pollyanna Sanderson, policy counsel with the Future of Privacy Forum, about whether the Biden Administration would likely consider implementing a country-wide privacy standard. Sanderson remarked, "the Biden team does not really have a huge learning curve. Lots of the folks who are involved were also involved in the Obama Consumer Privacy Bill of Rights, and they are coming back into the room and can pick up where they left off, noting that with Biden's arrival, a similar approach and tone are expected."

Regan (2020) discussed congressional oversite of online platforms by reviewing congressional committees responsible for developing legislation. She found recognition of the failure of the law to keep pace with technology in her review of congressional proceedings. Her review revealed concern that the small cadre of technology platforms rely on one another, and they control news, advertising, and technology to monetize transactions. Her concern about data platforms' roles was that limited data protection guidelines could lead to exploitative and exclusionary conduct by platforms (p. 205). Regan noted that congressional discussions about creating legislation were primarily partisan, and when congressional committees were fragmented in their support, policy solutions were less effective. She also reported more bipartisan support for identifying the problem, but solution discussions were partisan and relied heavily on industry input from platforms themselves.

Though the change in administration may signal a change in appetite for more privacy regulation, Congressional partisanship may still impact US ability to establish meaningful privacy regulation, especially if platform networks continue to exert influence in their favor. Regan noted that technology platforms have also increased their lobbying spending to continue to exert their position in the system (p. 220). Lastly, in July 2020, India introduced legislation that clarifies nonpersonal data use and establishes a framework to address issues that arise using nonpersonal data (Hunton Privacy Blog, 2020). These new and potential clarifications about the unrestricted use of nonpersonal data indicate a change in the international privacy perspective.

The above review shows an international move toward a more comprehensive nation-based privacy regulatory framework. However, since much of the regulation focuses on traditional data classifications, they still may not be as effective in light of the growing changes in data produced by devices.

Traditional data protection methods: Data classifications: owned, processed, sourced, and linked

Though the "personal" data classification is still effectively regulated in the medical arena, technological innovation has made the classification of "nonpersonal" data less effective at preventing identification. Moreover, even DNA is not entirely personal since its identity can be derived from family members who share DNA (Kearns and Roth, 2019). Consumers are said to use the privacy calculus theory to calculate the trade-offs between the value of personal data and its use (Pentina et al., 2016). However, Cofone (2020) suggests the trade-offs are nothing more than a take-it-or-leave-it option for data owners, with the only option being opting out.

Data that has been processed to remove identification-layered attributes is classified as anonymous (gathered without personal identifiers), anonymized (personal identifiers removed), and pseudonymized (a pseudonym used in place of personal attributes). The GDPR relies on these classifications to indicate to users which data is subject to regulation (Finck and Pallas, 2020). The GDPR's descriptions for categorizing include the tension between risk-based approaches and absolute standards' approach and how transformation techniques effectively change personal data to nonpersonal data. Under the GDPR, anonymous and fully anonymized data is not regulated. Once data has no personal identifiers, it is considered unowned, and others are free to use the data.

Data is also categorized based on sources of personal interaction with devices or between devices. Much of the device interaction data is categorized as metadata, which is defined as data that contains information about other data captured through machine and human interactions with devices (Agarwal et al., 2020). Since metadata is not based on personal attributes, explicit consent and privacy protection were thought unnecessary. However, views about the use of metadata have changed. The International Committee of the Red Cross classified the collection and sharing of metadata as a humanitarian crisis (ICRC, 2018). They discuss military use of metadata, suggesting that without using personally identified data, gatherers of metadata can learn all they want to know about a given situation because of surveillance evolution (p. 22). Initially, IP addresses were not considered personal data under the GDPR; however, in the *Breyer* case, the court applied the Data Protection Directive determining that the person or entity that owns the IP address can lawfully obtain sufficient additional data to link the information to a person's real world identity, notwithstanding the objective definitions of the GDPR (Borgesius, 2017, p. 137).

Big data is a repository of unstructured data generated from multiple devices and from sharing and combining arrangements from third-party information brokers that are continuously augmented with new data. Relational database methods transform the data into decision-making insights that are of great value to businesses. However, there are emerging privacy concerns surrounding this data (Ylijoki and Porras, 2016). Big data is very valuable because it reduces data mining costs (Kraft, 2020; Martin, 2015; Surbakti et al. 2020).

Trace data is a record of activity gleaned from online information systems (Stier et al., 2020, citing Howison, Wiggins, and Crowston, 2011). However, software algorithms using as few as 15 personal attributes from trace data have been used to identify individuals (Kosinski et al., 2013). In addition, based on the results of an FTC study on data brokers in 2014, Rostow (2017) reported that the largest data broker, Acxiom, has an average of over 3,000 data segments (categories of data) on every US consumer, even selling data to other consumers without knowledge and consent.

Since the advent of location data, linking location data is a popular form of its use. Global Positioning Systems (GPS) in most smartphone architecture situate the data point in the context of other identified data points that can lead to the identity of the person carrying the device (Wang and Loui, 2009). In the United States in 2016, the FTC announced a settlement with Inmobi, a mobile advertising app, challenging its location practices of tracking device location without user permission. Inmobi built a geolocating database and could infer device location by tracking device connection with wi-fi networks. Combining or linking digital trace data and accumulated digital location data points, collectors can use this information to build a location-based identity profile without knowing who was carrying the device (Boutet and Gambs, 2019). Boshell (2019) give a startling description of how location data is gathered, used, and sold to many collectors, aggregators, and others. The authors warn that "the use of multiple systems to track location, and the use of data analytics to combine location data with other personal data, enables both the identification of anonymous data and the compilation of comprehensive and precise profiles of tracked individuals" (p. 6). They suggest that the current privacy regime cannot be achieved since the permissible overcollection of location data is not purpose-driven. Collectors are free to imagine how to use and monetize data for the secondary market. As Hand (2018) notes, data is not necessarily consumed when gathered, and it can be reused without being consumed or diminished (p. 179). As shown, the current classification scheme with current regulatory guidelines has not gone far enough to prohibit users from identifying individuals and using their information without their consent. However, as discussed below, data scientists have addressed many of these concerns, though hackers often find ways around these new technological protections.

Privacy-based tools supporting current regulations: Informed consent

The app development community is actively engaged in developing technology-based solutions to some of the ethical concerns identified in this study. Some of these solutions are captured below and provide a starting resource for what may be available to keep data nonpersonal and provide more effective informed consent. A "robustness" standard can maintain data and information anonymity to make it stable against data attacks (Pfitzmann and Hansen, 2010, p. 11). App developers have incorporated "differential privacy," which introduces "noise" into the data set so that inferences can be drawn about the data as if personal data were used (Xiong et al., 2020). Synthetic data models are also being used to create databases that simulate real data without the need to expose individual data for analysis (El Emam et al., 2020).

Ashrafi and Ng (2009) explain that often data can be subject to reidentification due to collusion attacks (data integration episodes) that undermine conventional methods of preserving anonymity. They proposed an anonymity protection protocol that manipulates service providers' location data to sufficiently alter it and prevent reidentification. Recent studies reflect the increasingly sophisticated ways that programmers are attempting to protect the anonymity of data gathered by mobile apps. Unfortunately, hackers and others eventually found a way to minimize the impact of a particular solution, requiring continually updated solutions (Cormode and Yi, 2020).

The discussion above supports the notion that regulatory protection using traditional data classifications is ineffective in protecting identification from device-created data. However, the utilization of the classifications by data scientists has provided methods that have successfully kept data private, improved informed consent, and restricted data use. However, technological innovation by these same data scientists has created additional opportunities for data usage and possible misuse. This phenomenon reflects the "cross-purpose" of technological innovation and privacy. Using Slaughter's network theory, the following section focuses on understanding how technological advances driven by "web" versus "chessboard" influences have enabled data platforms to simultaneously act as nonstate actors, influential networks, and business concerns in the privacy landscape.

Entanglement of the Chessboard and Web—Slaughter's Perspective

The backdrop of this discussion needs to be briefly mentioned here, as it is related to the volume where this chapter sits. Acharya and Buzan (2019) described a change in international relations scholarship that includes shifting nation-state power dynamics, signaling the rise of other nation-states into an international relation conflict profile. The authors suggest that as other nation-states become more prominent on the international scene, the "West" will play a less influential role in establishing the political discourse. Anne Marie Slaughter (2017) focuses on a similar aspect of international relations concerning the inclusion of different perspectives. According to Slaughter, Thomas Schelling's book, the *Strategy of Conflict*, has been the standard strategy used by nations in international relations. Slaughter describes Schelling's strategy as a chessboard with moves and countermoves to determine the winner of a zero-sum game. Slaughter argues that diplomats have primarily used this strategy to interface with other countries, and with them, nations adopt specific behaviors to address national conflict or develop relationships. Though Slaughter believes that chessboard actions play a vital role, she argues that network activities growing alongside chessboards should be included in international relations strategies. Slaughter lays out a comprehensive analysis of networks' activities alongside traditional international relations strategies to describe interactions between hierarchical structures (governments) with networks developed by interest-based groups. She also describes the emerging role of data scientists as nonstate actors to describe a more comprehensive view of international relations, which is used here to understand network-based effects on data privacy.

According to Slaughter, networks represent nodes (individuals or other groups) in a relational system whose viability is understood by their structure and network position. Node structure and vulnerability are determined by how their connections with other nodes are organized. Hierarchically structured nodes support multiple connections; however, the whole network can be disrupted if the central "node" is attacked. Decentralized networks with no centralized node can be "scale free" and robust against random failure but cannot manage intrusions that spread unchecked through its connections. Finally, distributed networks are clusters of individual connected nodes that are resilient to direct attacks on the center and can isolate intrusions through directed information flow to protect the whole.

Moreover, Slaughter notes that network theory describes the power of networks based on the centrality of a network or its connectedness. Centrality is a critical measurement of the power of network nodes. Using the four centrality measures, she notes that degree centrality (number of connections) is related to social power. In the international setting, she suggests that smaller states can maximize their position relative to larger states through social power. Closeness centrality is a measurement of how close one node in the network is to another. Another type of centrality is betweenness centrality measured by computing the distance between nodes in the network. It can influence interactions between nodes and even "broker" their transactions. Eigenvalue centrality is another measure of a node's influence on a network, specifically when other nodes in the network have high eigenvalue centrality. In alignment with Slaughter's perspective, network theory, specifically node centrality, can be used to understand the effectiveness of the roles of specific stakeholders in the privacy landscape.

An application of these structural attributes to data platform networks reveals the complexity of describing how data platform networks exist in the privacy protection network. For example, data platform's structural attributes as a part of the technology network can appear hierarchical, decentralized, and distributed because their role supports, captures, regulates, and permits data collection throughout its internal systems (data platform terms and conditions) and external affiliations (the FTC asking that data platforms change the standards based on the outcomes of litigation). Additionally, its power to admit or deny access to its systems demonstrates the closeness, betweenness, and eigenvalue centrality of its network. Moreover, data platforms can determine the parameter of what can be or cannot be private based on their operationalization of privacy standards.

The power of network centrality

Network theory presents many different measures to capture node centrality (Ghalmane et al., 2018). It is also well settled that node centrality is a proxy for importance (Dablander and Hinne, 2019), and certain nodes are so important that they can influence entire ecosystems. Nodes with few other nodes within their network and with many connections are considered hubs. Hubs are considered "spreaders" and are critical to network viability.

To understand hub centrality, Wang et al. (2017) developed an efficiency centrality that captures the influence that a hub contributes to a complex network's efficiency. The authors define the efficiency-centrality of a node by "removing it from a weighted network and then compare the network efficiency's degree change before and after removal." The authors note that if a spreader node is removed, connected edges may dissolve, and closeness centrality will be affected. However, what if the spreader owns the network? Lui et al. (2012) combine control theory and network science to understand how driver nodes control the whole network. Network control seems to be a product of a nodes' ability to maintain a system's controllability.

The literature does not directly discuss data platform controllability and centrality. However, efficiency and controllability are necessary network measures for future exploration.

Network theory is also helpful in explaining community-based node-led networks that use network power to support their groups. Iranzo et al. (2020) used a network perspective in socioeconomic systems. They propose that the interconnection of small communities may give rise to complex socioeconomic structures, arguing that the process "is driven by the local behavior of the members of different networked communities that contact each other exclusively guided by self-interest or following a combination of individual and collective motivations" (p. 2). Their model suggests that "eigenvector centrality" can emerge from these interactions, based on the notion that "the interaction of simple ensembles toward larger and more complex structures will only be feasible through the self-interest of individuals that act regardless of the fate of their own community" (p. 3). The authors suggest the largest eigenvalue grows with the number of nodes and links, and "serves as a proxy for the network strength and the rate at which knowledge is generated." They suggest their model can be applied to scenarios in which nodes transiently explore new connections and abandon them if the result is unsatisfactory (p. 9). Though they use a mathematical analysis that supports their model, it is being used here as a basis for understanding how disparate "interest" groups might use network methods to organize around important topics, especially those that cannot easily use "chessboard-type" solutions. Using Iranzo and colleagues' model, this part of the chapter will discuss the Safecity network related to its network development around helping sexual assault victims through its crowdsourcing app.

Example 1—Network centrality of data platforms

The influence of data platforms (Platforms), such as Apple and Google, as nonstate actors has been discussed in courts and governments. Varshey (2020) reported on a Federal District Court in Washington, DC that dismissed a case where plaintiffs argued that Platforms are quasi-state actors because they regulate their public Platforms requiring more of a nexus between Platform and state action. This case shows that the legal definitions cannot fully recognize the influence that these organizations wield. There is much discussion about the roles and actions of digital Platforms. Gorjón Rivas (2019) discusses concerns about the Platform's harms to society; Cammaerts and Mansell (2020) discuss a country's reliance on Platform self-regulation. Busch (2020) discusses the different Platforms' roles as market intermediaries and regulatory intermediaries, controlling contracts, defining community guidelines, implementing feedback mechanisms, and reputational enforcement. He argues that these roles have benefits to regulators by describing ways that these platforms can help. Moreover, Blanke and Pybus (2020) suggest that Platforms are also ecosystems that decompose and recompose themselves and can shift the economic dynamics of competition and monopolization. Moreover, Platforms influence may control the nonregulated space where no privacy or informed consent is required.

Another perspective on data platforms by Plantin et al. (2018) explains the dual nature of commercial platforms that supports innovation and creativity while their constrained participation channels profit the Platform's creators. They note that "changing political sentiment has created an environment in which platforms can achieve enormous scales, co-exist with infrastructure aided by providing more competitive alternatives to governmental infrastructures, and in some cases compete with or even supplant them." They suggest (citing Edwards et al., 2007) that Platforms are centrally designed and controlled systems that look more like a network or web, linking independently developed and maintained systems. Their study suggests that these Platforms have become infrastructures.

App platforms are also responsible for data security. Data security is another privacy-related issue confounded by the fact that application platforms like

Google and Apple participate in gathering and sharing app data and are also responsible for policing applications that use their services. Even though much of the data shared is not considered personal, there are still significant privacy concerns. App platforms include many data-sharing agreements, many unknown to users, and sometimes even app designers. Brandtzaeg et al. (2019) conducted a study to understand certain apps' prevalence to share collected data through platforms with third-party domains. They studied apps that transmitted personal information such as email addresses, advertiser IDs, device IDs, Facebook IDs, and GPS locations with six hundred different primary and third-party domains, sharing this data continuously. The FTC has cracked down on websites and data brokers that required users to provide their location and then automatically shared their locations to address privacy issues related to data sharing without the users' permission. They have also prosecuted fake pop-ups requesting permission to share locations designed to skirt the regulation electronically (Reardon et al., 2019). Consistent with the Platform's aforementioned role as a regulatory intermediary, the FTC has also begun to require platforms to engage in more policing of apps on the platforms.

Using network theory, data platforms' influence in the data privacy regulatory scheme becomes clearer. A network hub's ability to regulate access to their systems, even by governments, shifts their power to address data privacy. Slaughter's framework further describes Platforms as nonstate actors. Similarly, Leiser and Murray (2016) call them business actors, acting as gatekeepers in a self-regulatory mode to police and deal with content across the Platform. Slaughter's identification of the "cultivator leader role" seems to fit the work of Platforms. Cultivators create environments for networks to flourish, delegate, empower, provide maintenance, and resolve conflicts. She states that "until platform systems and their programmers become like commodities, they will determine network make-up and decide under which standards individuals can participate" (p. 56). Slaughter's perspective also suggests that Platforms lead innovation networks that provide communities of practice and are producers of value (p. 76). As we will see in the brief discussion of COVID-19 apps, Platforms' use of their network connections to solve problems is vast, and their overall network influence is growing. However, the positions that Platforms take can be constrained by their profit motive.

Contact tracing for COVID-19: Web versus Chessboard Influence

Contact tracing apps were made available in early March 2020. The literature has exploded with news, specifications, and emerging privacy concerns around developing contract tracing apps. Many articles review and compare contract tracing apps. Other articles explain the benefits and drawbacks of specific app designs related to protecting user privacy. For example, TraceTogether, an app developed in Singapore, used a centralized method of collecting and notifying individuals where the government collected and stored personal and nonpersonal data. In several articles, the authors reported that the app's success was because of citizens' great trust in the government.

According to Veale (2020), an EU consortium group that included academicians and industry professionals addressed issues with a centralized contract tracing app design. They created a decentralized open protocol and codebase called Decentralized Privacy-Preserving Proximity Tracing (DP-3T) system for the EU that needed to comply with Apple and Google platforms. However, the academics left the group when it was clear that industry members were also attempting to include code for their centralized systems. When the consortium failed, Apple and Google proposed a solution called Exposure Notification that uses DP-3T code and a Bluetooth solution but was missing code needed for centralized platforms. Several authors expressed concerns that governments that adopt the Apple/Google (AG) solution set a dangerous precedent with ethical implications. Lanzing (2020) noted that the AG partnership allows platforms to "shape the domains." He also noted that AG's closed solution lacks ethical transparency. Nabben et al. (2020) note that the government lacked digital preparedness having to rely on providers instead of appropriate government expertise. Rowe (2020) noted that the government's acceptance of AG is tantamount to using a technical solution to address a social problem, noting specifically the "the world we build with technology incorporates irreversible trends that are a part of the digital transformation" (p. 6). However, Veale's (2020) description of the interaction between governments and the AG partnership is most informative. He noted that in agreeing to the AG app, the EU failed to use the legal systems under their control to address privacy and consent issues. He notes that these tech giants were treated as states in this interaction, "treating them as diplomatic interlocutors rather than firms operating under national laws" (p. 38).

This example shows that data platforms may exert efficiency centrality because of their role concerning the data privacy scheme. The platform's ability to substitute their systems for the government's preferred system indicates how influential they have become in designing and carrying out privacy-related protection. This perspective underscores the importance of regulating data platform roles into a scheme that appropriately identifies the regulatory space consistent with balancing the greater good. Slaughter joins Rowe's (2020) observation stating that "network power is held primarily by programmers: those who design the network, set the protocols, rules, structures and how the information flows and who can join" (p. 199). Without nation-state regulation, data platforms will continue to be the primary influencer and regulator of data privacy in domestic and international environments.

Example 2—Web-based ecosystems with eigenvector centrality

Smartphone applications have also enabled users to address societal problems, even when the data being collected is sensitive, and the data comes from potentially vulnerable populations. Safecity's app and its community ecosystem are examples of a unique network structure that uses its network to solve societal issues. A full description of the smartphone app and its results can be found in the chapter in this volume authored by Lea and D'Silva. The app collects anonymous stories and incident locations from individuals. Through informed consent best practices, members can access the app community on the Safecity website to support others and receive tips about unsafe locations. The locations pin incidents without information about persons.

However, the network ecosystem goes beyond the victims that share stories and the owners of the app. Members include individuals and communities and, in some cases, police departments. Communities and police departments can be viewed as separate nodes, connecting to the Safecity node to support the shared goal of reducing sexual assaults in communities and understanding victim-related aspects of sexual assault not captured through "chessboard" means. Iranzo et al.'s (2020) model suggests that Safecity's ecosystem (app, website, and leaders) is the catalyst that increases eigenvector centrality of the connections made with individuals, communities, and police departments joined together to address place-based sexual violence. In communities where it has been launched, it has positively impacted residence through a community-enabled process. Measuring this type of eigenvector centrality in the Safecity-related communities where it has been deployed would provide additional insights.

Additionally, the app design supports its privacy-preserving mission by not sharing data through its platform-related agreements. If police department partners receive data, it receives deidentified information to capture sexual assault prevalence, but only as a community stakeholder. As the app builds its footprint internationally, the local communities will maintain their local community connections, while data prevalence is combined to depict global trends. Communities that participate evolve into ecosystems because of the continual use of individual members for reporting assaults or accessing the system to steer clear of areas where assaults have occurred. Without the smartphone app, the data could not be used to understand dangerous locations in communities and understand international prevalence based on data trends.

Discussion

Though data privacy regulation exists through nation-state regulation, technological advancements have made regulation less effective in preventing disclosure. Web networks have emerged that have influenced how privacy is defined and policed. In some instances, like the COVID-19 tracing apps, data platforms substituted the government's preferred privacy methodology for one they designed. Even though data scientists, app developers, and data platforms work diligently to provide methods to gather informed consent and increase control over the data individuals provide, the Platform's role in data networks contributes to both the problem and the solution. The privacy protection role of governments seems to have been data platforms acting in quasi-government roles because of the innovation and infrastructure they provide for privacy protection.

This chapter supports Slaughter's identification of how different networks' work impacts privacy, primarily that "chessboards" have not fully addressed the issues created by technological advances or demonstrated their understanding that privacy protection is itself an ecosystem. Holt and Malčić (2015) explain that "the privacy ecosystem affects all users, providers, and distributors of digital data," pondering whether the "rules of engagement" in this ecosystem will be determined by government regulations or by private practices such as those employed by digital content platforms (e.g., Google, Apple) and Internet service providers (ISPs).

The brief mention of agency related to privacy suggests that emerging technology may provide needed solutions in the form of self-sovereign-based identity. Ishmaev (2020) reviews the literature on digital identity as a part of understanding whether the promise of self-sovereign identity comports with the notion of self-sovereign agency. He supports the tenants of self-sovereign identity as the type of agency that creates a level of ownership of one's identity across the Internet. However, he warns that technologically operationalizing moral standards does not mean that the term reflects the usual social meaning. Further, he notes that settling for a technology solution does not mean that ethical protection has been achieved. His concern is that allowing data scientists to define self-sovereignty is akin to how data scientists have identified privacy, making the process equivalent to the goal. But, again, if data scientists' definition determines ethical standards, the question is: Are they writing new standards with their interpretation?

The good news is that emerging technology does support an individual-managed privacy solution using Blockchains. Blockchain technology integrates the benefits of transaction-by-transaction permission without the fear of identity disclosure. Blockchain methods are network methods in that they segregate network requirements into nodes and enable those nodes' connections to interact in a way that preserves privacy and control. Blockchains are popular because of their ability to mask identity and contract tracing (Xu et al., 2020). It will be interesting to see whether the promise of Blockchains becomes the vehicle that returns both ownership and control of "personal" data to individuals.

Finally, to understand the future of a distributed Internet (as opposed to the current centralized one), Poblet describes an example of using distributed technologies and digitally enabled mobilization in Spain in 2004. Large-scale activism of decentralized methods enabled hackers and community participants to thwart governmental attacks on citizens and their Internet systems. She commented that "the overall vision of the decentralized web aims at re-decentralizing the Internet with architectures and tools that allows its users greater self-sovereignty in terms of data access, ownership, privacy, security and preservation of digital memory." However, Poblet asserted, and this author agrees, that without strong governments to establish and manage decentralized networks' rules, individually controlled privacy promises may not be achieved.

Conclusion

The most important conclusion of this study is that international laws and industry guidelines are continually changing. However, as the United States fails to assume a leadership role in international privacy, other nonstate actors with international connections may drive the privacy landscape. The goal of the study was twofold. First, the study reviewed the literature revealing that US regulators' roles are essential to regulate data platforms and establish appropriately balanced ethical data regulation schemes. Second was to understand Slaughter's perspective that reveals US regulators' inaction, the gaps in chessboard-related regulation, and the entrance of web-networked groups filling the void. Without regulatory guidance, some networks can use their roles to gain an unfair, unethical advantage and an uneven, tangled global policy about gathering and using data. Slaughter's framework provides a better way to understand the complexities of data privacy and possibly provides a road map for understanding data platform networks and socioeconomic networks on how the notion of privacy will be understood in the future.

Conflicts of Interest

I worked with the Safecity team to help include best practice informed consent provisions in their app and website. A part of this chapter's focus was to inform the Safecity owners about the state of international regulation for collecting data using smartphone apps. I also sit on Safecity's advisory board. I am not paid by, nor do I receive any compensation from Safecity.

Limitations

In this study, the comparison between networks and network theory descriptions is just a preliminary step in evaluating the state of privacy internationally. Network centrality can be quantitively measured, and node weights can be determined. Since this chapter's goal was to integrate Slaughter's framework to understand network influences on privacy, the next step would be to chart data platform networks to understand their influence on the privacy ecosystems.

References

Acharya, A., 2018. *Constructing Global Order: Agency and Change in World Politics.* Cambridge: Cambridge University Press.

Acharya, A., and Buzan, B., 2019. *The Making of Global International Relations.* Cambridge: Cambridge University Press.

Agarwal, A., Yadav, O., Saxena, R., Singhal, S., Sharma, S. (2020) "Protecting User Privacy on Social Media by Metadata Removal," *UGC Care Journal* 19(16), p. 7. ISSN: 2320-0693.

Ashrafi, M. Z., and Ng, S. K., 2009, June. "Collusion-Resistant Anonymous Data Collection Method." In *Proceedings of the 15th ACM SIGKDD International Conference on Knowledge Discovery and Data Mining*, pp. 69–78.

Blanke, T. and Pybus, J., 2020. "The Material Conditions of Platforms: Monopolization through Decentralization." *Social Media+ Society*, 6 (4), pp. 1–13.

Borgesius, F. Z., 2017. "The Breyer Case of the Court of Justice of the European Union: I.P. Addresses and the Personal Data Definition." *European Data Protection Law Review*, 3, p. 130.

Boshell, P. M. (2019) "The Power of Place: Geolocation Tracking and Privacy. Business Law Today." Retrieved on June 1, 2020, from https://businesslawtoday.org/2019/03/power-place-geolocation-tracking-privacy/.

Boutet, A. and Gambs, S., 2019, November. "Inspect What Your Location History Reveals about You: Raising User Awareness on Privacy Threats Associated with Disclosing His Location Data." In *Proceedings of the 28th ACM International Conference on Information and Knowledge Management*, pp. 2861–64.

Brandtzaeg, P. B., Pultier, A., and Moen, G. M., 2019. "Losing Control to Data-Hungry Apps: A Mixed-Methods Approach to Mobile App Privacy." *Social Science Computer Review*, 37 (4), 466–88.

Busch, C. (2020) "Self-regulation and Regulatory Intermediation in the Platform Economy." In *The Role of the EU in Transnational Legal Ordering*. Cheltenham: Edward Elgar.

Butler, A., 2017. "Whither Privacy Shield in the Trump Era." *European Data Protection Law Review*, 3, p. 111.

Cammaerts, B., and Mansell, R., 2020. "Digital Platform Policy and Regulation: Toward a Radical Democratic Turn." *International Journal of Communication*, 14, pp. 20, 135–54.

Cisco Annual Internet Report (2018–2023) White Paper (2020) Retrieved July 15, 2020, from https://www.cisco.com/c/en/us/solutions/collateral/executive-perspectives/annual-internet-report/white-paper-c11-741490.html.

Cofone, I. (2021) Beyond Data Ownership. Available at SSRN 3564480. 43 *Cardozo Law Review* 101.

Congressional Research Service. 2019. Retrieved from https://fas.org/sgp/crs/row/R45 584.pdf.

Cormode, G., and Yi, K., 2020. *Small Summaries for Big Data*. Cambridge: Cambridge University Press.

Dablander, F., and Hinne, M., 2019. "Node Centrality Measures Are a Poor Substitute for Causal Inference." *Scientific Reports*, 9 (1), pp. 1–13.

Digital Single Market Commission. "Regulation on the Free Flow of Non-Personal Data." May 29, 2019. https://ec.europa.eu/digital-single-market/en/free-flow-non-personal-data (accessed November 20, 2020).

Edwards, P. N., Jackson, S. J., Bowker, G. C., and Knobel, C. P. (2007) Understanding Infrastructure: Dynamics, Tensions, and Design. Report of a Workshop on "History & Theory of Infrastructure: Lessons for New Scientific Cyberinfrastructures"'.

El Emam, K., Mosquera, L., and Hoptroff, R., 2020. *Practical Synthetic Data Generation: Balancing Privacy and the Broad Availability of Data*. Sebastopol, CA: O'Reilly Media.

Fadler, M. and Legner, C., 2020. Who Owns Data in the Enterprise? Rethinking Data Ownership in times of Big Data and Analytics. In ECIS. Twenty-Eigth European Conference on Information Systems (ECIS2020), Marrakesh, Morocco.

Federal Trade Commission (2014) Data Brokers Call for Transparency and Accountability. Retrieved on August , 2020 from https://www.ftc.gov/system/files/documents/reports/data-brokers-call-transparency-accountability-report-federal-trade-commission-may-2014/140527databrokerreport.pdf.

Fefer, R. F., 2019. *Data Flows, Online Privacy, and Trade Policy*. Congressional Research Service.

Finck, M., and Pallas, F., 2020. "They Who Must Not Be Identified-Distinguishing Personal from Non-Personal Data under the GDPR." *International Data Privacy Law*, 10(1), pp. 19–14.

Ghalmane, Z., El Hassouni, M., and Cherifi, H., 2018, October. "Betweenness Centrality for Networks with Non-overlapping Community Structure." In *2018 IEEE Workshop on Complexity in Engineering (COMPENG)*, pp. 1–5.

Gilbert, F. 2020. https://cloudsecurityalliance.org/blog/2020/06/30/united-states-mexico-canada-agreement-digital-trade-provisions-nafta-2-0-meets-the-internet/.

Gorjón Rivas, S. (2020) "Digital Platforms: Developments in Their Regulation and Challenges in the Financial Arena." *Economic bulletin/Banco de España* [Artículos], n. 4.

Hand, D. J., 2018. "Aspects of Data Ethics in a Changing World: Where Are We Now?" *Big Data*, 6 (3), pp. 176–90.

Holt, J., and Malčić, S., 2015. "The Privacy Ecosystem: Regulating Digital Identity in the United States and European Union." *Journal of Information Policy*, 5, pp. 155–78.

Hummel, P., Braun, M., and Dabrock, P. (2021), "Own Data? Ethical Reflections on Data Ownership." *Philosophy & Technology* 34, 545–72. https://doi.org/10.1007/s13 347-020-00404-9.

Hunton Privacy Blog. 2020. Retrieved from https://www.huntonprivacyblog.com/ (accessed March 24, 2020).

International Committee of the Red Cross (ICRC) and Privacy International (2018) The Humanitarian Metadata Problem: "Doing No Harm" in the Digital Era. https://privacyinternational.org/report/2509/humanitarian-metadata-problem-doing-no-harm-digital-era.

Iranzo, J., Pablo-Martí, F., and Aguirre, J., 2020. "Emergence of Complex Socioeconomic Networks Driven by Individual and Collective Interests." *Physical Review Research*, 2 (4), p. 043352-1.

Ishmaev, G. (2021) "Sovereignty, Privacy, and Ethics in Blockchain-based Identity Management Systems." *Ethics and Information Technology* 23, 239–52. Retrieved on June 23, 2020, from https://doi.org/10.1007/s10676-020-09563-x

Jensen, M., 2013, June. "Challenges of Privacy Protection in Big Data Analytics." In *2013 IEEE International Congress on Big Data*, pp. 235–38.

Kearns, M., and Roth, A., 2019. *The Ethical Algorithm: The Science of Socially Aware Algorithm Design*. Oxford: Oxford University Press.

Kessler, J., 2019. "Data Protection in the Wake of the GDPR: California's Solution for Protecting 'the World's Most Valuable Resource.'" *Southern California Law Review*, 93, p. 99.

Kosinski, M., Stillwell, D., and Graepel, T. (2013) "Private Traits and Attributes Are Predictable from Digital Records of Human Behavior." *Proceedings of the National Academy of Sciences of the United States of America* (April 9) 110(15): 5802–5. doi: 10.1073/pnas.1218772110.

Kraft, M., 2020. "Big Data, Little Privacy: Protecting Consumers' Data While Promoting Economic Growth." University of Dayton Law Review, 45, p. 97.

Leiser, M. R., Murray, A. D., Brownsford, R., Scotford, E., and Yeung, K., 2016. The Role of Non-state Actors and Institutions in the Governance of New and Emerging Digital Technologies." In *The Oxford Handbook of Law, Regulation, and Techn ology*, ed. R. Brownsford, E. Scotford, and K. Yeung, pp. 670–704.

Liu, Y. Y., Slotine, J. J., and Barabási, A. L., 2012. "Control Centrality and Hierarchical Structure in Complex Networks." *Plos one*, 7 (9), p. e44459.

Martin, K. E., 2015. "Ethical Issues in the Big Data Industry." *MIS Quarterly Executive*, 14, p. 2. https://ssrn.com/abstract=2598956 (accessed October 2, 2020).

Miller, A. R., 1969. "Personal Privacy in the Computer Age: The Challenge of a New Technology in an Information-Oriented Society." *Michigan Law Review*, 67 (6), pp. 1089–1246.

Mobile Health Act Interactive Tool. Retrieved from: https://www.ftc.gov/tips-advice/business-center/guidance/mobile-health-apps-interactive-tool (accessed September 23, 2020).

Mourby, M., Mackey, E., Elliot, M., Gowans, H., Wallace, S. E., Bell, J., Smith, H., Aidinlis, S. and Kaye, J., 2018. 'Are 'Pseudonymised' Data Always Personal Data? Implications of the GDPR for Administrative Data Research in the U.K." *Computer Law & Security Review*, 34 (2), pp. 222–33.

Mulligan, S. P., Freeman, W. C. and Linebaugh, C. D., 2019, March. Data Protection Law: An Overview. In R45631. Congressional Research Service. https://crsreports.congress. gov/product/pdf/. https://crsreports.congress.gov/product/pdf/IF/IF11 207 (accessed May 3, 2020).

Nabben, K., Poblet, M., and Barca, J. C., 2020, October. "What Is Known from a Network?: Digital Contact Tracing, Privacy, and Pandemics in the Digital Age. Digital Contact Tracing, Privacy, and Pandemics in the Digital Age." COVID-19 Response Working Paper Series.

Paper, C. W. 2020. "Cisco Visual Networking Index: Global Mobile Data Traffic Forecast Update, 2018–2022."

Pentina, I., Zhang, L., Bata, H., and Chen, Y., 2016. "Exploring Privacy Paradox in Information-Sensitive Mobile App Adoption: A Cross-Cultural Comparison." *Computers in Human Behavior*, 65, pp. 409–19.

Pfitzmann, A., and Hansen, M. (2010) "A terminology for Talking about Privacy by Data Minimization: Anonymity, Unlinkability, Undetectability, Unobservability, Pseudonymity, and Identity Management." Retrieved on August 13, 2020, from http://dud.inf.tu-dresden.de/Anon_Terminology.shtml.

Plantin, J. C., Lagoze, C., Edwards, P. N., and Sandvig, C., 2018. "Infrastructure Studies Meet Platform Studies in the Age of Google and Facebook." *New Media & Society*, 20 (1), pp. 293–310.

Privacy Shield. 2016. 81 FR 51041

Reardon, J., Feal, Á., Wijesekera, P., On, A. E., Vallina-Rodriguez, N., and Egelman, S. (2019) "50 Ways to Leak Your Data: An Exploration of Apps' Circumvention of the Android Permissions System. USENIX Security Symposium." Retrieved on May 1, 2020, from https://www.usenix.org/conference/usenixsecurity19/presentation/reardon.

Regan, P. M., 2020. "Three Arenas of Congressional Oversight of Online Platforms: Competition, Privacy, and Content." *Wayne Law Review*, 66, p. 193.

Ropek, L. 2020. "Privacy Policy and the Biden Presidency: A Promising Outlook." https://www.govtech.com/security/privacy-policy-and-the-biden-presidency-a-promising-outlook.html (accessed September 2, 2020).

Rostow, T., 2017. "What Happens When an Acquaintance Buys Your Data: A New Privacy Harm in the Age of Data Brokers." *Yale Journal on Regulation*, 34, p. 667.

Rowe, F., 2020. "Contact Tracing Apps and Values Dilemmas: A Privacy Paradox in a Neo-Liberal World." *International Journal of Information Management*, 55, p. 102178.

Rustad, M. L., and Koenig, T. H., 2019. "Towards a Global Data Privacy Standard." *Florida Law Review*, 71, p. 365.

Slaughter, A. M., 2017. *The Chessboard and the Web: Strategies of Connection in a Networked World*. New Haven, CT: Yale University Press.

Stier, S., Breuer, J., Siegers, P., and Thorson, K., 2020. "Integrating Survey Data and Digital Trace Data: Key Issues in Developing an Emerging Field." *Social Science Computer Review*, 38(5), pp. 503–16.

Stier, S., Breuer, J., Siegers, P., and Thorson, K., 2020. *Integrating Survey Data and Digital Trace Data: Key Issues in Developing an Emerging Field*.

Surbakti, F. P. S., Wang, W., Indulska, M., and Sadiq, S. (2020) "Factors Influencing Effective Use of Big Data: A Research Framework." *Information & Management*, 57(1), pp. 103–46.

Tovino, S. A., 2020. "Mobile Research Applications and State Research Laws." *Journal of Law, Medicine & Ethics*, 48 (1 suppl), pp. 82–86.

Tracol, X., 2020. " 'Schrems II': The return of the Privacy Shield." *Computer Law & Security Review*, 39, p. 105484.

United States (2004) The Health Insurance Portability and Accountability Act (HIPAA), *Public Law*, pp. 104–91. (Washington, DC), U.S. Dept. of Labor, Employee Benefits Security Administration. http://purl.fdlp.gov/GPO/gpo10291.

Varshney, N. (2020) Tech Companies Aren't "State Actors," Judge Dismisses Conservative Bias Lawsuit Against Facebook, Twitter, Google, Apple. Retrieved on May 3, 2020, from https://www.yahoo.com/now/tech-companies-arent-state-actors-121424420.html.

Veale, M., 2020. *Sovereignty, Privacy, and Contact Tracing Protocols*. Oxford: Meatspace Press.

Wang, S., Du, Y., and Deng, Y., 2017. "A New Measure of identifying Influential Nodes: Efficiency Centrality." *Communications in Nonlinear Science and Numerical Simulation*, 47, pp. 151–63.

Wang, J. L., and Loui, M. C., 2009, May. "Privacy and ethical issues in location-based tracking systems." In IEEE International Symposium on Technology and Society, pp. 1–4.

Xiong, X., Liu, S., Li, D., Cai, Z., and Niu, X. (2020) "A Comprehensive Survey on Local Differential Privacy." *Security and Communication Networks*, Volume 2020 |Article ID 8829523 Retrieved on August 31, 2020, https://doi.org/10.1155/2020/8829523.

Xu, H., Zhang, L., Onireti, O., Fang, Y., Buchanan, W. J., and Imran, M. A., 2020. "BeepTrace: Blockchain-Enabled Privacy-Preserving Contact Tracing for COVID-19 Pandemic and Beyond." *IEEE Internet of Things Journal*, 8 (5), pp. 3915–29.

Yakovleva, S., and Irion, K., 2020. "Pitching Trade against Privacy: Reconciling E.U. Governance of Personal Data Flows with External Trade." *International Data Privacy Law*, 10 (3), pp. 201–21.

Ylijoki, O., and Porras, J., 2016. "Perspectives to Definition of Big Data: A Mapping Study and Discussion." *Journal of Innovation Management*, 4 (1), pp. 69–91.

Chapter 7

ETHICAL CONSIDERATIONS AROUND CROWDSOURCING STORIES OF SEXUAL ABUSE AND HARASSMENT IN PUBLIC SPACES: THE SAFECITY INDIA STORY

Suzanne Goodney Lea and Elsa Marie D'Silva

Introduction

In 2012, Safecity.in devised an innovative solution to shed light on a persistent problem: the sexual harassment and assault of individuals—mostly, but certainly not entirely women—in public places. This is one of several phenomena categorized as a "dark figure of crime" (Biderman and Reiss, 1967; Coleman and Moynihan, 1996). These are crimes that tend to be markedly underreported in official statistics, and these unreported incidents can impede our understanding of all types of crime in many parts of the world where bribery of police may be required just to report a crime or where professionalization standards governing policing are still emergent. But such underreporting is rampant globally in the case of sensitive crimes that carry with them a significant stigma even for the victim (Kamruzzaman, 2016). Safecity.in developed a mechanism by which any individual on the planet could anonymously share having experienced an incident of sexual harassment or assault on a singular global platform so that the incident would then be mapped on a global interface using Ushahidi.com's revolutionary approach to crowdsourcing data from members of the public. In our case, a primary goal was to expand our understanding of the locational aspects of gender-based violence as place has increasingly become a unit of analysis for better understanding of criminal incidents and behaviors (Meares, 1997; Weisbunr et al. 2008). Within a few years, an app was developed to enhance and expand upon the web-based reporting platform, and it has been shared in many different communities so that people in more places can make reports. When enough people report in a concentrated area, hot spots of activity can be identified.

In the advent of the COVID-19 pandemic and the eruption of Black Lives Matter protests in the United States and, now, globally, we have had to pivot the use of our platform so as to better incorporate and represent broader aspects of safety in public places as they relate to gender-based violence: that is, including (1) reporting on domestic violence as this becomes more of a public problem as more women and children are forced to shelter in place with possible abusers; (2) incorporating aspects of racial and ethnic overtones into the reporting of gender-based violence occurring in public places—with the inclusion of the capacity to denote when such incidents are propagated by authority figures; and (3) including an option to report online harassment/stalking, because we know from informal discussions and some more recent reports that incidents that might have occurred in physical public spaces are now migrating to our virtual communities as more and more of us move our interactions with family, friends, and colleagues online. Tcherni et al. (2016) suggest that there is likely a good deal of crime hiding online, and their article looks specifically at property crimes occurring in cyberspace. We expect we will generate a similar article about gender-based crimes within the next year or so of collecting these data on our platform as we suspect that there is a good deal of it happening and an uptick since the COVID-19 pandemic began.

Though our platform mainly collects these data for mapping of location/place as a possible critical component of sexual assault, the actual reports that are shared provide unexpected details and, thereby, unanticipated benefits. This chapter explores some of the ethical and practical considerations we have engaged in considering how to more effectively engage these additional insights that the data reported on the app provides as well as to address issues regarding ownership of these types of data. We believe that, given that the data is generated by the people and for the people, the people themselves own the data—and this is an innovative approach in an era of algorithms, some of which can codify and even weaponize patterns of oppression (Noble, 2018). It is precisely for this reason, the same which inspired Ushahidi, that we feel such data must be open source and accessible to all people, and we conclude by offering our reflections as to why this is so essential when collecting data that a government cannot or will not collect.

Background to the Creation of the Safecity.in Platform

In December 2012, a young woman, Jyoti Singh, was gangraped multiple times on a private bus in Delhi and left to die of her injuries on the side of the road (Roychowdhury, 2013; Nigam, 2014; Lodhia, 2015). The incident caused an uproar in India and abroad. Just as we are now seeing in the United States the response to the alleged murder of George Floyd by police in Minneapolis, Minnesota (Hill et al., 2020), people in India took to the streets and demanded justice. In fact, in 2012, just as now in many US cities, a curfew was imposed in Delhi as the crowds were unprecedented. In Mumbai, there were demonstrations and candlelight vigils. But perhaps most importantly, people started to open up more about their own experiences of sexual harassment and abuse—even by those who, until then, had not talked about the incidents as communities or made formal complaints to authorities.

As the second author listened to the news and the stories friends were sharing, she began to wonder how many such incidents might be occurring throughout India. However, it was not very easy to find much information about the number of cases in India—or even relevant information from which we could interpolate the numbers. The one statistic that kept coming up repeatedly was from UN Women (Besheer, 2019): one in three women around the world, on average, experience sexual violence at least once in their lifetime. It is an oft-quoted statistic, but we really have no way of confirming it. It also seemed unlikely that it was reflective of what was happening in India, as stories shared with the second author informally and in community discussions suggested that possibly most of the women and girls—and not a few men and boys—had some experience to share. And, indeed, a survey of women and girls throughout India found that 90 percent of women and girls in the country report having experienced at least one incident of sexual harassment or assault in a public place during their lifetimes (Gaynair, 2013).

As so, the second author decided to launch Safecity.in, a crowd map which was modeled along the lines of HarassMap Egypt. The intention was to help women and girls document their experiences of sexual violence anonymously so as to be able to have information that authorities and individuals could use to estimate numbers and clusters of incidents. Our crowd map was created on the open source Ushahidi platform, which was free. As a volunteer collective, we had to keep costs low, and so this was a useful tool that allowed us to launch our site quickly and with the least amount of overhead costs. We created a basic website with information on legal resources, the crowd map, and an associated reporting form. The crowd map clusters individual stories as red pinpoints (dots) on the map, noted by location. The more stories that are reported for a given location, the larger the red dots become (indicating clusters of incidents), thus making it easy to visualize the data. Users could read and comment on the reports as well as query the data on the map by category.

Structure the Reporting Platform to Make It Accessible and Engaging

As the stories trickled in, the number of dots grew in number and size. From the start, we received a lot of press coverage so there was a constant inflow of stories from all parts of India, confirming that sexual harassment is indeed a widespread and nearly universal problem—particularly for women. We intentionally kept the reporting form simple and easy to use with just a few fields to complete: click one category or more, enter the location of the incident and date and time of the incident, and provide a brief description of what happened. There was no mandatory requirement to sign up on the site or leave one's name or email address. The description field was free-form text, and some people wrote a lengthy note, while others just put in one word: harassed. Several people also used the comment section to offer solidarity and help. Some even offered to walk with one woman who complained of having to pass a group of intimidating men every day on her way to work. Another offered to visit the site of harassment to check on loitering drug addicts (as was mentioned in that particular report).

Many women (and some men, though it is our impression from many workshops and discussions that male-directed sexual abuse is less likely to occur in public settings) reported incidents that happened decades prior, suggesting that some people may experience a personal benefit by being able to share their story in what they feel is a meaningful way. This detail of data provides much more insight into what happened, and this is critical information for helping us to understand such incidents more deeply so that we can better prevent them. Survivors tend to be very committed to wanting to prevent what happened to them from ever occurring to anyone else. Thus, we are now working to add a survey component to our app so that we can collect and learn from such details.

One of our prior analysis efforts of our data (Lea et al., 2017) taught us that even relatively sparse data can provide insight into things like strategies that work well in different settings, as we can examine a setting, look at an array of responses and identity patterns and associated outcomes to various approaches to such incidents. We do not put a time limit as to when an incident needed to have occurred for it to be reported on the platform. A recent survey of Maryland sexual assault hotlines by the first author revealed that after 18- to 25-year-olds, the most common group calling these hotlines are those women aged 40–50. All of the hotlines reported the same trend. Those that she spoke with who were working in the survivor-facing field managing hotlines and answering calls hypothesize that this is a result of the #MeToo movement emboldening more women to come forward and share their stories. These sorts of added insights generating from this data have led us to reevaluate and greatly expand our informed consent procedures so as to better protect the people who report incidents. For instance, if you provide enough detail in your account, you could put yourself at risk as it is mapped to a particular place. We excise any identifying data, but if one knows a neighborhood, it is always possible that one might recognize an incident, or even a person, based upon some detail in the account. We need people to understand that risk—and that is part of owning something. It becomes a collaborative undertaking as the residents become our partners. None of this works without accounts, and we owe it to those who trust us and report on our platform to make them well aware of the risks and protect them as best we can.

Still, we have been finding that many people were reticent to report on a digital platform. We explored this issue by engaging teams of students in sharing the app within their communities. What we learned was fascinating: many women, especially younger ones dealing with a more recent incident, were quite disinclined to report an incident at all. Others found the technological nature of the reporting tool to be demoralizing, with one remarking that she found the experience "more me alone than #MeToo." We have been working with Data Duck LLC to engage their expertise in enhancing the empathy of technology, especially as a tool for reporting these sorts of incidents. Most people do not feel comfortable reporting sexual violence at all (Binder, 1981; Sable et al., 2006), but a female police officer can be helpful, as can a well-trained sexual assault hotline worker. But, just as with an anonymous hotline, it would seem like technology would make a person wanting to report an incident feel more at ease doing so as they do not even have to talk with a person, but in fact, it seems as though a stranger—but still a human person—is easier to talk to than a machine interface. Having a detailed and personable informed consent disclosure is somewhat helpful as the effort anticipates and addresses some of the anxieties a person might have when reporting. But we have just received a grant from Vital Voices to give this question a much closer look. We will be engaging many survivors in several locations to better understand whether or not they sought help or reported the incident to authorities at the time; where, when, and how they sought help, if they did; and why they elected to seek assistance in the way(s) that they did.

While we have noticed how profoundly difficult it can be to report incidents of sexual harassment and, especially assault, the data collected on the Safecity. in platform, which consists of individual reports detailing simply what happened, the location where the incident took place, and the date and time when it occurred, raises validity concerns for some people. Anonymous reporting is encouraged, but it is exceedingly rare that an incident that is reported raises validity concerns for us, which is a charge often raised regarding, in particular, women's reports of sexual assault and harassment. Notably, Lisak et al. (2010) found in an analysis of 10 years of reported cases of sexual assault that only 5.9 percent were false reports. Still, false reporting is a legitimate concern regarding any crowdsourced data (Barbier et al., 2012). On our platform, validity is checked by examining patterns. The platform is designed to identify locations in which reported events cluster. As such, accounts in certain quadrants tend to echo one another. If one occurrence is quite different than the locational pattern, it raises a validity concern, but in now over 12,000 incidents reported, only a small handful of cases (fewer than 10) have ever raised such a concern.

Practical Change Driven by and for the Community

Encouraged by the response to the crowd map and requests from people who wanted to volunteer in some way, we decided to set up localized teams in Delhi and Mumbai to create awareness of the issue and the reporting platform. In Mumbai, we worked with a local group that was trying to mobilize communities to address violence in public spaces. Over a six-month period and after several hundred interviews, focus group discussions, and information fairs in a local park, we focused upon an oft-reported issue: "chain snatching" or petty robbery. We decided to narrow our focus to working on a small area of 10 streets and had regular meetings to collect data and discuss options for solutions. The community-driven solutions ranged from a signature campaign, engagement of the police, installation of CCTV cameras at key points that showed up in the data, education of the larger community, a whistle protocol for the security personnel, and a communication tree protocol for the residents across the 10 streets. The intervention was a success, as there were no further robberies reported over the next three years in that location, and this increased the confidence among the residents to walk down their streets without fear. And that is the goal of our work. If all people cannot feel safe traversing their own community's public spaces at any time of day, then that society is, ultimately, not practicing democracy as democracy requires universal access to all of the public commons—physical and virtual.

In Delhi, we had college students from IP University, Dwarka, who reached out and wanted to work with us. They were enraged by the gang rape of Jyoti Singh and wished to work on making their college campuses safer. The volunteers mobilized themselves and other students to create awareness. Together they collected about six hundred reports of incidents by reaching out to people and encouraging them to share their story. They identified some of the trends showing up in the data and engaged with transport officials, civic authorities, and their own campus administration. They individually reported that their confidence levels in accessing public spaces was increased and that they felt an increased sense of community. Moreover, survivors who may have felt alone and ashamed began to experience a recentering of their identities (Demerath, 2006): I am not alone. There are many who have experienced the same.

We have worked in many different neighborhoods across different cities in India, Kenya, and in a handful of other countries. Data has shown us that context matters. We are already seeing trends emerge based on the physical features of the location and the contextual use of the space. For example, in Mumbai, the railways are a primary form of transport as millions of commuters use them daily. Therefore, most of the hotspots reported are along the railway lines, at entrances and exits to the railway stations, or on the overhead bridges or the auto and taxi stands outside the station. Those connection points provide last-mile connectivity for area commuters to reach their final destinations. Some railway stations that have bad lighting and limited space have more incidents being reported, indicating that there is a correlation to lighting and the use and size of a space. In Delhi, a commercial area like Connaught Place, which is crowded during the day, has a higher number of cases of groping and touching as the crowd provides anonymity for the perpetrator. In contrast, a residential area like Malviya Nagar might have a higher case of chain snatching or petty robbery as women are seen as easy targets for such attacks—and, indeed, women routinely assess the potential danger of being sexually assaulted based on their social location (Valentine, 1992).

Understanding the impact of the time of day, location, use of space, and basic amenities available is clearly critical in planning the allocation of resources—as well as instituting policies and decision-making protocols. For much of human history, such decisions were top-down, planned endeavors. Government and government agencies surveyed needs and planned ways to address them. Eventually it became possible to survey people directly and create focus groups to garner a more individualized perspective on social needs. But, as Anne-Marie Slaughter (2018) argues in *The Chessboard and the Web: Strategies of Connection in a Networked World*, the digital age decentralizes and democratizes access to information—and the ability of information to readily flow from citizens to policy makers. A couple of years after we had launched Safecity.in, we were informed that the police in Mumbai were already referring to our crowd map for data. So, we started sending bimonthly data dashboards to the Mumbai, Delhi, and Goa police forces. Subsequently, we have been informed that Bangalore and Pune police also use our crowd map for data to drive their patrol decisions.

Insights into Place as a Critical Unit of Analysis for Bringing the Dark Figure of Gender-Based Violence into Focus

Place as a unit of analysis for understanding criminal behavior has greatly expanded our capacity to reimagine crime dynamics far beyond individuals and their interactions and motivations (Meares, 1997). Technological tools such as crowd-sourced, crime-mapped data greatly expand our capacity to collect violent-incident data for that has long been underreported (Weisburd et al., 2008). Indeed, perhaps the dark figure of crime reflects a society's disinclination to want to see certain kinds of violence, either that affecting marginalized persons or that which the state itself may be propagating. New technological tools that allow us to make place a more plausible unite of analysis have also helped to move the field toward a more subtle understanding of how exactly routine activities and interactional patterns intersect with one's social location to create hot spots of victimization (Brantingham, 2011; Weisburd, 2012).

Pain et al. (2001) contended that the ways in which gender intersects with public and private spaces, including the very designation of public and private, are gendered. Whitman (2007) added a consideration of how geographies can also be gendered with regard to fear, echoing Valentine's (1992) earlier study. Indeed, women often report having many strategies for negotiating public spaces safely (Gaynair, 2013; Bhatt et al., 2015; Lea et al., 2016), and that prompts us to want to better understand how public and private spaces—physical and virtual—associate risk and vulnerability. This is why we are very curious to see what we will learn about the prevalence of gender-based violence in virtual spaces. We suspect that we will need to identify and name whole new categories of violent, aggressive, and/or threatening behavior.

Researchers have begun to look more broadly at the definition of public space to make it explicit enough to clarify which behaviors are welcome, allowed, wanted, or forced within it (Ceccato, 2016; Lea et al., 2016). Clearly defined boundaries between public and private spaces decrease crime opportunities and improve upon the perceived safety of insiders (Ceccato, 2016). We suspect that physical transitional spaces, specifically, are important as they increase one's exposure to vulnerability, and events such as COVID-19 bring new attention to these transitional dynamics. When people are forced to stay at home with a potential abuser, as is too often happening under the COVID-19 epidemic—which is why we have added domestic violence as a marker on our maps—this becomes a public problem as, arguably, the state and its people bear responsibility for protecting people who are put at risk (often women and children) for abuse or sexual exploitation. We aspire to better understand the nature of permeability within physical virtual public spaces, especially as it relates to traditional private-space protections. With better insights, victims, communities, and law enforcement might reconsider their conceptualizations of the protective effect of boundaries within physical and virtual public and private spaces, coming to a better understanding of the unique vulnerabilities inherent to both settings. Slaughter's (2018) concept of a loss of privacy due to the surveillance state that has emerged since 9/11 and as closed-circuit monitoring has become affordable and thus widespread suggests a double-edged sword: yes, we lose privacy but we gain security. This was the same argument made for increased surveillance at airports and elsewhere after 9/11. By this point, as corporate entities have vastly expanded their digitally based surveillance, does any expectation of privacy remain?

Ownership of the Data: From the People, for the People

While the collection and analysis of data are important, it is also important to make the data available back to the community and the individuals who provided it. Our data is open source so that anyone can access them freely and without cost on our website, replicating the example that Ushahidi established. We have had individuals use our data to stay safe and better understand the area in which they are living, working, or visiting. Communities have used our data to find local solutions to address issues like staring, commenting, stalking, and so on. Having data has allowed them to engage with the police and demand better surveillance or shifts in patrol timings, to compel civic authorities to fix broken toilets and streetlights, and to educate authorities as to how to make college campuses safer.

This has resulted in many parents feeling more confident in letting their children—and in particular their daughters—access an education, as reported by our community partners. Our aim now is to scale up the collection of data, both in terms of what data we collect and who is aware of and thereby able to engage our platform so as to use it to report incidents. Such efforts will encourage more women and girls to speak up and break their silence. We also work to educate and encourage men and boys to be active bystanders—as well as to report incidents they witness or experience. We would like to integrate our data via dashboards that integrate with formal civic government systems so that there can be a more effective allocation of resources, better design of public spaces, and quicker responses to address incidents of sexual violence. For example, our reporting tool would be a great asset for deploying blue emergency phone stands on walking paths, as it would allow planners to identify where such a stand would be most useful in a given area. This also cuts down on the need for random patrols, as communities can put emergency stands in places in which an incident is more likely to occur. Police could then more quickly be drawn to the relevant location. This, then, more efficiently deploys community resources.

A final consideration is that, when data is collected not by police but by more disinterested municipal or university partners, it can ensure a broader approach toward making the data collected accessible and useful to people in the community. Issues like sexual assault and racial targeting/harassment often go unaddressed—especially if there is no data to demonstrate a pattern of incidents, as these incidents tend to affect persons who belong to marginalized and/or disempowered groups in their communities. Police are not always so motivated to want to collect data that draws attention to patterns of discrimination within the broader societal context. Collecting data from the ground up by going directly to residents of a community, by contrast, is democratizing as it makes evident whatever issues exist. However, it is only possible to see such data and the associated insights if the area residents participate by reporting incidents. They are agreeing to share something personal and private to them. As such, the amassed insights that generate from sharing those data should belong to them and everyone else who shared, as they very much have a direct, personal stake in the manifestation of those data. And many of the people who report to us have noted that they are intent on having their awful experience of being victimized potentially help others not be.

Police Use of Deadly Force: When the State Wishes Not to Collect Data

Police use of deadly force is a topic that, like gender-based violence, has received fairly substantial attention in the criminology and criminal justice literatures, and even now globally since the murder of George Floyd at the hands of officers resulted in the Black Lives Matter protests spreading throughout Europe and elsewhere. Still, this attention has generated little change in the collection of such data or in policies set by local leaders. Arguably, the lack of data makes it much easier for local leaders to not redress policies. Some police use of deadly force cases garner national or even international media coverage, but rarely do even those cases result in policy change. Even when such incidents are caught on tape, such as the infamous Rodney King case, or are exceedingly violent, such as the 41-shot assault on Amadou Diallo who was unarmed and simply reaching for his wallet, or the suffocation death of George Floyd in May 2020, which led to a massive, international spate of Black Lives Matter protests, the officers involved are rarely, if ever, held criminally liable for the shootings—nor are protocols changed (Thomson-DeVeaux et al., 2020).

To identify and document a social problem, however, one needs data by which to describe and, ultimately, define the problem. For this reason, state authorities are generally reticent to release information about potentially controversial activities and situations—or to systematically collect data that might demonstrate biases or systematic mistreatment of citizens or some subset thereof. The former Soviet Union, China, and other such authoritarian governments have been characterized by their efforts to control information about the government and its actions. Other "liberal democratic" nations have been more creative in their efforts to manage their images. Rather than attempt to control the distribution of unflattering information, France, for instance, collects no information at all about the racial characteristics of individuals being held within its prison system (Tournier, 1997). The only distinction they make is between French citizens and "foreigners." French authorities claim that this is a progressive effort, asserting that their society is "beyond" concerning itself with racial differences. And, yet, a much larger percentage of the corps Française who herald from an Arabic or African heritage find themselves languishing within the rather archaic French prison system.

In the United States, Brazil, and elsewhere, authorities use more of a French approach with regard to use of force by police authorities against citizens. Though formal reports are, of course, filed when such incidents occur, these are kept only by the specific agency involved in the incident. Until recently, there has existed absolutely no means by which to index this information on a national scale; that is, there has been no clearinghouse for this sort of information—even in the case of lethal use of force. No national reporting agency such as the Federal Bureau of Investigation, which collects and retains the Uniform Crime Report (UCR) data, or the Bureau of Justice Statistics (BJS), which collects extensive criminal justice data, collects and compiles data on police violence against citizens. This has made it very difficult to identify systematic patterns or inequalities that impact police officers' decisions to use force.

What information we have in the United States as to the extent of this phenomenon is discernible, for the most part, only indirectly. There are but two means by which to assess how many people are killed by police officers while the officers are on duty. One could search for news articles, and at one point since such incidents might typically have been reported upon in at least the local paper, but local papers have been gutted by the digital age so that many communities do not even have a local paper—or have one that is supported by a very skeletal staff. Over the last five years the Washington Post had been maintaining a database of police use of deadly force incidents, nationwide, but much of the coding of this data is not terribly nuanced. However, original articles are linked so that additional information can be derived. That said, many times the initial information is incomplete, and the Post does not always update the information. Alternatively, one could look at the Center for Disease Control's (CDC) records for statistics on "deaths by legal intervention," which is the technical term for being killed by a police officer or other agent exercising state authority (DeGue et al., 2016). The CDC publishes summaries of this data every few years. But the state exercising its authority is a serious matter and thus should be something that is well-monitored and routinely reported as is any crime data such as homicides or burglaries. Tools such as crowd mapping provide new means to collect and analyze this kind of data and would help greatly in making the case for greater public accountability.

By that logic, one could argue that technology that allows for crowdsourcing data combined with resources such as organizations devoted to civic dialogue and deliberation places us at a game-changing moment, socially. To put it in Slaughter's (2018) terms: it is now quite possible to use web-driven, decentralized data to change social structures. State authorities enjoyed immense power when politics internally and internationally worked like a chessboard, but the digital era has leveled the playing field. Perhaps this is why the world has seen an authoritarian turn. Decentralization of information access and data generation has likely unsettled many leaders across the globe—Myanmar, India, the United States, and Russia have all recently seen massive protests in the face of markedly authoritarian leadership. Protesters have used social media to organize, and governments have been quick to try to curtail or monitor such organizational innovations. Democracy empowers everyday people and draws them together, and this can unsettle leaders who might like to retain broad and absolute authority. Members of a society now have the means to collaboratively engage various social issues and render their deliberative considerations to policy makers so that a more direct democracy is possible (Lea and Rahman, 2020). This would offer a way to move people from pouring their outrage into the streets by providing a means for them to have their concerns and ideas for change be heard by policy makers.

Crowd mapping and dialogue would offer people another tool for documenting the extent of the problem, arming them with the hard evidence needed to give weight to their concerns and force policy makers to take seriously their ideas for change. Typically, policy makers have dismissed such feedback (Robinson-Jacobs, 2020), but if it were systematically integrated into a city, region, or national governance system, people living in a country or a state, local community, or even a neighborhood could be engaged and have a say in how their locality is governed. Safecity.in has demonstrated very well how such input can make a real, significant difference. But, for that to happen, the data must be used to empower the people in a community, meaning that the data serves as a starting point—an initial barometer of a social problem that can be seen via clusters of reports and then returned to the community for remediation. This is but one additional example of a social problem for which data, which could now be generated by the people for the people, could make a dramatic impact on awareness and thus inspire policy change.

Conclusions

We contend here, using the example of the ongoing Safecity.in effort, that crowd-sourced data presents some unique opportunities for insights that can greatly enhance governance of a society by empowering residents, survivors of gender-based violence, and would-be allies (bystanders) to change their society for the better. Something as simple as a crowd-sourced map can make visible the dark figure of crime. The state itself does not always want to see these data, but without them, there is little way to make useful, directed changes in a society. It is for this reason that we propose that such data, as they are furnished by the local population, must belong to that community so that the community can better understand itself and its governance and make needed changes to itself. We have the tools to do this. We now simply need to apply the will.

References

Barbier, G., Zafarani, R., Gao, H., Fung, G., and Liu, H. (2012) "Maximizing benefits from crowdsourced data," *Computational & Mathematical Organization Theory*, 18 (3), pp. 1–23.

Besheer, M. (2019) "UN: Sexual violence affects 1 in 3 women globally," VOA News, November 25 [online]. Available at https://www.voanews.com/middle-east/un-sexual-violence-affects-1-3-women-globally (accessed July 6, 2020).

Bhatt, A., Menon, R., and Khan, A. (2015) "Women's safety in public transport: A pilot initiative in Bhopal," Embarq India, pp. 7–65 [online]. Available at http://www.wrirosscities.org/sites/default/files/Final_Report_30072015.pdf (accessed May 3, 2017).

Biderman, A., and Reiss, A. (1967) "On exploring the 'dark figure' of crime," *Annals of the American Academy of Political and Social Science*, 374 (1), pp. 1–15.

Binder, R. (1981) "Why women don't report sexual assault," *Journal of Clinical Psychiatry*, 42 (11), pp. 437–38.

Brantingham, P. (2011) "Crime and place: Rapidly evolving research methods in the 21st century," *Cityscape: A Journal of Policy Development and Research*, 13 (3), pp. 199–203.

Ceccato, V. (2016) "Public space and the situational conditions of crime and fear," *International Criminal Justice Review*, 26 (2), pp. 69–79.

Coleman, C., and Moynihan, J. (1996) *Understanding Crime Data: Haunted by the Dark Figure*, Buckingham: Open University Press.

DeGue, S., Fowler, K., and Calkins, C. (2016) "Deaths due to use of deadly force by law enforcement: Findings from the national violent death reporting system, 17 states, 2009–2012," *American Journal of Preventative Medicine* 51 (5S3), pp. S173–S187.

Demerath, L. (2006) "Epistemological identity theory: Reconceptualizing commitment as self-knowledge," *Sociological Spectrum*, 26 (5), pp. 491–517.

Gaynair, G. (2013) "ICRW survey: 95 percent of women and girls consider New Delhi unsafe," International Centre for Research on Women [online]. Available at http://www.icrw.org/media/news/icrw-survey-95-percent-women-and-girls-consider-new-delhi-unsafe (accessed May 7, 2017).

Hill, E., Tiefenthäler, A., Triebert, C., Jordan, D., Willis, H. and Stein, R., 2020. How George Floyd was killed in police custody. *New York Times*, 31.

Kamruzzaman, M. (2016) "A criminological study on the dark figure of crime as a sociological bulk of victimization," *American Journal of Business, Economics and Management*, 4 (4), pp. 35–39.

Lea, S., D'Silva, E., and Asok, A. (2017) "Women's strategies addressing sexual harassment and assault on public buses: An analysis of crowdsourced data," *Crime Prevention and Community Safety*, 19 (3–4), pp. 227–39.

Lea, S., and Rahman, E. A. (2020) "Fourth track diplomacy: It's time has come," *Journal of Dialogue Studies, Special Issue: Rethinking Dialogue in the Age of New Challenges and Opportunities*, 8, pp. 51–66.

Lisak, D., Gardinier, L., Nicksa, S. C. and Cote, A. M., 2010. "False allegations of sexual assault: An analysis of ten years of reported cases." *Violence against Women*, 16(12), pp. 1318–34.

Lodhia, S. (2015) "From 'living corpse' to India's daughter: Exploring the social, political and legal landscape of the 2012 Delhi gang rape," *Women's Studies International Forum*, 50, pp. 89–101.

Meares, T. (1997) "Place and Crime," *Chicago Kent Law Review*, 73, p. 669.

Nigam, S. (2014) "Violence, protest and change: A socio-legal analysis of extraordinary mobilization after the 2012 Delhi gang rape case," *International Journal of Gender and Women's Studies*, 2 (2), 197–221.

Noble, S. (2018) *Algorithms of Oppression: How Search Engines Reinforce Racism*. New York: New York University Press.

O'Donohue, W. T., Elliott, A. N., Nickerson, M. and Valentine, S. (1992) "Perceived credibility of children's sexual abuse allegations: Effects of gender and sexual attitudes." *Violence and Victims*, 7(2), pp. 147–55.

Pain, R., 2001. "Gender, race, age and fear in the city." *Urban Studies*, 38(5–6), pp. 899–913.

Pain, R., Grundy, S., Gill, S., Towner, E., Sparks, G., and Hughes, K. (2005) "So long as I take my mobile: Mobile phones, urban life and geographies of young people's safety," *International Journal of Urban and Regional Research*, 29 (4), pp. 814–30.

Robinson-Jacobs, K. (2020) "NAACP urged Minneapolis police to ban neck restraints," NBC News.com. Available at https://www.nbcnews.com/news/nbcblk/naacp-urged-minneapolis-police-ban-neck-restraints-suspects-years-ago-n1209646 (accessed June 1, 2020).

Roychowdhury, Poulami (2013) "'The Delhi gang rape': The making of international causes," *Feminist Studies*, 39 (1), pp. 282–92.

Sable, M., Danis, F., Mauzy, D., and Gallagher, S. (2006) "Barriers to reporting sexual assault for women and men: Perspectives of college students," *Journal of American College Health*, 55 (3), pp. 157–62.

Slaughter, A. (2018) *The Chessboard and the Web: Strategies of Connection in a Networked World*. New Haven, CT: Yale University Press.

Tcherni, M., Davies, A., Lopes, G., and Lizotte, A. (2016) "The dark figure of online property crime: Is cyberspace hiding a crime wave?" *Justice Quarterly*, 33 (5), pp. 890–911.

Thomson-DeVeaux, A., Rakich, N., and Butchireddygari, L. (2020) "Why it's so rare for police officers to face legal consequences," FiveThirtyEight. Available at https://fivethirtyeight.com/features/why-its-still-so-rare-for-police-officers-to-face-legal-consequences-for-misconduct/ (accessed June 4, 2020).

Tournier, P. (1997) "Nationality, crime, and Criminal justice in France," *Crime and Justice, Ethnicity, Crime and Immigration: Comparative and Cross-National Perspectives*, 21, pp. 523–51.

Weisburd, D. (2012) "Bringing social context back into the equation: The importance of social characteristics of places in the prevention of crime," *Criminology & Public Policy*, 11, p. 317.

Weisburd, D., Bernasco, W., and Bruinsma, G., eds. (2008) *Putting Crime in Its Place*. New York: Springer.

Whitman, J. L. (2007) "Understanding and responding to teen victims: A developmental framework." *The Prevention Researcher*, 14(1), pp. 10–14.

Chapter 8

PROTECTING PRIVACY IN A SEXUAL ASSAULT PREVENTION PROGRAM

Lynne Chandler-Garcia and John C. Riley

Over 30 years ago the FBI documented sexual assault on college campuses as being a widespread and significant threat (Koss et al., 1987), and although a plethora of reduction programs have been introduced, the distressing reality is that few have empirically demonstrated a reduction in prevalence (Vladutiu et al., 2011). The US Air Force Academy (USAFA) is a case in point. For almost two decades, a myriad of sexual assault prevention programs have been introduced to the USAFA, but the rates of unwanted sexual contact have not decreased (The Department of Defense SAPRO ODEI, 2019).

The authors of this chapter are professors in the Department of Political Science at the USAFA, who served as leaders for a nontraditional program aimed at preventing sexual assault at the Academy. As political scientists, they had no special training in victim advocacy or counseling, and neither professor saw themselves as someday spearheading any sexual assault reduction efforts. Nor did either fathom how hard it would be to test and implement a new program at the Academy. This chapter is a reflection on their unlikely story.

As part of their duties in advising and teaching, both professors found themselves meeting with victims often crying in their respective offices. With little professional training on these matters, the professors could do little more than listen sympathetically and walk the distraught cadets to a helping agency. There was a desire to help. Fortuitously, the professors met with two former members of the Sexual Assault Prevention and Response (SAPR) office, who had recently conducted a small pilot test of the Enhanced Access, Acknowledge, Act (EAAA) sexual assault resistance program. EAAA, which consists of four 12-hour sessions, has demonstrated significant results in reducing campus assaults among college females. Together they formed a small team to implement the EAAA program on a larger scale and to conduct further research of the evidence-based program to a military academy.

It is this effort to test the efficacy of bringing EAAA to the USAFA that informs this chapter's insights into gender, privacy, and the military. It was heartening to see how earnest all elements of the USAFA community were in wanting to end sexual assault, and it also was gratifying to see how vigilant the USAFA leadership was at protecting cadet privacy. These two goals, however, did not always neatly align.

Understanding the pattern of behaviors and testing the efficacy of the EAAA program required gathering data from the cadets. In some cases, these data could have been used to sanction cadets under the military justice system. Therefore, a set of rules and procedures had to be developed whereby data was carefully deidentified, secured, and trust among all parties was fostered. It was a constant struggle to equip the female cadets with a set of skills that might help them prevent an assault, without stigmatizing them, and simultaneously protecting their privacy.

Overview of Military Academies

Cadets and midshipmen at the US Military Service Academies (MSA) hover between the twin worlds of academia and military service. They are students with homework and exams; at the same time, they go through military training with the goal of commissioning as officers in the US military upon graduation. These young military members are free to pursue romantic interests, but, at the same time, they also are subject to the Uniform Code of Military Justice (UCMJ) and unique USAFA regulations that dictate some of the parameters of these intimate relationships. For example, cadets cannot be married or have dependents.

In many aspects, these military students are similar to the 18- to 23-year-olds undertaking undergraduate education at civilian institutions across the nation; in many other ways, these students are very different. An unfortunate commonality is that the problem of sexual assault is equally alarming at both military and civilian institutions, and some of the same tactics have been deployed at both types of institution to combat the problem. At the same time, the military nature of academies means there are some fundamental differences in culture that affect how programs are implemented and how privacy is protected.

The Problem of Sexual Assault on Campus and within Military Units

Among undergraduate students across the nation, approximately one in five females is the victim of sexual assault or rape during her college career (Cantor et al., 2015; Krebs et al., 2007). Between one-third to one-half of university women have experienced some type of sexual coercion (Koss et al., 1987; DeKeseredy and Kelly, 1993; Simpson and Senn, 2003). In the vast majority of assaults against women, the perpetrator was male, and in approximately 90 percent of the cases, the victim knew the alleged offender ("Most Victims Know Their Attacker," 2008).

At the USAFA, the statistics for sexual assault for the period June 2017 through April 2018 were slightly lower but on trend with the national average, with 15.1 percent of female cadets experiencing unwanted sexual contact and 5.5 percent experiencing completed penetration since June 2017. Both rates were significantly higher than the rates reported in 2016 (The Department of Defense SAPRO ODEI, 2019). Similar to civilian schools, of the USAFA females who experienced uninvited sexual contact, a majority (95%) indicated that the alleged offender was male, and 63 percent reported that the alleged offender was another USAFA cadet.

Discovering ways to eliminate or at least reduce the problem of sexual assault on campus is critically important because not only is assault an offense against the dignity and sovereignty of the victim, but sexual assault causes numerous negative effects, including social, physical, psychological, and academic problems (Koss et al., 1994; Eisenberg et al., 2009; Carey et al., 2018). Sexual trauma has been associated with anxiety, depression, and eating disorders, among a host of other issues (Eisenberg et al., 2009). Military academies need to be especially in tune with these negative consequences because effects on the victim are acute for women serving in the military. Female veterans who experienced sexual assault during their military service report significantly more physical issues, including pelvic pain, menstrual issues, back pain, and headache, than female veterans who were not victimized and have a much higher probability of depression, panic disorder, and alcohol abuse (J.-C. Surìs et al., 2004). Women who have been sexually assaulted in the military are nine times more likely to develop PTSD than nonvictimized female service members (J.-C. Surìs et al., 2004). When compared to civilian victims of sexual assault, women who were victimized within the military had higher rates of depression and alcohol abuse, and self-reported greater physical pain and impaired social functioning (A. Surìs et al., 2007). A study of female military sexual assault victims revealed that assault ruptures a victim's identity as a military member, as the victim no longer feels included within their military unit. Instead, they are likely to sever ties with the military (Bonnes, 2019). Surìs et al. (2007) point out that when assault occurs within a military unit, the trust the woman has for her unit is shattered, and the protective barrier provided by the unit is no longer available. Further, because victims who report may experience retaliation, may be looked down upon for seeking mental health care, and might be considered undeployable, these victims often remain silent in order to protect their careers (Himmelfarb et al., 2006).

Given the critical problem of sexual assault within college campuses, including military academies, academy leadership has devoted considerable time, money, and manpower to implementing programs that would help alleviate the problem. At the same time, however, concerns of retaliation and career jeopardy loom as considerable issues for women seeking support and help after an assault. Thus, any program implemented by military organizations must seek to carefully balance programming with the need to protect individual privacy.

Privacy within the Military

From routine drug tests to possible inspections during basic training, once someone enters the US military, a degree of privacy is immediately sacrificed. That is not to suggest that military members' lives are open books—they are not. Rather, the question of setting aside the right to privacy is raised when an individual's right potentially undermines the military mission. To this end, sexual orientation and sexual assault have been at the center of the storm over privacy in the military.

In many ways, President Clinton's famous "Don't Ask Don't Tell" directive encapsulated some of the salient issues surrounding the privacy debate; a service member could be gay, lesbian, or bisexual as long as they did not disclose their sexuality, and the military would tolerate their sexual orientation as long as it did not find out about it (Department of Defense, 2015). As the self-titled "Godfather of the Act" puts it, the belief was "unit cohesion is not helped by sexual diversity" (De La Garza, 2018). Although repealed in 2011, much of the same logic informs the government's decision to ban transgender people serving in the military. For example, when justifying the ban, the Department of Defense concluded "that accommodating gender transition could impair unit readiness; undermine unit cohesion, as well as good order and discipline" (Department of Defense, 2018, p. 7). Put another way, a person with gender dysphoria may serve in the military, as long as they do so privately, meaning they are not diagnosed with the condition or take corrective medical steps. In situations of homosexuality and gender dysphoria, the military member maintains privacy—indeed the Department of Defense mandates that these factors not be made public—but the "right" to privacy is not necessarily established or guaranteed.

Protecting privacy in sexual assault situations is especially important because a lack of privacy is often a barrier to reporting. According to Directive 6495.02, "The DoD seeks increased reporting by victims of sexual assault. A system that is perceived as fair and treats victims with dignity and respect and promotes privacy and confidentiality may have a positive impact in bringing victims forward to provide information about being assaulted" (2013). Despite this pledge, military members are skeptical that privacy will be maintained. Data from the 2015 RAND Military Workplace Study revealed that only 22.3 percent of women strongly agreed that the military would protect their privacy in the event of a sexual assault (Gore et al., 2015).

Thus, sexual assault prevention programs for military members must mitigate this problem of distrust. Group programs are a natural setting for victims to share their experiences (Ahrens et al., 2007). Therefore, coordinators must ensure that information shared in the program will not be leaked to anyone outside of the program. This assurance will not only build faith in the military; it will encourage participants to share their experiences, if they so desire.

To formally report a sexual assault within the military, a victim may issue either a restricted or unrestricted report. The intent of a restricted report is to allow a victim to disclose the crime confidentially and receive the medical care and counseling he or she needs without triggering an official investigation. For the purpose of public safety, the installation commander is notified, but the victim's identity remains anonymous (US DoD SAPR, n.d.a). Alternatively, the victim may file an unrestricted report and initiate an official investigation. In this case, the military investigation will proceed, the commander will be informed of the details of the assault, and information only will be "disclosed to personnel with official 'need to know'" (US DoD SAPR, n.d.b).

Anyone in a victim's chain of command is a mandatory reporter. Thus, if a mandatory reporter hears about an incident either directly or indirectly, s/he is required to report the incident. It is imperative that in a military-run prevention program, coordinators and instructors are not within the direct chain of command of any participants, because that would create a mandatory reporting situation. Victims participating in the program may not desire to formally report an assault, and requiring them to participate with someone in their chain of command could force a report against their wishes. It is also imperative that participants do not leak information shared during a session, which could find its way to someone within the victim's chain of command. In instances of sexual assault, the role of the commander takes on special importance because the commander has responsibility to protect subordinates and ensure that breaches of the law are met with justice. These two responsibilities can come into conflict where a commander is trying to investigate an allegation of misconduct within the unit. The commander may request access to confidential reports in order to investigate a sexual crime, which may, in turn, violate the victim's privacy. For instance, even with restricted reports, commanders may ascertain the identity of the victim or "demand to know the parties" of the case (Hansen 2011, p. 554). In some cases, commanders have inappropriately pressured the Special Assault Referral Centre or the Victim Advocate to release details about the case.

An unrestricted report triggers an official law enforcement investigation and very often a defense by the perpetrator. Victims may worry that information shared within a group setting or on a survey associated with program research may be subpoenaed as evidence in a criminal case. The simple act of signing a consent form may make a person fear a loss of anonymity (Fontes, 2004). Although there are statutes preventing this confidential information from being shared, this is a constant concern in a prevention program.

An unrestricted report might create negative knockoff effects as well. For example, the report to a commander may require that he or she separate the victim and the perpetrator until the military investigator can review the details of the report. That may take weeks—and effectively make the victim the outcast of the unit (Hansen 2011, p. 576). Separating the victim and perpetrator is particularly hard to do within a military unit where military members live in barracks or, in the case of military academies, within dorms. The military has acknowledged that assaults in barracks are a particularly vexing problem (Mulrine, 2012). Women who are still in contact with their attackers may fear reprisal for participating in a study where the nature of the attack could become known to others (Fontes, 2004).

Fear of ostracism is perhaps a greater obstacle than formal command relationships. Fellow service members may see a fellow service member making a report, witness a member seeking medical attention, overhear a conversation, or learn about the assault via a number of methods. This may subject the victim to unwanted scrutiny, stigmatization, derision, or even further attack. In a 2010 survey of military members, 71 percent of women who experienced unwanted sexual conduct said they did not report the incident because they did not feel the report would be kept confidential. Focus groups further revealed victims feared they would be stigmatized and labeled within their units. Although retaliation is strictly prohibited, 54 percent of respondents in a separate poll stated that they did not report because they feared retaliation from perpetrators or friends (Gore et al., 2015).

Turning to military academies, many of the same issues apply. Military academies need to promote unit cohesion and discipline, while protecting the privacy of cadets seeking to report or attain treatment after an assault. To simulate life in the military, cadets are organized into squadrons in which they live, eat, sleep, and perform a variety of military leadership roles and training tasks. Squadrons are very close-knit, with privacy taking a second place to cohesiveness.

It is important to note that cadets take an oath to uphold the honor code: "We will not lie, steal, or cheat, nor tolerate among us anyone who does. Furthermore,

I resolve to do my duty and to live honorably (so help me God)." The toleration clause has unique privacy implications. That is, if a cadet witnesses another cadet breaking the code, he or she does not have the right to keep the instance to themselves. This can create tremendous pressure on a cadet, who may fear they may be removed from the Academy for failing to report a violation.

At the same time, a conflicting pressure is the social ostracism or even retaliation that often comes with reporting on a fellow cadet. As a USAFA professor explains, "I hear it in my classroom. 'Hey, so and so, they're shunned now because they reported on their brother or their sister in their squadron and now everyone is hosed.' So they're known as the snitch now. That's the kind of retaliation we're facing" (Barry et al., 2017, p. 95).

Cadets cite a lack of privacy as a significant barrier to reporting at USAFA, explaining that close quarters fueled rumor mills and increased the visibility of reports. Victims fear damage to their reputations, ostracism, and even retaliation from members of their unit, if they speak out or report an assault. A female sophomore explained that by reporting, "You could ruin your reputation. If somebody sees you as 'Oh, she got them in trouble for this,' and they didn't think he deserved it, then that rumor spreads and you're known as an untrustworthy person" (ibid., p. 91).

At the USAFA, privacy considerations take on additional dimensions as almost every aspect of cadet life comes under constant scrutiny. For example, cadet dorm rooms are subject to frequent inspections, and something as simple as an unauthorized candle or plant can lead to significant consequences. Morale, Wellness, and Health Inspections can be particularly intrusive as all locked drawers and trunks are opened and items, such as medications, feminine hygiene, or sex-related items, can be reviewed. Four-degree cadets (freshmen) must keep their dorm room doors open throughout most of the day, and it is common for upper-class cadets to pop-in to see if standards are being met, all of which leads cadets to sometimes comment that "they have no home at USAFA."

All of these considerations must be taken into account for military-based prevention programs. When conducting sexual assault prevention programs and associated research, a central principle is to do no harm to participants. There are several ways that participants potentially could be harmed. First, communication during a program session, or even participating in the program itself, could jeopardize a victim's anonymity. Participants must be carefully counseled concerning maintaining the privacy of their fellow participants. The physical location of the program must be carefully considered (Rosoff, 2018). The location needs to be easily accessible but also private enough that conversations cannot be overheard. If the program is voluntary, others should not be able to easily witness participants entering or leaving the location so that victimization is not deduced.

Personnel conducting sexual assault programs and research must ensure participants that confidentiality will be maintained, and information collected during the course of the program will be protected. Survey methods that protect anonymity, such as computer-administered surveys, tend to produce higher estimates for sensitive subjects than in-person interview methods (Farris et al., 2015). When taking surveys, participants should not be able to see another person's paper or screen (if administered electronically).

Finally, there is a worry that the content of the program and associated survey questions may be upsetting or triggering to victims. Questions from validated instruments such as the Sexual Experiences Survey feature probing questions as to the nature, timing, and frequency of assault. Asking victims to recount those incidents may force them to relive their trauma. Further, asking participants in a study to disclose sensitive information could be seen as an invasion of privacy. Numerous researchers have investigated this problem and have found that while women with histories of sexual victimization have immediate negative emotional reactions to research questions, most participants do not feel retraumatized after participating in surveys or interviews. In fact, most victims report positive experiences after participating in scientific research that they feel is important and worthwhile (Walker et al., 1997; Edwards et al., 2009; Yeater et al., 2012; Gómez et al., 2015).

Although these issues plague the closely knit and thoroughly scrutinized culture of military units, the Department of Defense does have a number of formal regulations to protect the privacy of victims. In civilian institutions, Title IX and the Family Education Rights and Privacy Act (FERPA) regulate privacy issues connected with sexual assault on campus. Title IX, which prohibits sexual discrimination in schools that receive federal funding, has been used to combat sexual assault as it requires schools to respond and investigate instances of sexual harassment and assault. Student victims are able to bring suit against public institutions that fail to address assaults. Military academies are specifically exempt from both Title IX and FERPA, which means that cadets do not have legal recourse to sue the institution.

FERPA requires that schools protect student records or any other information directly related to a student, including reports of assault. FERPA's application to military academies is nebulous. While the USAFA registrar states, "FERPA permits disclosure to USAFA officials with legitimate educational interest in the records being sought" (Office of Student Academic Affairs & Academic Registrar, n.d.), access to cadet records is easily attained by faculty and USAFA leadership. For instance, faculty can instantaneously call up a cadet's grades, college entrance scores, and any probations they may have incurred. The intent is to give a whole-of-effort support of cadet development, but one of the consequences is virtually zero academic privacy between cadets and staff.

Findings: Testing EAAA at USAFA

In 2003, a sexual assault scandal shook the USAFA to its core (Bingham, 2003) and, in very short order, the Academy attempted to transform its culture from an institution that "punished victims" to a place where sexual assault prevention and response was one of its highest priorities (Holmquist, 2019). As it now stands, the SAPR office has a very visible presence, and cadets as well as the faculty and staff continuously complete a virtual cornucopia of training that ranges from "awareness briefings" that last a full day to "bystander intervention" courses. Unfortunately, despite these efforts, the Academy has failed to meet its goal of reducing, let alone eliminating, sexual assault and harassment.

The Annual Report on Sexual Harassment and Violence at the MSA is part of a congressionally mandated exercise to measure the prevalence of sexual assault at the military academies. The findings are hardly encouraging. At the USAFA in the 2017–18 academic year, 29 sexual assaults were reported (20 unrestricted and 9 restricted), 46 percent of the female cadets reported that they experienced sexual harassment, and unwanted sexual contact among female cadets rose from 11.2 to 15.1 percent (The Department of Defense SAPRO ODEI, 2019). Testifying to Congress, the USAFA superintendent, Lieutenant General Jay Silveria, concluded, "These results are unacceptable [...] Where we have fallen short, it is our responsibility to take active ownership of these shortcomings and work aggressively to correct them. I am disheartened and frustrated by the results, but I will not rest until we get this right" (Silveria, 2019).

It was at approximately this point when a small team of researchers, initially working out of the USAFA SAPR office with faculty later joining, began exploring the possibility of bringing the EAAA sexual assault resistance program to the USAFA.

At the University of Windsor, Charlene Senn developed the EAAA program for first-year female college students. Drawing heavily on successful rape self-defense strategies and cognitive ecological models on women's responses to sexual assault, Senn developed an innovative four-unit course that sought to improve women's ability to assess and acknowledge the risk of sexual assault, defend themselves with Wen-Do techniques, and develop strategies for sexual communication (Senn et al., 2015).

The results from the EAAA program were impressive. In as little as six months, the EAAA program significantly reduced the incidence of completed rape by 58.2 percent. Moreover, the program continued to be efficacious up to 24 months. Attempted rape was also dramatically reduced over the entire 24-month period, with effects ranging from 55.8 to 71.8 percent. EAAA is effectively the gold standard for collegiate sexual assault reduction programs

(Senn et al., 2017, p. 155). However, it was far from clear whether the program would be a good fit at USAFA or other MSA.

Some of the concerns centered on basic administrative questions that proved to be hardly trivial. For instance, at the USAFA, every day—and virtually every hour—of the 47-month curriculum is deliberately constructed. When would a 15-hour program be scheduled, and would it come at the cost of another program? More fundamental concerns focused on equality and efficacy. Would it be fair to mandate a program only for female cadets? Would the female cadets see EAAA as just more training that they had to complete or, worse yet, would they feel targeted? The female freshmen class is perhaps the most vulnerable population at the USAFA, and the researchers were very concerned that by changing the schedules for female freshmen, and at times requiring them to wear different uniforms, they would be adversely singled out.

Moreover, the extent to which EAAA would be effective at the USAFA was not clear. For instance, all cadets already receive combat arms training and the USAFA culture does not resemble typical college campuses. Would the exercises that were designed to debunk rape myths and promote healthy dialogue about sexual relations resonate with young adults who are already developing a military mindset?

Finally, concerns over cadet privacy were of seminal importance. From ostracism for participating in the program, to leakage of personal information, to securing data collected from the program, privacy concerns dictated much of how the course was implemented.

The research team's solution was to make cadet privacy and safety a sacrosanct principle. Moving cautiously, the team created safeguards at every step. At the same time, however, the team was testing the program at USAFA and needed to gather data to assess the effectiveness of the program. Therefore, at every turn, the requirement to protect a military member's privacy butted against the countervailing need to gather data that were fundamental to a sexual assault prevention program.

The first steps in protecting privacy involved securing the surveys. To effectively assess the course, the cadets would have to take a series of surveys that asked exceptionally personal questions ranging from previous sexual relations to alcohol and drug use. Although all of the surveys were validated by other institutions, the nature of the questions could be jarring, especially to those who might be victimized. Further, since the cadets are subject to the UCMJ and unique USAFA operating instructions, any admission to certain activities could be interpreted as confessing to having committed a prohibited activity or a crime. The potential consequences could range from punishment at USAFA (such as marching tours) to disenrollment and criminal sanctions.

To protect data, the researchers utilized a Health Insurance Portability and Accountability Act (HIPAA)-compliant, web-based instrument that deidentified all collected data. Due to concerns over subpoenas, Freedom of Information Act inquiries, and other requests for information, it was imperative that data collected could not be traced to an individual cadet. The team explored possibilities, such as using a code to log in to the online survey tool, having a third party store login credentials, and not collecting IP addresses. Because the concern over tracing identifiable information was so great, the research team ultimately decided to only collect information in the aggregate, with all questions disassociated from each other. Not having student-level data meant that some statistical computations were not possible, but the protection of privacy was deemed more important than the research gains from individual-level data collection.

The next set of privacy concerns involved the logistics of administering the surveys. Because the survey was online, it could easily be administered in a cadet's dorm room. However, given the personal nature of the questions, the team was concerned that cadets receive support from the SAPR helping agency, if necessary. Therefore, the cadets were scheduled to take the surveys in an auditorium where cadets could be spaced out so that they could not see one another's computer screens. The SAPR office provided counsellors to assist, if the questions triggered any of the participants.

The next challenge was ensuring questions didn't violate policy. Because of the "Don't Ask, Don't Tell" policy, the military is not allowed to ask questions about sexual orientation. Therefore, even though these questions were part of the validated surveys, questions involving homosexuality or bisexuality were deleted. The second set of survey questions that the team scrutinized involved underage drinking. Asking these questions puts cadets in a bind: If they answer the question truthfully and say they have engaged in underage drinking, they are admitting to violating the law; if they lie and say they have not consumed alcohol, they are violating the USAFA honor code. Because alcohol is a significant contributor to sexual assault, it was imperative that data be gathered on this topic. Thus, the team decided to keep the questions but not associate answers to respondents so that the information could not be traced to an individual student.

Privacy challenges also presented in the training of cadets by volunteer instructors. Two points are worth underlining. First, the instructors were purposefully matched with a group of cadets who were not in their chain of command, so that they would never be in the position of being a mandatory reporter. Therefore, cadets could feel free to share their experiences without inadvertently triggering a military investigation. Second, the military officers did not wear their uniforms during the training. The cadets were made aware of the instructor's background and role at the Academy—and this proved to be an important element in establishing trust. However, a deliberate effort was made to minimize the officer's hierarchical position. In military parlance, every effort was made to make this an educational experience and not a training exercise.

Instructors cautioned cadets to refrain from sharing personal details about past victimization and, instead, to focus on the preventative measures of the curriculum. Inevitably, however, personal details were shared in the group setting. Instructors repeatedly stressed the closed-door nature of the class. Thought also was put into the venue for the classes. USAFA has several locations where cadets can report assault and seek support. Some locations were easily accessible to encourage cadets to seek the help they need, but these locations suffer from high visibility that reduces cadet privacy. Other locations are much more remote but are more difficult to access on foot. To mitigate both of these concerns, a classroom in the primary education building was chosen. This easily accessible room was not labeled. Thus, cadets could be seen entering and leaving, but no one knew that this was an EAAA class and, thus, it seemed to be class as usual.

Two separate pilot tests were conducted. The first test consisted of a small group of female volunteers, who received the course at an off-site location. The second pilot was composed of approximately half the entire freshman female class, and it was conducted throughout their first fall semester. The results were very encouraging, and they led the researches to apply for a Congressionally Mandated Medical Research Grant to reduce sexual assault and harassment.

Interestingly, even though preliminary data were very encouraging, the program was almost canceled at several critical junctures. The question of implementing a new (in some people's view, a "radical") program for only females at the USAFA raised ethical concerns with almost all parties. The research team has thus far moved the program along by tying policy conversations to empirical findings. Do the cadets find the program to be worthwhile? Are myths about rape being debunked? Ultimately, the most important question is whether the prevalence of sexual assaults and harassment decreases over time. If so, then the program ought to be supported; if not, alternatives must be sought out.

Finally, it is important to note the impact the COVID-19 pandemic had on this program. The research team had scheduled EAAA training and assessment for the second half of the freshman women cohort during the Spring 2020 semester. However, when the lower three classes at USAFA were sent home in early March 2020, all training was canceled for the semester. Although the cadet wing has returned for the Fall 2020 semester, uncertainty surrounding the pandemic has led the research team to continue to suspend EAAA training until Spring 2021. The hope is that with proper social distancing and following the guidelines outlined by the CDC, training will restart.

Lessons Learned

Maintaining privacy was a foundational principle that proved to be a necessary prerequisite to establishing trust with all the participants. The concern about collecting data that might lead to severe consequences under the military justice system is fairly unique to USAFA, but any civilian school will have the similar challenge of earning participants' trust. The question on the EAAA assessment surveys and the conversations had in the classrooms can be exceptionally personal, and the program will be effective only if the participants are forthright and honest. Of course, none of this is possible with the prior belief that the data will be held in strict confidence.

Using a HIPAA-compliant survey instrument was an important step in gaining the cadets' trust. However, equally important was the role that other cadets played in validating the program. Very early in the process, the researchers turned to upper-class men to speak to the participants and ask that they give the course their full attention. Cadets also volunteered their time and helped bring meals to the participants, and they were seen helping complete other administrative tasks. It is true that at the USAFA, cadets tend to rely very heavily on their fellow cadets for guidance, but the idea of fellow students establishing an environment of trust could prove pivotal for any civilian school.

Equally importantly, trust had to be established with the USAFA administration. In this case, it had to flow both ways. From the administration's perspective, EAAA represented a relatively high-visibility and high-risk program. Not only is there congressional oversight, but any mishaps might easily garner media attention. Moreover, the administration had to firmly believe in the value of the EAAA program, if they were going to make room in the cadets' schedules. This, in turn, led the researchers to place additional emphasis on methodological transparency. To this end, the team brought in a distinguished visiting professor, who could examine the methods and interrupt the findings without any institutional bias.

The research team also had to trust that the administration would not display any undue influence or try to connect the data with individual cadets. Again, the HIPAA-complaint instrument went a long way in providing this security, but it was important that the administration paid for the instrument. By spending considerable money on an instrument that prohibited anyone's ability to connect an individual to specific responses, it helped a culture in which everyone made cadet privacy the highest priority.

Conclusion

The case of bringing EAAA to a MSA offers an exceptionally interesting window into the intersection of gender and privacy. At the academies, there is pressure on all the cadets to adopt a warrior culture and survive the rigors of military life. Survival strategies vary, but a popular one is to blend into the crowd and do one's best not to bring unwanted attention onto oneself. With this as a context, we can ask, "Is it ethical to bring EAAA to USAFA and only train female cadets?"

Perhaps the most frequent criticism that the research team received was that it was unfair (both to the men and women) to only offer EAAA to women. On the one hand, the team recognizes that only offering training to a subgroup of female cadets during the pilot tests may have called attention to these women. If so, an aspect of their privacy might have been compromised. However, if EAAA is adopted and all freshmen women complete the training, then this will become less of an issue. Additionally, the question of new types of training for male cadets is under investigation as well. The long-term plan is that all cadets receive an equal amount of training and that all programs be evaluated with a rigorous methodology.

There is also the charge that by only training women, EAAA violates a basic US military tenet that calls for servicemen to set aside a degree of individuality and adopt a common identity. At precisely the most foundational period, freshmen year, EAAA training singles out the women from the men.

This critique, however, is only potentially damaging if one defines the common military identity along the exceptionally narrow guise of a genderless lens. Of course, this is not how the military operates. If it did, it would not have different uniforms for the different sexes, and it would not use the terms like "Ma'am or Sir." These dress standards and customs and courtesies are part of the larger socially constructed process that marks the differences in the genders in the military. The service members ought to be able to retain their masculinity or femininity and still be a soldier, sailor, marine, or airman.

Unfortunately, sexual assault and harassment is a problem that touches both sexes. EAAA is designed specifically to empower women from being assaulted by men. The academies would benefit greatly if men, who too often are also sexual assault victims, had a program tailored for them. It is far more inclusive to be united in the goal of ending sexual assault than to have a common program with poor results.

Whether or not the USAFA makes EAAA part of its permanent curriculum is still an open question. It is likely to take another two to three years of testing before a determination is made. However, what has become clear to the research team is that the USAFA—from the cadets who volunteered to support the EAAA program to every level of leadership—is committed to ending sexual assault and harassment.

References

Ahrens, Courtney E., Rebecca Campbell, N. Karen Ternier-Thames, Sharon M. Wasco, and Tracy Sefl. 2007. "Deciding Whom to Tell: Expectations and Outcomes of Rape Survivors' First Disclosures." *Psychology of Women Quarterly* 31 (1): 38–49. https://doi.org/10.1111/j.1471-6402.2007.00329.x.

Barry, Amanda, Natalie Namrow, Jason Debus, W. Xav Klauberg, Hunter Peebles, and Marsh Harper. 2017. "2017 Service Academy Gender Relations Focus Groups." OPA Report 2017-039. Office of People Analytics.

Bingham, Clara. 2003. "Code of Dishonor." *Vanity Fair*, December 2003. https://www.vanityfair.com/news/2003/12/airforce200312.

Bonnes, Stephanie. 2019. "Service-Women's Responses to Sexual Harassment: The Importance of Identity Work and Masculinity in a Gendered Organization." *Violence against Women*, September, 1077801219873433. https://doi.org/10.1177/1077801219873433.

Cantor, David, Bonnie Fisher, Susan Chibnall, Reanne Townsend, Hyunshik Lee, Carol Bruce, and Gail Thomas. 2015. "Report on the AAU Campus Climate Survey on Sexual Assault and Sexual Misconduct," September, 288.

Carey, Kate B., Alyssa L. Norris, Sarah E. Durney, Robyn L. Shepardson, and Michael P. Carey. 2018. "Mental Health Consequences of Sexual Assault among First-Year College Women." *Journal of American College Health* 66 (6): 480–86. https://doi.org/10.1080/07448481.2018.1431915.

De La Garza, Alejandro. 2018. "'Don't Ask, Don't Tell' Was a Complicated Moment for Gay Rights: Many of the Same Issues Remain." *The Time*, July 19, 2018. https://time.com/5339634/dont-ask-dont-tell-25-year-anniversary/.

DeKeseredy, Walter, and Katharine Kelly. 1993. "The Incidence and Prevalence of Woman Abuse in Canadian University and College Dating Relationships." *Canadian Journal of Sociology/Cahiers Canadiens de Sociologie* 18 (2): 137–59. https://doi.org/10.2307/3341255.

Department of Defense. 2015. "Department of Defense Instruction 1304.26."

———. 2018. "Department of Defense Report and Recommendations on Military Service by Transgender Persons." https://www.lambdalegal.org/sites/default/files/legal-docs/downloads/dkt._216-2._dod_report_and_recommendations_feb_20181.pdf.

Edwards, Katie M., Megan C. Kearns, Karen S. Calhoun, and Christine A. Gidycz. 2009. "College Women's Reactions to Sexual Assault Research Participation: Is It Distressing?" *Psychology of Women Quarterly* 33 (2): 225–34. https://doi.org/10.1111/j.1471-6402.2009.01492.x.

Eisenberg, Daniel, Ezra Golberstein, and Justin B Hunt. 2009. "Mental Health and Academic Success in College." *B.E. Journal of Economic Analysis & Policy* 9 (1): 1–35. https://doi.org/10.2202/1935-1682.2191.

Farris, Coreen, Lisa H. Jaycox, Terry L. Schell, Amy E. Street, Dean G. Kilpatrick, and Terri Tanielian. 2015. "Sexual Harassment and Gender Discrimination Findings: Active Component." In *Sexual Assault and Sexual Harassment in the U.S. Military*, edited by Terry L. Schell, Andrew R. Morral, and Kristie L. Gore, 31–54. Volume 2. Estimates for Department of Defense Service Members from the 2014 RAND Military Workplace Study. RAND Corporation. https://www.jstor.org/stable/10.7249/j.ctt15sk8jf.12.

Fontes, Lisa Aronson. 2004. "Ethics in Violence against Women Research: The Sensitive, the Dangerous, and the Overlooked." *Ethics & Behavior* 14 (2): 141–74. https://doi.org/10.1207/s15327019eb1402_4.

Gómez, Jennifer M., Carly Smith, Marina N. Rosenthal, and Jennifer J. Freyd. 2015. "Participant Reactions to Questions about Gender-Based Sexual Violence: Implications for Campus Climate Surveys." *EJournal of Public Affairs* 4 (2): 39–71. https://doi.org/10.21768/EJOPA.V4I2.75.

Gore, Kristie L., Kayla M. Williams, and Bonnie Ghosh-Dastidar. 2015. "Beliefs about Sexual Assault and Sexual Harassment Prevalence, Prevention, and Progress." In *Sexual Assault and Sexual Harassment in the U.S. Military*, edited by Kristie L. Gore, Andrew R. Morral, and Terry L. Schell, 55–60. Volume 2. Estimates for Department of Defense Service Members from the 2014 RAND Military Workplace Study. RAND Corporation. https://www.jstor.org/stable/10.7249/j.ctt15sk8jf.13.

Hansen, Emily. 2011. "Carry That Weight: Victim Privacy within the Military Sexual Assault Reporting Methods." *Journal of John Marshall Computer & Information Law* 28 (4): 43.

Himmelfarb, Naomi, Deborah Yaeger, and Jim Mintz. 2006. "Posttraumatic Stress Disorder in Female Veterans with Military and Civilian Sexual Trauma." *Journal of Traumatic Stress* 19 (6): 837–46. https://doi.org/10.1002/jts.20163.

Holmquist, Jeff. 2019. "USAFA Continues Search for Effective Sexual Assault Education Programs." Checkpoints, December 2019.

Koss, Mary P., Christine A Gidycz, and Nadine N Wisniewski. 1987. "The Scope of Rape: Incidence and Prevalence of Sexual Aggression and Victimization in a National Sample of Higher Education Students." *Journal of Consulting and Clinical Psychology* 55 (2): 162–70.

Koss, Mary P., Lori Heise, and Nancy Felipe Russo. 1994. "The Global Health Burden of Rape." *Psychology of Women Quarterly* 18 (4): 509–37. https://doi.org/10.1111/j.1471-6402.1994.tb01046.x.

Krebs, Christopher P., Christine H. Lindquist, Tara D. Warner, Bonnie S. Fisher, and Sandra L. Martin. 2007. "The Campus Sexual Assault (CSA) Study," December, 111.

"Most Victims Know Their Attacker." 2008. National Institute of Justice. September 30, 2008. https://nij.ojp.gov/topics/articles/most-victims-know-their-attacker.

Mulrine, Anna. 2012. "Pentagon Dilemma: More Privacy in Barracks Linked to More Sexual Assault." *Christian Science Monitor*, June 26, 2012. https://www.csmonitor.com/USA/Military/2012/0626/Pentagon-dilemma-More-privacy-in-barracks-linked-to-more-sexual-assault.

Office of Student Academic Affairs & Academic Registrar. n.d. "Official Notice Concerning Your Student Records." US Air Force Academy.

Rosoff, Cari B. 2018. "Ethics in College Sexual Assault Research." *Ethics & Behavior* 28 (2): 91–103. https://doi.org/10.1080/10508422.2017.1333001.

Senn, Charlene Y., Misha Eliasziw, Paula C. Barata, Wilfreda E. Thurston, Ian R. Newby-Clark, H. Lorraine Radtke, and Karen L. Hobden. 2015. "Efficacy of a Sexual Assault Resistance Program for University Women." *New England Journal of Medicine* 372 (24): 2326–35. https://doi.org/10.1056/NEJMsa1411131.

Senn, Charlene Y., Misha Eliasziw, Karen L. Hobden, Ian R. Newby-Clark, Paula C. Barata, H. Lorraine Radtke, and Wilfreda E. Thurston. 2017. "Secondary and 2-Year Outcomes of a Sexual Assault Resistance Program for University Women." *Psychology of Women Quarterly* 41 (2): 147–62. https://doi.org/10.1177/0361684317690119.

Silveria, Jay. 2019. Statement of Lieutenant General Jay B. Silveria, USAF Superintendent of the United States Air Force Academy Before the Subcommittee on Military Personnel Committee on Armed Services United States House of Representatives.

Simpson, Amber, and Charlene Y. Senn. 2003. "Sexual Coercion and Sexual Assault: Are the Effects on Hostility Gender Specific?" *Guidance & Counselling* 18 (3): 111–17.

Surís, Alina, Lisa Lind, T. Michael Kashner, and Patricia D. Borman. 2007. "Mental Health, Quality of Life, and Health Functioning in Women Veterans: Differential Outcomes Associated with Military and Civilian Sexual Assault." *Journal of Interpersonal Violence* 22 (2): 179–97. https://doi.org/10.1177/0886260506295347.

Surís, J.-C., P.-A. Michaud, and R. Viner. 2004. "The Adolescent with a Chronic Condition. Part I: Developmental Issues." *Archives of Disease in Childhood* 89 (10): 938–42. https://doi.org/10.1136/adc.2003.045369.

The Department of Defense SAPRO ODEI. 2019. "Annual Report on Sexual Harassment and Violence at the Military Service Academies Academic Program Year 2017–2018."

US DoD SAPR. n.d. a. "Restricted Reporting." Accessed July 27, 2020. https://www.sapr.mil/restricted-reporting.

———. n.d. b "Unrestricted Reporting." Accessed July 27, 2020. https://www.sapr.mil/unrestricted-reporting.

Vladutiu, Catherine J., Sandra L. Martin, and Rebecca J. Macy. 2011. "College- or University-Based Sexual Assault Prevention Programs: A Review of Program Outcomes, Characteristics, and Recommendations." *Trauma, Violence, & Abuse* 12 (2): 67–86. https://doi.org/10.1177/1524838010390708.

Walker, E. A., E. Newman, M. Koss, and D. Bernstein. 1997. "Does the Study of Victimization Revictimize the Victims?" *General Hospital Psychiatry* 19 (6): 403–10. https://doi.org/10.1016/s0163-8343(97)00061-3.

Yeater, Elizabeth, Geoffrey Miller, Jenny Rinehart, and Erica Nason. 2012. "Trauma and Sex Surveys Meet Minimal Risk Standards: Implications for Institutional Review Boards." *Psychological Science*, May. https://doi.org/10.1177/0956797611435131.

CONCLUSION

Colette Mazzucelli, James Felton Keith, and Andrea Adams

Acharya and Buzan's (2019) GIS 1.2 predictions suggest a change in the power dynamics between core and periphery countries where there will be a wide diffusion of wealth, power, and cultural influences. The GIS 1.2 also evidences shifting global dynamics where global capitalistic issues exist in different ideological settings. The authors predict rapid technological advancements that support nation-state activities. Non-nation-state data scientists and data platforms influence domestic and international behavior. Similarly, Slaughter's description of web networks suggests that intentional, organic, and uncivil actors participate in international relations alongside chessboards. She suggests these technological advances facilitate network actions, thereby empowering communications among participants, yet subject to the interests of data platform structures.

The first three chapters respond to the initial question this volume raises. Brevard's comparative analysis, specifically, looking at the right to privacy in the People's Republic of China and the United States, was able to show parallels between China's overt desire to track movement, actions, and decisions of its citizens, to the United States' covert practices through the Patriot Act to do the same. She aimed to show the similarities between the People's Republic of China and the United States, notably regarding information technology and surveillance. Since both export their technologies and use device data mining in Big Data, Brevard argues that the United States may be leaning toward the Peoples Republic of China's authoritarian tendencies. Acharya and Buzan indicate that in GIS 1.2, nation-state actions in scientific knowledge and technology will be influenced by uncertainty, in that the trajectory and contours of the Internet are undetermined. This uncertainty has significant implications for inclusionism given its specific individual/community orientation as well as technology's insidious and pervasive influence in the lives of more and more people across the world. The PRC–US relationship at the apex of global international society 1.2 is increasingly subject to forces that are well beyond the scope of nation-state influence with considerable implications for agency as this pertains to the daily lives of their respective populations.

Ehmke's chapter focuses on regulating online disinformation, that is, fake news, as her analysis questions the greater risk to democracy: fake news or the measures to control the flow of information. Her study focuses on limiting freedom of expression using legal methods to regulate problematic speech in a journalistic context. Ehmke notes that Internet and social media platforms consistently permit individuals with fewer credentials to have the protection of journalists. Here again, data platform standards conflict with chessboard legal schemes. Ehmke, however, argues that the current legal environment needs to address the current media ecosystem. Her study is indicative of a lagging chessboard response to network-based activities, which is consistent with Slaughter's strategy. In terms of inclusionism, Ehmke's chapter asks us to revisit a fundamental question: What rights are our communities owed? Specifically, can we derive structure from the agency of individuals? To what extent may individuals lead in the ecosystem that Ehmke's chapter analyzes? The limitations on agency in this context are the crux of the matter.

Cameron's description of the effect of geopolitics on Iran's COVID-19 response explicitly links Slaughter's perspective on how chessboard strategies of Iran and the US policy-driven sanctions affect Iranian citizens during the pandemic. She argues that addressing global crises requires a focus on global citizen well-being. She explains how politics influenced the governmental response and that sanctions influence the government's ability to provide humanitarian aid for citizens. Politics also drives Iran's rejection of humanitarian assistance from the United States and has not allowed Western relief organizations to operate in the country. Further, Iran's government has not been able to address online misinformation about the pandemic. In a recent article about the pandemic, Slaughter and LaForge (2021: 157) write,

> The response to the COVID-19 pandemic is only one example of how global actors, not states alone, drive solutions to complex problems. Although it would have been preferable had efficient central governments organized a coherent response to the pandemic, the distributed response on the part of others demonstrated just how much problem-solving talent exists outside the state. Moreover, as some countries become more nationalist, parochial, and captured by special interests, opening up the international order to global actors is the best way to reform the order in the absence of a major state-led initiative.

Slaughter and LaForge's recent comment support Cameron's perspective in that it describes Iran's decision not to allow global assistance as the reason for the significant harm to its citizens. This study also supports the notion that when chessboards lack resources or the political will to shed ideological stances in the face of shared-fate global concerns, there may not be other options to protect citizens. This chapter's findings speak to the ways in which inclusionism fills a gap in the international relations literature. Inclusionism is a lens that addresses state limitations when confronted with the challenges of shared-fate concerns for individual citizens as well as a larger community, which is cosmopolitan in nature give its presence beyond the borders of any one state.

Acharaya and Buzan discuss "the making of global international relations" in a way that takes into consideration countries that are emerging at the center of an evolving society, which includes a diverse array of actors previously ignored in traditional analyses, most notably the various strands of realism analyzed extensively in the Western literature (Doyle, 1997). The People's Republic of China is at the center of the transition occurring in global international relations. The chapters in section two of this edited volume speak to the tensions between, on the one hand, the core of Western international relations theories and those that speak to race, gender, the postcolonial and the environmental, as well as Western and non-Western international relations perspectives, including indigenous voices around the world, anchored increasingly in local experiences during the COVID-19 pandemic. It is no coincidence that each chapter references social constructivism in its analysis given the bridge function of this lens between realism and liberalism in the Western core. Postcolonialism, feminism, and race theories, as well as environmental stewardship, often challenge the assumptions of their more frequently cited theoretical counterparts. The research into minority abuses of Uyghurs in Xinjiang by Davis speaks to identity questions in the People's Republic of China as the Party's capacity to develop surveillance technology to control the population over an expansive territory deepens. Taiwan's response to the COVID-19 pandemic, including extensive references to personal data collection, further differentiates its identity from that of the People's Republic of China.

The absence of references to personal data in most international relations analyses of the PRC's emergence as a rising power or Taiwan's steadily evolving identity separate from that of China is notable in the literature. While Taiwan may be considered on the periphery, China is entering the semi-core owing to its rapid economic development over the past several generations. Such is the breadth and depth of China's influence, largely through its One Belt One Road (OBOR) state capitalist initiative. OBOR challenges the Washington Consensus, which drives a liberal capitalist globalization process. This evolution is acknowledged increasingly by periphery countries in search of which model for development to import, state or liberal capitalist, especially given the impact of the COVID-19 pandemic on their stagnant or weak economic growth. Likewise, Taiwan's quest to establish its own identity distinct from that of the PRC speaks to its ongoing search for an evolving role in the various networks that Slaughter analyzes while bearing in mind the absence of a vocabulary to explain the emerging importance of the web in diplomacy, as the world endures the dynamics of a postpandemic era. Inclusionism aims to build a vocabulary that is relevant in this postpandemic environment in the making by taking into its lexicon the knowledge and practices of the non-Western, the indigenous: in other words, those actors at the edge of international relations who remain invisible or whose voices are marginalized in discussions that occur in global international society 1.2. The challenge in this context is a recognition that the evolution of technology explained in this volume risks making those actors presently invisible in GIS 1.2 visible in ways that are harmful to local identity and tradition. The risk is that their voices may only be heard as the echo of larger forces that remain well beyond their ability to control.

The focus on additional levels of analysis in the ethics of personal data collection in international relations illustrates tensions between the PRC and Taiwan in a different way. Identity politics leaves its mark on the making of global international relations. In this volume's call for increasing distribution of agency in the name of inclusionism, the authors of this conclusion recognize the need to reconsider Slaughter's call for a new vocabulary of the web.

The COVID-19 pandemic gives Taiwan the opportunity in its personal data-driven response to emphasize its specificity vis-à-vis the People's Republic of China. The pandemic response makes clear that Taiwan's experience is that of a distinct community despite the Chinese Communist Party's (CCP's) determination to pursue a policy of reunification looking ahead to 2049. Taiwan's experience, as the Lee chapter explains, is that of a vibrant democracy. It is clear, given the PRC's actions in Xinjiang, that Taiwan's experience is that of a distinct community. In her chapter, Davis elaborates on the lack of data to account for the breadth of human rights abuses in China against the Uyghur people since 2016. She recommends a constructivist approach to hack The Party in China. Davis aims to allow the reader to account for the power dynamics at play—the potential Thucydides Trap regarding the United States as well as the few options available to Uyghurs. Her approach tries to account for The Party's agency to incite change in the present situation.

Inclusionism, in the context of international relations and environmental stewardship, which includes human participations in designed space, is specifically a hack on systems that stifle the agency of individuals. Constructivism is an avenue of opportunity for the inclusionist argument that individuals have an intrinsic value and that institutions, including The Party, are only well formed when they continually compel their individuals to self-identify the functional needs of the institution. While constructivists Martha Finnemore (1996) and Alexander Wendt (1999) challenge neorealism's conceptualization of the distribution of material capabilities by agents in an international structure, they hold that social structure is "ontologically prior to and generative of agents." Furthermore, social structure creates actors; it is not created by them (1996). An inclusionist would argue that the evolution of identifying personal data and the new reality that the data of our lives are not separate from our lives have made the immaterial capabilities of humankind into something material. Moreover, a socially constructive, meaning cultural value, system is in fact the newest driver of material or what we should call a technologically deterministic, or tangible, value system.

The plight of Uyghur individuals has a direct impact on the health of the Chinese environment, as they compel actors to identify material gaps from inside and outside of that environment. Per inclusionism honoring their intrinsic value would require a global system that prioritizes the distribution of goods, both products and services, to all identifiable individuals as they exercise the discovery of their personal agency from the community with which they stem. Adequate human engagement must be at the center of good environmental stewardship. Per the introduction to this volume, we insist that individuals are at their best when they identify with a community and communities are only at their best when they identify all their individuals. This truth is at the core of the notion that people have an intrinsic value.

In the chapter by Adams, agency is a mechanism of identifying culture. She looks at people as operating systems via their cell phones and how they communicate decision via their devices—real-time replicas of our agency. Adams' chapter describes how the United States, during the Trump Administration, refused to regulate beyond innovation-oriented strategies to protect data privacy, which seems to align with the "West versus the Rest" protection-oriented positioning, yet possibly misunderstanding data privacy's neorealistic implications. Using Slaughter's networks strategies, Adams points out that, without regulatory recognition of the role of networks, individual agency is still constrained through a consent-only privacy protection strategy. However, she notes that the notion of constrained agency may not reflect the reality that smartphones have delivered increased global agency in the COVID-19 tracking and ecosystem development. Adams shows how the US government has opted to engage Data Platforms, that is, "Supernodes," to ensure regulatory compliance assuming international leadership in the privacy space. By describing a Data Platform as nonstate actors behaving like nation-states, Adams conveys that this reality sits in defiance of Waltz's notion of state actors. The lack of

US regulation, clearly defining Data Platform roles, allows these Supernodes to exist as part of and subject to the US government.

Taken in their entirety, the chapters in this volume contrast the reality between the actions of a nation-state's security and that of the individual's social media identities applied to a nation-state's security. The additional chapters in the closing section by Garcia and Riley at the USAFA and Goodney Lea and D'Silva documenting the context in India elaborate on the identification of women's trauma from sexual assault in a nation-state's closed and open security system, respectively. The military police in the USAFA and the local police forces of India adhere to two different organizational cultures, per their locales and their functional roles in their locale's security apparatus. The USAFA teaches that all cadets adopt a warrior culture and survive the rigors of military life. Survival strategies vary, yet a popular one is to "blend into the crowd and do one's best not to bring unwanted attention onto oneself." The difference between the chapters from Garcia–Riley and Goodney Lea–D'Silva is one between exploring genderless uniformed personnel and segregation of genders, respectively. The functionality of stewardship differs from private to public organizations; yet the use of personal data to identify the needs of participants continues to help those organizations evolve in this era.

The USAFA introduced the Enhanced Access, Acknowledge, Act (EAAA) sexual assault resistance program to scrutiny to the extent that EAAA was unfair to both men and women. In these efforts the American military has questioned the very design of uniform differentiation from male to female and addressing superiors with the prefix "Ma'am" or "Sir"; all of this was happening during the same timeline that American citizens of transgender experience were shunned from military service by the former president of the United States: the gender lines are blurred through the scrutiny of a methodology like the EAAA. In India, crowd-sourced data presents some unique opportunities for insights that can greatly enhance governance of a society by empowering residents, survivors of gender-based violence, and would-be allies (bystanders) to be visible. The Safecity geomapping software-as-a-service (SaaS) application transformed the policing practices of notably dangerous regions of Delhi, a city of more than 18,000,000 people.

When applying this research to the seamingly hybrid environment, namely, the *technologically-constructive* reality of inclusionism, where the social constructivist ranks are not pitted against the technological determinist ranks, it is necessary to acknowledge that technologies come in three rigid forms: methodologies, hardware, and software.

Methodologies	Hardware	Software
Processes	Able to touch	Unable to touch

Tech is anything that we make: even the lives we make. The oldest types of tech humanity and humanoids might reference are hammers in the form of sticks or stones (hardware), human-made fire from hardware (software), and language (methodologies). The methods we use to communicate experiences with hardware–software are our greatest technologies, at least, from a usability standpoint. Law is a tech. Policy is a tech. Text is a tech. Our ability to communicate everything that we can and cannot touch to the next generation is empowered by that underlined information tech. We are currently in a post-Information Age. We mean that we have identified what can be information. We have identified all matter, even the dark matter, and endeavor to place a data point on everything that matters, until it all does. Data and further personal data are not the new oil or water, data is the new matter. Data is everything that we think matters; in our efforts to include everyone in the interconnected relations of our international community, we must identify the agency of their individual experience, down to the data points, to save our collective life and enhance our environmental stewardship potential.

Acknowledgment of people by the data-points transforms our thinking away from nature, state, and system, the original images of international relations. This volume expands the concept of race with reference to the legacy of colonialism and the persistent inequalities in the world deepened by the uneven impact of the COVID-19 pandemic on countries around the globe. Its chapters bring in non-Western perspectives from China and Iran as well as India to bring diverse voices into our understanding of why it is significant to consider the ethics of personal data collection at the edge of international relations, thereby deepening our understanding of the immersion in the local. The contributions in this volume speak to what Finnemore highlights, namely, tensions and cultural feedback from periphery to core, which is a less explored direction in the literature of international relations as a discipline.

By framing inclusionism in a more specific International Relations/international relations, theory/practice context, Mazzucelli's ideas about the successor lens to environmental stewardship relate to the way nature must be brought more centrally into the conflict analysis discourse. For example, we are called as citizens of the planet to consider the ways in which indigenous voices are raised in global discussions about the pandemic. The indigenous voices have much to contribute given their unique experiences of the interactions between different species, human and nonhuman, and nature. Their concerns are raised specifically in discussions among members in the Fletcher community learning together during an Executive Education online seminar, "2021—A Super Year for Sustainable Development Diplomacy," taught by Dean Rachel Kyte, which features commentary by Hindou Oumarou Ibrahim, an environmental activist and geographer who is the coordinator of the Association of Peul Women and Autochthonous Peoples of Chad (AFPAT) as well as the codirector of the pavilion of the World Indigenous Peoples' Initiative and Pavilion during COP21, COP22, and COP23. In the volume's afterword, Dean Joshua Cooper reiterates these concerns, thereby extending the reflections introduced by Secretary-General Azza Karam in the foreword.

As Niall Ferguson argues (2021), globalization needs circuit breakers, namely, social networks that must address the fragility demonstrated by the spread of COVID-19, to cite India at present as just one example. The other aspect of inclusionism that Mazzucelli observes in the specific International Relations/international relations context relates to the nature of data in economic terms. Unlike oil or other material resources, data is, as Slaughter and McCormick state, "nonrival"—"used simultaneously and repeatedly by any number of firms or people without being diminished" (*Foreign Affairs*, 2021). This context opens greater possibilities for more people in a greater number of countries around the world to be on the grid over time unless states acting as gatekeepers close off that access to billions, that is, the CCP in China, the BJP in India, and the clerics in Iran. This challenge to the spread of democracy is a constant theme developed by various contributors in this volume, which prompts further research inquiry to elaborate on inclusionism looking ahead.

Moreover, the rapid spread of the pandemic in India with tragic results for that country, Asia, and the world must be understood in the context of a traditional religious festival, *Kumbh Mela*, as the BJP also seeks further to consolidate its political influence through mass election rallies. Secretary-General Karam's foreword highlights the nature of the twenty-first-century dilemma humanity faces:

> At worst, threats facing our world at present are significantly amplified by our very environment, Planet Earth, struggling to survive. Today we deal not only with a global pandemic: its moral, financial, and cultural ramifications abound. The Novel Coronavirus hit our world at a time when each and all our institutions, political, economic, financial, and social, are lame, or limping along, with their credibility tarnished by all manner of human weaknesses. Not least of these is an amplification of multiple forms of intersecting discrimination combined with a deficit of ideology as well as leadership. Our religious institutions are as tarnished as all others. Some suffer from a ludicrous sense of territoriality, internal and externally oriented struggles for power and influence amid theological disputes, racism, sexism, political corruption [...] the list is endless. Our institutions, created to be the means of liberation, egalitarianism, economic and financial sustainability, and accountability, have become, possibly, our Achilles' heel. If the multi-governmental is struggling, it is because of the Darwinian

prevalence of the survival of the fittest—rather than the ethos of collaboration and connectivity.

The data about the nature of this irresponsible governmental behavior in India is not readily accessible. It is the inequalities during the pandemic that personal data captures, which ask for intersectional analysis and the new vocabulary, building on Slaughter's observation, to address the inequities that are the concern of inclusionism. The realities of a new millennium prompt this volume to question Waltz from the vantage point of what presently occurs in our postpandemic world. The end of the twentieth-century bridge to the early twenty-first is in the changed nature of conflict—primarily from interstate to largely intrastate. Inclusionism speaks to this revolution in liberal, capitalist-oriented globalization, which cuts into the hierarchical pyramid of power that defined the short twentieth century, 1914–[1989] 1991. This volume questions the nature of society as civil and global, particularly as the COVID-19 pandemic renders the majority increasingly marginalized and the chaos in most of the developing world is instrumentalized. Just as the international system continues to expand with more states than ever in the United Nations, Waltz's structural realism incessantly calls for the interstate system to contract. In contrast, this volume introduces reflections that speak to conflict in a postpandemic era, which poses distinct challenges to the maintenance of peace as more than simply the absence of war, particularly in local environments.

Neorealism in the twenty-first century focuses narrowly, exclusively on the People's Republic of China and the United States at the apex of the pyramid; yet the impact of the COVID-19 pandemic calls for the distribution of more agency as democracy, experienced with a small "d," calls for the evolution of humanity. Humanity in the twenty-first century is less white, as human security is more concerned by issues related to race and gender. These changes in humanity stem from colonial legacies of empires in history as well as the postcolonial interplay of present-day globalization and the enduring overlays of imperialistic control. These overlays persist in the education systems, bureaucratic structures, and personal connections of government elites in developing countries. Data platform activities also support Slaughter's description of what the authors term Supernodes, which have their own infrastructure and wield extraordinary power in the network structures that connect users to other networks employing their services. This volume's analysis supports Slaughter's description of how these Supernodes behave differently from chessboards, seem to act as chessboard equals, and whose activities international relations scholars must consider in future research inquiries looking ahead in this century.

References

Acharya, A., and Buzan, B. (2019) *The Making of Global International Relations: Origins and Evolution of IR at Its Centenary*. Cambridge: Cambridge University Press.

Doyle, M. (1997) *Ways of War and Peace*. New York: W.W. Norton.

Ferguson, N. (2021) *Doom: The Politics of Catastrophe*. New York: Penguin Press.

Finnemore, M. (1996) *Norms, Culture, and World Politics: Insights from Sociology's Institutionalism* [online]. Available at https://home.gwu.edu/~finnemor/articles/1996_institutionalism_io.pdf, George Washington University Press, p. 333 (accessed March 15, 2021).

Slaughter, A.-M., and LaForge, G. (2021) "Opening Up the Order: More Inclusive International System." *Foreign Affairs*, 100 (2) [online]. Available at https://www.foreignaffairs.com/articles/world/2021-02-16/opening-order (accessed April 26, 2021).

Slaughter, M., and McCormick, D. (2021) "Data Is Power." *Foreign Affairs*, 100 (3), [online]. Available at https://www.foreignaffairs.com/articles/united-states/2021-04-16/data-power-new-rules-digital-age (accessed April 26, 2021).

Wendt, A. (1999) *Social Theory of International Politics*. Cambridge: Cambridge University Press.

AFTERWORD

Dean Joshua Cooper,
International Training Center for Teaching
Peace and Human Rights (Geneva)

Building Forward in Beauty and Balance: A Decade of Action Rooted in Human and Indigenous Rights

We are in the decade of action to save our planet and the people that inhabit our Island Earth. Even the world's top diplomat knows we are far from respecting indigenous knowledge rooted in respect for nature. The UN secretary-general calls for a truce today in the war on nature and calls for new relationship building on indigenous wisdom to nurture our world.

UN Secretary-General Antonio Guterres said in the foreword of *Making Peace with Nature*, "Our war on nature has left the planet broken. This is senseless and suicidal. The consequences of our recklessness are already apparent in human suffering [...] and the accelerating erosion of life on Earth."

UN Secretary-General Guterres recognizes humanity is capable of changing views based on new values, citing, "By transforming how we view nature, we can recognize its true value. By reflecting this value in policies, plans and economic systems, we can channel investments into activities that restore nature and are rewarded for it."

"Making peace with nature is the defining task of the coming decades. We must seize the opportunity presented by the COVID-19 crisis to accelerate change. This year, several major international conferences, including on climate change, biodiversity, and desertification, provide an opportunity to increase ambition and action [...] Our central objective is to build a global coalition for carbon neutrality."

"An inclusive world at peace with nature can ensure that people enjoy better health and the full respect of their human rights so they can live with dignity on a healthy planet."

The pandemic provides a point of reference regarding what really matters the most and challenges all measurements we cherish as meaningful. Inclusionism, as defined by Mazzucelli, Keith, and Adams in this volume, integrates nature into world affairs and places the indigenous wisdom of environmental stewardship at the core of international relations while demanding a decolonization of all minds on behalf of a genuine grassroots global justice movement.

When we are not too busy making a living, there is a reimagination of the good life and how we can all contribute to a better world. Development becomes much deeper. We begin to challenge current practices and narrow definitions exploring beyond economic measurements toward well-being and culture those contributions to development of the self and the larger society.

We are one world. Our connectivity is evident in the challenges and changes facing humanity and our Island Earth. Our collective destiny depends on our ability to advocate and advance a legal as well as a human rights-based approach cherishing our diversity and commitment to dignity for all.

We must understand that humankind has rights to clean air, water, and a healthy environment. In this context, we must consistently and diligently protect our core civil and political rights—freedom of thought, expression, opinion, culture, peaceful assembly and partake in government—to guarantee humanity has a home for the future.

Our actions are grounded in the understanding that we are more important than me as we learn how to be fully human while listening to Indigenous Peoples across the Pacific and beyond. We have so much to learn together. We must listen, learn, and then lead in new direction. Pacific Islands Peoples share dedication to human dignity and personhood with the awareness of how we should all treat each other.

Indigenous methodologies provide deeper comprehension of our world. Indigenous ancestral wisdom supports modern science, providing path to what we must do. Together we must recognize the cosmology through service and stewardship of our Island Earth. Deep science and spirituality explain the relationship with the Earth. We can better comprehend if we listen to the indigenous stories and songs as well as experience the dancing and dreaming. Nature cannot be considered as the "Other." Nature is us. More importantly, our collective existence depends on how we care for nature.

During the pandemic, we have occasions to practice more of what we would preach and teach around the planet about rights and responsibilities in daily practices. We can help each other and heal our Earth. Unity is required with a commitment to human rights and social change rooted in diversity and dignity. Equality and equity must be the ethos for our multistakeholder, multicultural, multidisciplinary, and multigenerational movement. As we aim to build forward better in beauty and balance, we must bring love to life. We must break down barriers and build bridges among all sectors of society as we shatter outdated silos. We must trust in transformative tenacity and indigenous tools willingly shared with the world so that we understand family is everything and everyone just as everywhere there is family. As the human family, we must respect and protect our earth, including its nonhuman species.

We must create educational centers like the one above Honolua Bay, far beyond teaching and learning, yet building tools for transcendent thinking. The educational centers must create connections, catalyze conversations, coordinate campaigns, and change conditions. Such centers can touch and transcend layers for liberation beginning in the consciousness, and then in the classroom, the campus, the community, the city hall, the capitols, and eventually our emerging global civil society. Our initiatives must have an intensity for infinity as we nurture nature. We must listen to intuition and welcome insights from around the world.

As we confront multiple crises of the moment, at least two forces face us. Our moral compass must guide us going forward. As navigators seeking nonviolence and nature, there are constellations that can guide our governments, companies, and civil society. One crisis, that of fundamentalism, feeds on fear, which is rooted in reactionary policies of fascist regimes maintained by authoritarianism, disaster capitalism, increased technology, intensive surveillance, and corporate control. Other social forces illustrate images of the world we hold dear and can already hear and hold in our hearts: human rights for all rooted in rule of law and love, democracy delivering dignity and dedication to diversity, a regenerative circular economy based on equity, high touch guiding emerging high-tech honoring indigenous traditional knowledge, and glocalization for peace and abundance generating good around the globe. Join us on this journey for justice and joy.

It is no exaggeration to say that the fate of the human experiment depends on the outcome of this voyage. We face benighted extinction or enlightened existence on the Island Earth.

CONTRIBUTORS

Andrea Adams, PhD, JD, MBA, is an assistant professor in the Crime Justice and Security Program in the College of Arts and Sciences at the University of the District of Columbia (UDC). Andrea is on the Advisory Board of the RedDot Corporation, the parent of the Safecity.in, a smartphone app. The Safecity app creates awareness of street harassment and provides a place for women and other disadvantaged communities to break their silence and report personal assault experiences. Andrea's work helps design the organization's informed consent, privacy, and security provisions of the app, and one aspect of her research agenda focuses on the ethics of smartphone app use. Andrea is a licensed attorney and has 25+ years of business experience in labor and employment law.

Celeste Brevard has a Bachelor of Science (BS) degree in International Business and Communications and is a recent graduate of NYU's Graduate School of Arts and Science's International Relations program. While there, she concentrated in International Law and focused on International Humanitarian Law, Women's Rights, Immigration, and the Environment among other fields. She is working as a policy fellow at the Syrian Emergency Task Force. She currently lives in California with her husband and dog.

Megan Cameron is a multilingual development practitioner and qualitative researcher with 5+ years of experience working for international development institutions in crisis and development contexts. Megan has a keen interest in sociopolitical development, a humanitarian focus, and international relations. Her education includes a master's degree in development studies from York University. She is passionate about empowering refugee, marginalized communities and children, and this passion has developed further through her field experience in Lebanon and Iran along with her academic interest in international development.

Joshua Cooper is an academic, advocate, author, analyst, and activist based in Hawaii. Joshua has created, crafted, and coordinated over 50 unique courses in multiple fields for 100 plus classes at the University of Hawaii. Cooper has been dean and professor at various International Human Rights Law programs in Europe, including Global Leadership Academy for Human Rights Advocacy. Cooper is CEO of The GOOD Group and executive director, Hawai'i Institute for Human Rights. Cooper holds positions of senior global advocacy manager; senior director of communications & community engagement; senior director of global governance & international initiatives; senior director of research, policy & law with multiple peoples' movements, NGOs, human rights defenders' associations. Cooper is cochair of Universal Periodic Review Task Force for US Human Rights Network and serves on the US Human Rights Cities Alliance national steering committee.

Mary Davis was born and raised in the southern United States, spending her formative years in the Atlanta suburb of Stone Mountain, Georgia. She studied Linguistics and French as an undergraduate student and later received a master's degree in linguistics. Outside of the classroom, Mary has traveled and lived in the Languedoc-Roussillon region of France as well as the Sichuan Province of the PRC, studying language, teaching English, and eating great food. Mary now lives in New York with her partner and twin sons, while working as an advisor at New York University to support the international student community. She is currently pursuing her second master's degree at NYU's Center for Global Affairs with interests in US–China relations and peacebuilding.

Elsa Marie D'Silva is the founder of Red Dot Foundation (India) and president of Red Dot Foundation Global (United States). Its platform Safecity crowdsources personal experiences of sexual violence and abuse in public spaces. Since Safecity started in Dec 2012, it has become the largest crowd map on the issue in India and abroad. She is listed as one of BBC Hindi's 100 Women and has won several awards including Government of India Niti Aayog's #WomenTransformingIndia award. In 2017, she was awarded the Global Leadership Award by Vital Voices in the presence of Secretary Hillary Clinton. She is a coeditor and author of *The Demographic Dividend and the Power of Youth* published by Anthem Press on behalf of the German Federal Foreign Office's Global Diplomacy Lab.

Sophia Ehmke, originally from Germany, finished her secondary education in the UK and graduated summa cum laude with a Bachelor of Law degree (LLB) in European Law and a Master of Law degree (LLM) in European Law with a specialization in market integration from Maastricht University, Netherlands. She is particularly passionate about human rights, migration, and asylum law and the new EU Digital Service Act. She has worked as legal officer for the Dutch chapter of a global NGO (Liter of Light) and is currently a *stagiare* at the European Parliament (DG European Parliamentary Research Service—EPRS) in Brussels, Belgium.

Lynne Chandler Garcia is associate professor of political science at the US Air Force Academy. Her areas of research include sexual assault at military academies, empathy and efficacy in political behavior, foreign policy, military operations, and the art of pedagogy for underprivileged learners. Before coming to the Air Force Academy, she served as a military analyst at the Combat Studies Institute, Fort Leavenworth, Kansas, where she coauthored a series of 11 books covering US Army operations in Afghanistan and Iraq. She received her PhD at the University of Maryland, College Park.

C. Ann Hollifield, PhD, is professor emerita at the University of Georgia in the United States. Her research focuses on media economics, management, and news media viability in changing market conditions, work that started while she was a Robert Bosch Foundation Fellow in Germany in 1991–92. In 2006, she founded the first graduate degree program in the United States in media analytics. She is the author/editor of seven books and nearly 50 other research articles and book chapters. She continues to work internationally as a consultant on news media viability research, and she currently is authoring a textbook on data analytics for media professionals. Prior to her academic career, she spent 15 years as a journalist and senior editor in newspapers and television.

Azza Karam, PhD, serves as secretary-general of Religions for Peace International. Prior to this, she served in diverse positions in the United Nations: as chair of *the United Nations Inter-Agency Task Force on Religion*; senior advisor on culture at the United Nations Population Fund; lead facilitator for *the United Nations Strategic Learning Exchanges on Religion-Development-Diplomacy*, coordinator of the UN's Global Interfaith Networks of 600 faith-based organizations; executive secretary for the UN Multi-Faith Advisory Council; and coordinator of UNDP's Arab Human Development Reports (2004–7). She has published scholarly works, since 1993, in several languages, on political Islam, gender, conflict and peacemaking, education, and transnational religious dynamics. She is also a professor of religion and development at the Vrije Universiteit of Amsterdam, the Netherlands.

James Felton Keith is an award-winning engineer and economist who was the first Black LGBTQ person to run for US Congress or any of America's federal offices. As an author and activist, his Data Unions redefined the labor movement and personal data as the natural resource driving all corporate productivity. As an entrepreneur, he established the first international standard certification for corporate diversity and inclusion and the first insurance policy for a lack-of-inclusion based on an "inclusion score." His biopolitical philosophy, inclusionism, is at the forefront of human rights advocacy and international relations, and each week he hosts the WHCR 90.3 FM radio show, Inclusionism, from NYC.

Suzanne Goodney Lea, PhD is CEO of Red Dot Foundation Global, https://reddotfoundation.org, which strives to make public spaces safer using crowd mapping and community engagement. Dr. Goodney Lea is an assistant professor of crime, justice, and security studies at the University of the District of Columbia in Washington, DC. Her academic research explores place as a unit of analysis for understanding crime, gender-based violence, police use of deadly force, and ways of engaging communities using new technologies and social engagement to enhance the safety of their neighborhoods and the effectiveness of their governance policies. Dr. Goodney Lea serves on the Board of Advisors for #DontMuteDC. She is coauthor of *Let's Talk Politics: Restoring Civility Through Exploratory Discussion*.

Jasmine Lee is an NYU international relations MA graduate. Currently Lee is a researcher at a Taiwan-based research group IORG (Information Operation Research Group) and the coeditor of an online media US–Taiwan Watch. Jasmine writes a column at the News Lens and is the joint author of an upcoming book *Why U.S. matters? A comprehensive analysis of Taiwan-U.S. relations* (Linking Publishing House, forthcoming).

Colette Mazzucelli, PhD, EdM, MALD is President (Academia), Global Listening Centre, and has taught since 2004 on graduate faculty, GSAS & SPS, at NYU New York, https://as.nyu.edu/faculty/colette-mazzucelli.html. She is Lead Series Editor, Ethics of Personal Data Collection, Anthem Press. A BMW Foundation Responsible Leader, Colette serves on the Advisory Board of Higher Education, Irish Tech Society, https://www.irishtechsociety.ie/. At Pioneer Academics, she teaches international relations (Europe) mentoring students across continents, https://pioneeracademics.com/. Colette is the author and/or editor of seven volumes, including *France and Germany at Maastricht*, https://www.amazon.com/France-Germany-Maastricht-Negotiations-Contemporary/dp/0815335938. Since 1993, her biography appears in numerous *Marquis Who's Who* publications, including *Marquis Who's Who in America* and *Marquis Who's Who in the World*, https://wwlifetimeachievement.com/2019/01/07/colette-mazzucelli/.

John Riley is professor in the Department of Political Science at the US Air Force Academy, where he teaches and conducts research related to international relations, human rights, and security in fragile states. Since rejoining the faculty in 2015, he has directed courses in genocides, mass atrocities, and geopolitics. Dr. Riley received his PhD in political science from the George Washington University. He is a coeditor for *American Defense Policy 9th Edition*, and his research has been published in such venues as *Terrorism, and Political Violence, Armed Forces & Society*, and the *Wisconsin Journal of International Law*.

INDEX

"Don't Ask Don't Tell" 174
#MeToo movement 158–59
1948 Genocide Convention 121

abuse clause 53–54
AC19 App 81
accountability xii, 17, 24–25, 48, 65, 79–80, 84–85, 106–8, 133–34, 165–66, 181, 196–97
Act on the Protection of Personal Information 111–12
Acxiom 138
advertising 41–42, 56–58, 60–61, 138–39
advocacy xiii, 9, 121, 122, 171, 199, 203, 205
Afghanistan 73–74, 204–5
AFPAT 195–96
Africa xii, xiii, 30–31, 99–101, 133, 164–65
agency vii, ix, 9–11, 12–14, 34–35, 36, 81, 109–10, 112, 123, 132–33, 147, 165, 171, 181, 189–90, 192–94, 195, 197, 205
agonistic realism; *see also* realism 9, 10–11, 12–13, 93, 115–16, 125, 191, 192–93, 197
AI 30–31, 36–37, 39–40, 41–42, 65
AIDS xiii
Air Force Academy 17, 171
algorithm 39–40
American vii–viii, 4, 33–34, 48, 69, 73, 76, 115, 194, 207
Amnesty International 121–23
anonymous 63–64, 134–35, 137–39, 146, 155, 157, 159–60, 175
anti-apartheid xii
Apple 2–3, 8, 30–31, 34–35, 111, 143–44, 145, 147
Armenian Genocide 116–17
artificial intelligence (AI) 30–31, 36–37, 39–40, 41–42, 65
Asia Pacific 133, 134

Asia Pacific Economic Cooperative's 134
Atlantic Council 77–78
Audrey Tang 96
authoritarian 23, 25, 26, 27, 41–43, 48–49, 117–18, 124–25, 164–65, 166, 189–90
authoritarian regime 25, 26, 27, 41–42
authoritarianism 1, 26, 28–29, 109–10, 201
Azerbaijan 71

Baha'i xi
balancing 49, 51–52, 56–58, 145–46
Bangalore 161
basic human security; *see also* human security 115, 122, 197
Beijing 36–37, 97, 98, 104, 118–19, 120–21
Belt and Road Initiative 26–27, 30–31
Biden Administration 136
big data 30–31, 37–38, 41, 138, 189–90
biodiversity 199
Black Lives Matter 40–42, 155–56, 164
blockchain technology 132–33, 147–48
blue emergency phone stands 163
Bluetooth technology 95–96
border tensions xiii
Bosnian 116–17
Brazil 1–2, 30–31, 165
Brexit 47
Buddhist xi
Bulgarian 99
Bureau of Justice Statistics (BJS) 165
Burton's Basic Human Needs theory 98
business innovation 132

cadet 17, 171–72, 173, 176–77, 178, 179, 180–84, 185, 194
California Consumer Privacy Act 24–25, 106–7

INDEX

campus; *see also* college 17, 160, 163, 171, 172–74, 178, 179, 180, 201
Canada 71, 99–101, 134, 135
carbon neutrality 199
case studies 1, 2–4, 5–6
censoring 36–37, 58
Central Bank of Iran 77
Center for Disease Control's (CDC) 165–66
Central Epidemic Command Center 95–96
chain of command 175–76
Charter on Citizens' Rights 82
Chessboard and the Web; *see also* chessboard and web or chessboards 7–8, 16–17, 132, 140–41, 147, 161, 189, 190
China xii, 1, 4–5, 14, 15–16, 21–22, 25, 26–32, 34–35, 36–38, 39–40, 41, 43, 70–72, 75–76, 77–79, 93–94, 95–96, 97–102, 104–5, 110, 111–13, 115, 116–19, 120–25, 133, 164–65, 189–90, 191–92, 195, 196, 197, 204
China Cables 121
Chinese Communist Party 15–16, 115, 118–19, 125, 192
Cholera 71–72
churches, Christian xiii
CIA 23–24, 36, 72
Cisco Visual Networking Index 133
civic participation 4–5, 15, 95–96
civil war xiii, 118–19
clean air 200
Clearview AI 41–42
climate change vii, 1–2, 13–14, 199
CNN 120–21
collaboration xii, 86, 96–97, 196–97
college; *see also* campus vii–viii, 17, 160, 163, 171, 172–74, 178, 179, 180, 201, 204–5
commercial 23, 27–28, 36, 41–42, 49, 56–58, 60–61
community vii, viii–ix, 2–3, 8–9, 12–13, 15, 17, 23, 36, 73–74, 96, 121–22, 139, 142–43, 146, 148, 157, 160, 163–64, 166, 167, 172, 189–90, 192, 193, 195–96, 201
confidential 175–76
conflict mitigation xiii

conflicts xi, 115, 118–19, 144
Congressional Research Services 133–34
connectivity xii, 160–61, 196–97, 200
constructivism; *see also* social constructivism 12–13, 94, 97, 104–5, 112–13, 124, 191, 192–93
contact tracing 2, 4–5, 75–76, 82, 83, 144–45
contactless payments 77
coronavirus; *see also* Covid-19, global pandemic vii, ix, xii, xiii, 1–3, 4–5, 8, 9, 10–11, 13–14, 15, 16–17, 77–79, 80, 81, 82, 83, 84, 85, 94, 98, 101–2, 104–5, 108, 112–13, 132–33, 144, 147, 155–56, 162–63, 182–83, 190–92, 195, 196–97, 199
corporate control 201
Council of Europe 50–51, 62–63
COVAX 77–78
Covid-19; *see also* coronavirus, global pandemic vii, ix, xii, xiii, 1–3, 4–5, 8, 9, 10–11, 13–14, 15, 16–17, 77–79, 80, 81, 82, 83, 84, 85, 94, 98, 101–2, 104–5, 108, 112–13, 132–33, 144, 147, 155–56, 162–63, 182–83, 190–92, 195, 196–97, 199
crime-mapped data 161–62
critical medical supplies 73
Cross Border Privacy Rules 134
Cross-border viii, 65, 111–12, 131–32, 133–34
Cross-Strait Conflict 93
crowd mapping platforms 2–3
crowdfunding campaign 104

Darwinian xii, 196–97
data collection vii, viii, 1, 2–3, 4–5, 15, 22, 31–32, 41–43, 83, 84–85, 141–42, 181, 191, 192, 195, 206
Data Duck LLC 159
data fundamentalism 39–40
data mining 39–40, 41, 42–43, 138, 189–90
data platform 141–42, 145–46, 148, 149, 189, 190, 193–94, 197
data privacy 6, 8, 16–17, 105–8, 109–10, 111–12, 131–34, 136, 140–41, 144, 145–46, 147, 148, 193–94

Data Protection Directive 138
declining birth rates 120–21
Delhi 156–57, 160–61, 194
democracy 1, 10–11, 14, 21–22, 23, 24–25, 32, 40–43, 48–49, 51, 56–58, 64, 97–98, 101, 105–6, 108, 110, 111–12, 117–18, 160, 166, 190, 192, 196, 197, 201
democratic regime 23–24
denominations, Christian xi
Department of Commerce 135
Department of Defense 17, 22–23, 25, 34–35, 171, 173, 174, 178, 179
Department of State 76, 101–2
desertification 199
development 1, 16–17, 22–23, 26, 33–34, 51, 61–62, 76–77, 93, 97–98, 101–2, 104, 105, 109, 111–13, 118–19, 132–33, 139, 178, 191–92, 200, 205
differential privacy 139
digital lives 8
Digital Single Market Commission 134–35
diplomat 199
disaster capitalism 201
discrimination xii, 11, 30, 59, 163–64, 178, 196–97
disinformation 49–51, 52, 59, 77–78, 190
domestic law 3, 54
DP-3T code 145
due diligence 63–64
duties and responsibilities 49, 57, 61–65

EAAA 171–72, 179–80, 182, 183, 184–85, 194
Ebola xiii
ECHR 15, 49, 51–52, 53–54, 55, 58–59, 62–63, 64–65
ecological justice 132
economic growth 69, 84, 111–12, 191–92
economic inequality 4–5
economic power 93
economic terrorism 73–74
ecosystem 3–4, 7–8, 12, 17, 62–63, 64–65, 132–33, 146, 147, 190, 193–94
ECtHR 15, 49, 51–52, 53–54, 55–58, 59–65
egalitarianism xii, 13, 196–97
elections 47, 49, 55–56, 57, 71–72

Enhanced Access, Acknowledge, Act (EAAA) 171, 194
enigmatic outsider 15–16, 115, 117
enlightenment 69
environmental stewardship 1–2, 7, 11, 191, 192–93, 195–96, 200
ethanol 77–78
ethics vii, viii, ix, 1, 2–3, 5, 7–8, 10, 36–37, 62, 192, 195
Europe 10, 24–25, 42–43, 49–52, 62–63, 64, 65, 77–79, 99, 101, 106–7, 164
European Commission 49–51, 111–12
European Court of Human Rights (ECtHR), 15, 49, 51–53, 54–56, 57–59, 59–61, 61–64, 64
European Union xiii, 1, 47, 65, 73, 75–76, 132–33, 134–35

facial recognition 29–30, 39–40
faith inspiration xi–xii
faith-inspired civic actors xi–xii
fake news 8, 15, 47–51, 52, 53, 54, 55, 56–63, 64–65, 190
Federal Bureau of Investigation (FBI), 39, 40, 171
Federal Data Protection Act 109
Federal Trade Commission 32–33, 133–34
Fletcher Community 195–96
forced sterilization 120–21
foreign affairs; *see also* global relations, world affairs 28–29, 101–2, 115, 125, 196
foreign policy 69, 74, 76, 79–80, 101–2, 116–17, 124–25
Fourth Amendment 24–25, 32, 33–34, 41–42
France 49–50, 56, 59, 62–63
freedom of expression 48–50, 51–52, 53–58, 61–62, 63–65, 97–98, 190
freedom of speech 47
fundamental right 49, 51, 64, 109
Future of Privacy Forum 136

gatekeeping 8
gender 1, 5, 13–14, 81, 109–10, 155–56, 162, 164, 167, 172, 174, 184, 191, 194, 197
gender-based violence 155–56, 164, 167, 194

General Data Protection Regulation 10, 134–35
genocide vii, 5, 15–16, 59, 115–17, 121, 124
geopolitics 69, 84–85, 190
Germany 49–50, 54, 55–56, 134–35
global civil society 201
global coalition 199
Global Data Privacy Regulation 6
global epicenter 72
global foreign policy paradigm 116–17
global information technology 14
global international society 5–6, 189–90, 191–92
global justice movement 200
global mobile data traffic 133
global order 69
global pandemic; *see also* coronavirus, Covid-19, global pandemic, pandemic ix, xii, 4–5, 13–14, 105, 196–97
Global Positioning Systems 138–39
global relations; *see also* foreign affairs, world affairs 69
Global Times, The 26–27, 30–31, 122–24
Globalization 1–2, 10–11, 85, 191–92, 196, 197
Goa 161
Google 30–31, 36–39, 41–42, 106–7, 143–44, 145, 147
Grassroots 121–22, 200
Great Firewall of China 27, 37–38
Greece 55–56, 99

HarassMap Egypt 157
Health Information Accountability Act 133–34
Health Insurance Portability Accountability Act 17
heritage 94, 164–65
Hindu xi
HIPAA 17, 181, 183–84
HIV xiii
Holocaust xii, 59
Hong Kong 28–29, 41–42, 99–102, 110, 112, 123–24
Hong Kong Autonomy Act 123–24
Huawei 30–31
human intelligence xii–xiii

human rights 2–3, 8, 9, 10, 15, 24–25, 26–27, 28–30, 36–37, 48, 49, 58, 73–74, 99–101, 107–8, 113, 116–18, 120–23, 124–25, 192, 200–1
human rights, (rampant) violations of xi, 116–17, 121–22
human rights-based approach 200
Human Rights Watch 28–30, 122
human security 115, 122, 197
human suffering 199
humanitarian aid 190
humanitarian crisis 138
humanitarian intervention 116–17, 118–19
humanitarianism 116–17

identity viii, 4–5, 9, 11, 14, 15, 21–22, 23–24, 81, 94, 96–98, 99, 101–2, 104–5, 109, 112–13, 117, 118–19, 120, 121, 134–35, 137, 138–39, 147–48, 158–59, 173–74, 175, 184, 191–92
ideological confrontation 93
ideology xii, 4–5, 74, 123–24, 196–97
inclusionism viii, ix, 1–2, 8–9, 10–11, 12, 13–17, 189–90, 191–93, 194, 195–96, 197, 200, 205
India 1–3, 5, 13–14, 137, 156–58, 160–61, 166, 194, 195, 196–97
indigenous knowledge 199
Indigenous Peoples xiii, 200
Industrial Age 97–98
Industrial Revolution 69
industry guidelines 148
infection risk map 82
information and communications technology 81
Information Capitalism 22–23
Information Communication Technology (ICT) 30–31
information environment 23, 25, 34–35
information power 22–23, 25
Informed Consent 5, 139, 140, 143, 146, 147, 148–49, 159, 203
Inmobi 138–39
intelligence services xii–xiii
intent 50–51, 55, 58, 64, 163–64, 175, 178
Inter-Religious Councils xi–xii

INDEX

Interference 21–22, 49, 50, 51–52, 53–54, 56–58
international banking system 73
International Committee of the Red Cross 138
international law 3
International Monetary Fund 76–77
International Relations ix, xiii, 1–2, 3–4, 5, 6, 7, 8–9, 11, 12–13, 14, 85, 94, 105–6, 115–16, 140–41, 189, 190–93, 195–96, 197, 200
Internet 6–8, 21–22, 24–25, 26–31, 33–36, 41, 43, 51–52, 53, 62–65, 107–8, 147, 148, 189–90
internet content filtering 27
internment camps 121, 125
interfaith dialogue xi–xii
interfaith movement xii
IP University 160
Iran 1, 2–3, 15, 69, 70–80, 81, 82–83, 84–85, 190, 195, 196
Iran Nuclear Deal 73
Iranian military 75
Iranian Cyber Police 83
Iraq 73–74
Italy 99

Jain xi
Jamestown Foundation, The 120–21
Japan xii, xiii, 75–76, 97–98, 111–12
John Hopkins University 80, 95
journalism 50, 51, 62
journalists 40–41, 43, 49, 61–62, 63–65, 102, 121, 122, 190
judicial review 58, 64
jurisprudence 51–52
justice 59, 65, 116–17, 121–22, 132, 156–57, 164, 165, 172, 175–76, 183, 200

Kenya 160–61
Khamenei, Ali 71–72, 75, 76, 77–78
Korea xii, xiii, 1–2, 122–23
Kuwait 75–76

Lancet, The 74
Latin America xiii, 133
leadership 4, 47, 75, 131–32, 136, 148, 166, 172, 174, 176, 178, 185, 193–94, 196–97

Lebanon 71
legitimate aim 55–58
Let Taiwan Help 101–2
liberalism 13–14, 93, 101, 105–6, 110, 115–16, 191
liberation xii, 196–97, 201
Libya 117

Ma Ying-jeou Administration 93
machine learning 30, 37–38
man-made wars xiii
mandatory reporter 175–76, 181–82
manifestly ill-founded 58
margin of appreciation 56–58, 60, 61, 64–65
marketplace of ideas 47–48
Mask app 82
materialist 97–98
Mechanistic Physics 69
media; *see also* social media xiii, 6–7, 9, 15–16, 25, 28–29, 39, 40–41, 47, 52, 53, 58, 59–60, 62–63, 64–65, 73–74, 83, 98–99, 101–2, 122–24, 164, 166, 190, 194
medical terror 73–74
MediCapt 5
medRxiv 78–79
meta-rhino 115, 117–18
metadata 9, 136, 138
methodology 5–6, 51–52, 125, 147, 184, 194
Mexico 30–31, 40–41, 134, 135
Microsoft 37–38, 39, 41–42
Middle East 75–76, 133
military 13–14, 17, 36–37, 55–56, 74, 75, 93, 112–13, 118–19, 121, 138, 172, 173–76, 177, 178, 179, 180, 181–82, 183, 184, 194
military capacity 93
military justice system 172, 183
Ministry of Health and Medical Education 81–82
misinformation 15, 50, 75–76, 77–78, 84, 85, 190
MIT 36, 106
Mobile Health Act Interactive Tool 133–34
modern science 200
Moms Against Poverty 75–76

multicultural 200–1
multidisciplinary 200–1
multigenerational 200–1
multistakeholder 200–1
Mumbai 156–57, 160–61
Muslim xi, 99–101
Mustaan 77–78

nation-states xiii, 6–7, 14, 86, 131–32, 140–41, 193–94
National Development Fund 76–77
National Health Insurance 95–96
National Institute of Standards and Technology 39–40
National Science Foundation (NSF), 36
national security 55–56, 78–80, 99–101
National Security Council 78–79
nationalism xiii, 6, 10–11
nationalistic rhetoric xiii
neorealist 8–9
neorealistic 193–94
Netherlands, the 99
network centrality 132–33, 149
Networked Age 105
New York Times, The 39–40
Nigeria 122–23
Nodes 9, 141, 142–43, 146, 147–48
non-interventionism 115
North Korea 1–2, 122–23
NSA 33–35, 36
nuclear arms race xi
nuclear holocaust xii
nuclear weapons 74

Obama Consumer Privacy Bill of Rights 136
ostracism 17, 176, 177, 180

Pacific Islands Peoples 200
Pakistan 71, 73–74
pandemic; *see also* coronavirus, Covid-19, global pandemic vii, ix, xii, xiii, 1–3, 4–5, 8, 9, 10–11, 13–14, 15, 16–17, 77–79, 80, 81, 82, 83, 84, 85, 94, 98, 101–2, 104–5, 108, 112–13, 132–33, 144, 147, 155–56, 162–63, 182–83, 190–92, 195, 196–97, 199
partial lockdown 75
Patriot Act 32, 33–35, 189–90

peacebuilding 124–25
peacekeeping groups xiii
Personal Data Collection 1, 2–3, 4–5, 15, 191, 192, 195
Personal Data Protection 107–8, 111, 112
Personal Information Protection Act 112
Pfizer 77–78
polarization xiii
policy analysis 115, 125
Polish 52
political corruption xii, 196–97
political integration 93
political speech 56–58, 60, 61
Pompeo, Mike 71–72, 73
populism 8
post-materialism 97–98
poverty xi, 75–76, 84
Power Five 117
Privacy Shield 135
proposition 25 42–43
proxy wars xi
public watchdog 62

Qing Dynasty 118–19
Qom 70–71, 72
quarantine 75, 81, 95–96, 108–9

racism xii, 196–97
rainforests xiii
rape myths 180
re-education camps 28–29, 31–32
realism; *see also* agnostic realism realist 8–9, 10–11, 93, 115–16, 191, 197
realist paradigm 93
relationship building 199
Relief International 75–76
Religions for Peace vii–viii, xi–xii, xiii
Remdesivir 104
Restricted report; *see also* unrestricted report 175
rule of law xi, 26–27, 42–43, 51, 201
Russia 10–11, 15–16, 49–50, 75–76, 117, 166
Rwandan 116–17

safecity 142–43, 146, 148–49, 194
sanctions 15, 30, 58, 69, 73–74, 75–76, 77, 83, 123–24, 180, 190

INDEX

SARS 15, 95–96
Satellite Imagery Analysis 122–23
second wave 75
Second World War 9, 69, 109–10
self-sovereignty 147, 148
sexism xii, 196–97
sexual assault hotlines, Maryland 158–59
Sexual Assault Prevention and Response (SAPR) 171
Sexual Assault Prevention Programs 171, 175, 177
sexual violence 5, 13–14, 146, 157, 159, 163
Sharp Eyes 27–28
Shiraz 71–72
Sikh xi
Singapore 30–31, 144–45
Sky Net 29–30
social change 200–1
social constructivism 94, 105, 112–13, 191
social constructivist 4–5, 105, 109, 194
Social Credit System 26–27, 29–30, 39
Social Identity Theory 94, 102
social media; *see also* media xiii, 6–7, 14, 15–16, 28–30, 39, 40–41, 47, 53, 58, 62–63, 65, 83–84, 85, 98–99, 101–2, 111, 166, 190, 194
social protest 11
Social Welfare Fund 77
socioeconomic 13, 69, 72–73, 142–43, 148
South Africa xii, 30–31
sovereign nations 69, 86
sovereignty 97–98, 110, 147, 148
spiritual transcendence xi, xiii
superpowers 93
surveillance xiii, 11, 14, 21–22, 23, 25, 26–29, 30–31, 32–35, 36–37, 41, 109–10, 138, 162–63, 189–90, 191, 201
surveillance capitalism xiii, 23, 25, 26, 43
surveillance evolution 138
surveillance technology 22, 24–25, 27–29, 30–31, 41, 191
Sweden 99
Syria 10–11, 48, 117

Taiwan 1, 2, 4–5, 11, 15, 93, 94–99, 101–5, 108–13, 191–92
Taiwan Social Distancing App 95–96

technological innovation 137, 140
Tedros, Dr. 104
Tehran 70–72, 75, 76, 81
third wave 75, 78–79
Thucydides Trap 117–18, 123, 192
Tibet 118–19, 120, 124
Title IX 178
Trump Administration 73–74, 123–24, 134, 135, 193–94
Trump, Donald 73, 132
Trumpism 1
Turkestan 118–19
Turkey 30–31, 56–58, 59, 71–72, 75–76, 121
Twitter 39–40, 83–84

UN Women viii, 157
undergraduate students 172–73
Uniform Crime Report (UCR) 165
unification; *see also* unity 93, 94, 104, 120
United Arab Emirates 75–76
United Kingdom (UK) 51–52, 57, 58, 62–63, 99
United Nations (UN) xiii, 5, 10–11, 73–74, 116–17, 121, 197
United Nations Charter 116–17
United Nations High Commissioner for Refugees 116–17
United States (US) 1, 4–5, 8, 9, 10–11, 14, 21–22, 25, 26–27, 28–29, 31–32, 33–35, 36, 41, 42–43, 51, 71–72, 73–74, 76, 77–78, 79–80, 93, 99–101, 106–7, 117–18, 123–24, 131–34, 135–36, 138–39, 148, 155–57, 165–66, 189–90, 192, 193–94, 197
unity; *see also* unification 3, 110, 200–1
unrestricted report; *see also* restricted report 175, 176
uranium enrichment 74
US Department of State 76, 101–2
US Privacy and Civil Liberties Oversight Board 135
US Supreme Court 51–52
user data 37–38, 41–42, 82–83
Ushahidi 155, 156, 157, 163
USSR 117–18
Uyghur 15–16, 27, 28–29, 115, 120–22, 123–25, 192, 193

Uyghur Human Rights
   Act 123–24
Uzbekistan 75–76

victim advocacy 171
victimization 177, 178, 182
violent-incident data 161–62
Vital Voices 159

war crimes 73–74
Washington Post 165–66
web networks 132, 147, 189
women's rights 5
world affairs; *see also* global relations, foreign affairs 200

World Health Assembly 101–2
World Health Organization 75–76, 77–78, 101–2
World Indigenous Peoples' Initiative and Pavilion 195–96
World Social Report 84

Xinjiang 11, 15–16, 27–28, 30, 115–24, 125, 191, 192
Xinjiang-Uyghur Autonomous Region 120–21

zero-sum game 140–41
zero-sum politics 8–9
Zoroastrian xi

CPSIA information can be obtained
at www.ICGtesting.com
Printed in the USA
JSHW041607151222
34934JS00001B/1